CHAUCER STUDIES XXXIX

IMAGES OF KINGSHIP
IN CHAUCER AND HIS RICARDIAN CONTEMPORARIES

The idea of kingship forms a recurrent theme in the poems of the so-called 'Ricardians', John Gower, William Langland, the *Gawain*-poet and Chaucer – unsurprisingly, during a period of considerable turmoil. This book aims to widen understanding of these poets through an examination of the theme in *Confessio Amantis*, *Piers Plowman* and the works of the *Gawain*-poet and then setting these against the works of Geoffrey Chaucer, the most well-known and well-read of the Ricardians. It brings the other poets' work into sharper focus, showing that despite a diversity in style and approach, common concerns and attitudes underpin all of the poets under consideration.

SAMANTHA J. RAYNER gained her PhD from Bangor University.

CHAUCER STUDIES

ISSN 0261-9822

Previously published volumes in this series
are listed at the back of this book

IMAGES OF KINGSHIP
IN CHAUCER AND HIS RICARDIAN
CONTEMPORARIES

SAMANTHA J. RAYNER

D. S. BREWER

© Samantha J. Rayner 2008

All Rights Reserved. Except as permitted under current legislation no part of this work may be photocopied, stored in a retrieval system, published, performed in public, adapted, broadcast, transmitted, recorded or reproduced in any form or by any means, without the prior permission of the copyright owner

The right of Samantha J. Rayner to be identified as the author of this work has been asserted in accordance with sections 77 and 78 of the Copyright, Designs and Patents Act 1988

First published 2008
D. S. Brewer, Cambridge

ISBN 978–1–84384–174–6

D. S. Brewer is an imprint of Boydell & Brewer Ltd
PO Box 9, Woodbridge, Suffolk IP12 3DF, UK
and of Boydell & Brewer Inc.
668 Mt Hope Avenue, Rochester, NY 14620, USA
website: www.boydellandbrewer.com

A CIP catalogue record for this title is available
from the British Library

This publication is printed on acid-free paper

Printed in Great Britain by
CPI Antony Rowe, Chippenham, Wiltshire

Contents

Preface	vii
Acknowledgments	ix
Introduction	1

1 Gower: The *Confessio Amantis* — 5

2 Langland: *Piers Plowman* — 35
    The Visio — 36
    The Vita — 52

3 The *Gawain*-poet — 61
    Pearl — 62
    Cleanness — 72
    Patience — 75
    Sir Gawain and the Green Knight — 76

4 Chaucer — 83
    The Dream Poems — 85
    Troilus and Criseyde — 110
    The Canterbury Tales — 122

Conclusion — 160

Appendix: Prologues to *The Legend of the Good Women* — 163

Select Bibliography — 165

Index — 173

This book is dedicated to Eileen Aitken

Ubi amor, ibi fides

Preface

This study explores the theme of kingship in the English works of the four major Ricardian poets, John Gower, William Langland, the *Gawain*-poet and Geoffrey Chaucer. Since 1971, when John Burrow defined the late fourteenth century as a distinct literary period, scholars have looked in increasing detail at the relationships that exist between the writers' works, and the comparisons have yielded much to enrich the field of medieval literary studies. It is a period marked by extraordinary political events, a fact that has recently generated work applying New Historicist theory to investigate the impact Richard II's reign had on the poets and their writing. This study, however, concentrates on the texts themselves, and attempts to identify whether, by following the theme of kingship through the work of each poet, a coherent response can be seen that can be called distinctly 'Ricardian'.

Acknowledgments

The research for this book has provided me with many challenges and comforts; it has accompanied me through several years of change, and has persistently benefited from the support and encouragement of people without whom it would never have been completed. Its faults are entirely my own, and without the sustenance of all those who have shown an interest in its development, there would have been a great deal more of them.

I would therefore like to offer grateful thanks to my family, especially my son Jack, who has grown up with this project; to friends whose belief has never faltered, particularly Helen Price, Dr Ralph Norris, Dr Raluca Radulescu, Emma Chippendale, Simon and Philippa Holloway, Paula Veysey-Smith, Vanessa, Lizzie and Catherine Field, Professor Graeme Harper and Father Brian Jones. For the patient listening, the advice, the babysitting, the cups of tea, the threats and cajoling, I thank you all.

I have benefited from suggestions from Dr Ad Putter, and would, in addition, like to record my thanks to members of the English Department at Bangor University, who have supported my pursuit of this research with such sustained patience and goodwill.

I would also like to thank Professor Norris Lacy for his gallant help finding an image for this book's cover, and Ken Hull, the artist, for allowing me to use it.

The debt of gratitude that dwarfs all others, however, is to Professor Peter Field. Accompanied by such a generous guide, this journey has been rigorously informative, constantly inspiring, and above all rewarding and fun. The 'ernest' and the 'game' have become inseparable elements under his expert direction, and I thank him for making the whole experience such a positive and a pleasurable one.

Introduction

> ... for within the hollow crown
> That rounds the mortal temples of a king
> Keeps Death his court, and there the antick sits,
> Scoffing his state and grinning at his pomp;
> Allowing him a breath, a little scene,
> To monarchize, be fear'd and kill with looks,
> Infusing him with self and vain conceit
> As if this flesh which walls about our life
> Were brass impregnable; and humour'd thus
> Comes at the last, and with a little pin
> Bores through his castle wall, and farewell king!
> Cover your heads, and mock not flesh and blood
> With solemn reverence: throw away respect,
> Tradition, form, and ceremonious duty,
> For you have but mistook me all this while:
> I live with bread like you, feel want,
> Taste grief, need friends: subjected thus
> How can you say to me I am a king?
>
> Shakespeare, *Richard II*, III ii 161–77

When John Burrow defined the poetry of the late fourteenth century as 'Ricardian', he linked it to the King in a way even he admitted was 'not perfectly apt'.[1] The period was an unstable one for England, as Richard II's rule took the country from one political crisis to another. The writers who lived through it reflect the shifting nature of their world in the range of styles they use and the attitudes they portray.

Though these styles are very different, the challenges that their works present actually allow for a more focused pursuit of specific themes. Studies in medieval literature, characterised at the beginning of the twentieth century by a mainly philological emphasis, have now become more historicist, with scholars pushing for more integration and co-operation with historians to show how interdependent literary and non-literary texts were during this period. This means that political and social aspects have now become much more widely debated, and work by critics such as Lee Patterson, Paul Strohm and David Wallace has been influential in placing medieval literature at the forefront of expanding new horizons in theoretical appreciations of the texts.[2] Strohm argues that

---

[1] J. A. Burrow, *Ricardian Poetry* (London, 1971) 2.
[2] See for example, Paul Strohm, *Hochon's Arrow* (Princeton, 1992) and *Social Chaucer* (Cambridge, MA, 1989); Lee Patterson, *Chaucer and the Subject of History* (Madison, 1991) and *Negotiating the*

2 *Introduction*

composed within history, fictions offer irreplaceable historical evidence in their own right . . . they offer crucial testimony on other, though no less historical, matters: on contemporary perception, ideology, belief, and – above all – on the imaginative structures within which fourteenth-century participants acted and assumed that their actions would be understood.³

As a result, concentration on a theme such as kingship releases the reader from the narrower confines of stylistic debate into a presentation of those 'imaginative structures' that show the texts' many points of interception with contemporary and non-contemporary ideologies.

Richard was a king of deep contradictions: there was 'an inconsistency at the heart of his rule',⁴ which eventually caused his deposition; these contradictions converge in the image of kingship that he was trying to promote. One leading historian's view is that:

The image he presented was of a remote, almost god-like ruler, but the reality, as [his subjects] experienced it, was one of extreme 'intimacy'. Through the actions of his retainers, Richard had interfered more in their daily affairs than any previous king. The tension in these images between 'distance' and 'intimacy' was never properly resolved.⁵

Despite the unusual way in which it is described here – 'intimacy' is not the word that generally comes to mind when talking about a relationship with a head of state – the tension it indicates was undoubtedly a reality. The quotation from Shakespeare's *Richard II* at the head of this introduction further illustrates this tension between appearance and reality; Richard indicates that beneath the desire to be 'impregnable' in his regality, he must nonetheless acknowledge that he is made of the same mortal flesh as all his subjects. This is a portrayal borne out by evidence historians have gathered about the king: his was an 'alien, even a provocative, style of rule – an "absolutist" experiment conceived out of its time and predestined to failure'.⁶ There was an insupportable divide between the divine and untouchable Richard portrayed in the Wilton Diptych, and the man who worked to implement policies that brought him into closer contact with the affairs of his people, but which ultimately made him unpopular and vulnerable to attack: he 'aspired to be an English Solomon, but in reality he was an English Rehoboam'.⁷

In the poetry of this time, the relationship between Richard and his people produced a more pronounced emphasis on the individual, and how that individual could and should act as part of a larger community. Burrow's conclusion was that

---

Past: The Historical Understanding of Medieval Literature (Madison, 1987); David Wallace, ed., *The Cambridge History of Medieval English Literature* (Cambridge, 1999).
3   Strohm (1992) 4.
4   Nigel Saul, *Richard II* (New Haven, 1997) 445.
5   Saul (1997) 445.
6   Nigel Saul, 'The Kingship of Richard II', in *Richard II: The Art of Kingship,* eds Anthony Goodman and James L. Gillespie (Oxford, 1999) 37.
7   Saul (1997) 465.

the chief characters of Ricardian narrative, then, achieve little of public consequence. Their achievements are of the private, even questionable kind which will not concern the historian.[8]

It is certainly true that the selected writers look at the issues of personal integrity and of disciplined self-governance, and that this in itself creates relevant points of debate about moral and spiritual images of kingship. However, and vitally for what follows here, I believe that in concentrating upon the individual's contribution to society, the major Ricardian poets also reveal much about attitudes to expectations surrounding the behaviour of kings, and the consequences of good and bad rule. This seems inevitable, given that the period during which all our poets were writing was constantly trying to redefine itself. The writers' efforts to find stable reference points or re-create the questions that were being asked about the nature of kingship provide the critical stresses of this work. As one recent study explains:

> During the reign of Richard II, the prestige of the English crown and the terms used to define that crown were in flux. The Rising of 1381, the challenge to the church voiced by John Wyclif that escalated from the early 1370s on, the tensions of war with France, and the personal and political difficulties Richard had in assuming a position of true sovereignty after his accession to the throne as a child in 1377 were all factors in what has been described as a long crisis of authority.[9]

All these elements ensured that kingship was often in the thoughts of Richard's subjects, and it is no coincidence that at this time there was a proliferation of texts on kingship in circulation for our writers to draw upon. These have been detailed elsewhere,[10] and emphasise issues to do with the nature of tyranny, the balance of secular and ecclesiastical power, the role of the king as law-giver, peace-maker, protector and provider for his people. The influence that these works have on the poetry of the Ricardian poets shows that 'kingship and the vernacular literary text were inextricably interdependent',[11] even though we have little evidence that Richard himself directly encouraged any of the writers he had at court to write on this subject or indeed any other. Burrow states quite unequivocally that, though the king was a man of cultivated tastes,

> he was never, despite his absolutist leanings, an arbiter or cynosure of poets, in the manner of Renaissance monarchs such as Elizabeth I.[12]

Nigel Saul confirms this view:

---

[8] Burrow (1971) 100.
[9] Lynn Staley, *Languages of Power in the Age of Richard II* (University Park, PA, 2005) ix.
[10] For example: Margaret Schlauch, 'Chaucer's Doctrine of Kings and Tyrants', *Speculum* 20 (1945): 133–50; Staley (2005) 76–147; Richard Firth Green, *Poets and Princepleasers: Literature and the English Court in the Late Middle Ages* (Toronto, 1980) 135–67.
[11] Larry Scanlon, *Narrative, Authority and Power* (Cambridge, 1994) 142.
[12] Burrow (1971) 2.

for a king who presided over a court of such literary distinction the absence of more extensive patronage is surprising; yet its lack cannot be gainsaid or denied. The many talented writers who thronged the court or who found employment there ... wrote largely for their own satisfaction, and not in response to royal encouragement.[13]

These works therefore exist as products of a court observed from within and without, and, in the case of Langland, definitely divorced from that environment. They manoeuvre and negotiate within the spaces that their authors create in the existing fabric of ideas. Burrow's hesitation in applying his tag of Ricardian is therefore justified, for the poets do not speak for Richard, nor do they work within the limits of his reign (Chaucer, the best-recorded of them, lived to see three English kings on the throne). However, they invoke the spirit of an age where uncertainty, change and reflection are current across all areas of life, and in that they are certainly representative of a Ricardian period.

This study will look at ideas of kingship in the work of the four major Ricardian poets: as a literary analysis, it will concentrate only on what can be found about kingship in the works themselves, without comparison to the many other contemporary texts that exist from this period dealing more or less directly with kings and their governance. This decision has been made purely on the grounds of space, as an examination of the minor poets of this period, or the Mirrors for Princes, or the actual historical evidence of Richard's reign would enlarge this book to unmanageable proportions. Similarly, an examination of the increasing popularity of romances about Arthur, the best-known of all legendary kings, has also reluctantly been excluded. These are studies for a later date, and should complement the core analysis here, which will try and show whether all four poets share common attitudes and approaches, or whether the differences are more striking features.

I will begin by looking in detail at Book VII of Gower's English work, the *Confessio Amantis*, as this establishes the widest exempla of references to kingship. This will be followed by an investigation of Langland's *Piers Plowman*, before I turn to the four poems ascribed to the *Gawain*-poet. The final chapter will examine closely the major works of Chaucer. My aim is to show that the instabilities of the Ricardian label can resolve themselves into some solid conclusions about the ways in which major poets of the period responded to kingship, and also to contribute a little to fulfilling Charlotte Morse's hope that

> Broadening Burrow's perspective to Ricardian studies, embracing the issues he addressed, and expanding beyond them [will give] us the flexibility to keep the aesthetic, rhetorical, political, ethical, spiritual, and intellectual dimensions of Ricardian writing alive in and to the culture we inhabit.[14]

---

[13] Saul (1999) 44.
[14] Charlotte C. Morse, 'From *Ricardian Poetry* to Ricardian Studies', in *Essays on Ricardian Literature in Honour of J. A. Burrow*, eds A. J. Minnis, Charlotte C. Morse and Thorlac Turville-Petre (Oxford, 1997) 344.

1

Gower: The *Confessio Amantis*

Gower's *Confessio Amantis* is a very substantial poem. Its eight books run to some thirty thousand lines, about twenty-five per cent longer than the *Canterbury Tales* as we have it. It survives in over forty manuscripts,[1] which preserve two main versions: the earlier recension dedicated to Richard II and the later, more critical of Richard's reign, dedicated instead to Henry of Derby, the future Henry IV. The earlier recension was written about 1390 and the later one about 1392–3.[2] The poem was immediately popular, and very soon translated into Portuguese and Spanish, an unusual and expensive undertaking. Caxton printed a version in 1483, and Shakespeare adopted Gower as a narrator in his *Pericles*, which also uses Book VIII of the *Confessio* as a source for the story of Apollonius.[3]

Gower wrote two other long poems, the *Mirour de l'Omme* (1376–9) in French and the *Vox Clamantis* (begun in 1377) in Latin. Like the *Confessio*, these are concerned with themes of individual virtue, legal justice and the administrative responsibility of the king.[4] The most heavily explored theme in all three poems is wise rule, which is seen from a fundamentally moral point of view, naturally expressed in religious terms. One leading Gower critic describes this concern as an understanding that:

> the king of England is akin to the king of the soul; the state of England is linked to one's sense of personal domain; and right rule is mirrored simultaneously through both sides of the equation. In such a reciprocal ontology, the one sees itself through the other. Each side, the personal and the social, has a king, with the other as counsellor, who, in the exchange, is nearly as crucial as the king himself.[5]

---

[1] See the *Confessio Amantis* in *The English Works of John Gower*, ed G. C. Macaulay, 2 vols. EETS, Extra Series 81–2 (London, 1900–1). Parenthetical references in the text of this chapter are by book and line.

[2] For the status of Gower's text in the *Confessio Amantis*, see Derek Pearsall, 'The Organisation of the Latin Apparatus in Gower's *Confessio Amantis*: The Scribes and their Problems', *The Medieval Book and a Modern Collector: Essays in Honour of Toshiyuki Takamiya*, eds Takami Matsuda, Richard A. Linenthal and John Scahill (Cambridge, 2004) 99–112.

[3] See the introduction to Macaulay's edition of the *Confessio Amantis*, and John Fisher, *John Gower: Moral Philosopher and Friend of Chaucer* (London, 1965) 303–9.

[4] Defined by Fisher 136.

[5] Russell M. Peck, 'The Politics and Psychology of Governance in Gower: Ideas of Kingship and Real Kings', in *A Companion to Gower*, ed. Siân Echard (Cambridge, 2004) 216.

In addition to the larger works, Gower's many small poems give further proof that he cared about poetic form as well as public issues, manipulating poetry's own laws in order to illustrate the importance of strict governance of self and state. This belief, which is persistent in all of Gower's works, has been highlighted by John Fisher, Gower's biographer, as 'the most striking characteristic' of the poet's accomplishment; the consequence, he suggests, is that Gower's three major poems can be seen as one continuous work.[6] The present study will examine how successfully Gower achieves this aim in the *Confessio Amantis*, with particular analysis of Book VII, which deals explicitly with kingship.

Recent scholarship confirms the importance of kingship in Gower; Siân Echard observes that 'it is obvious that Gower concerned himself with right rule, of the individual and of the state, throughout his poetic career and in all his languages',[7] and Robert Epstein remarks that Gower's 'preoccupation with royal power is integral to his understanding of poetry and his relatively elevated conception of the role of the past'.[8] Recently Lynn Staley has commented that Gower joins 'two narratives exploring the nature of personal and national (or regal) authority'.[9] Gower reinterprets the past through Biblical, classical, romance and historical tales, and this is carefully integrated with the story of Amans and his quest to understand love in the *Confessio*. Indeed, the Prologue opens with a statement about the nobility of the kings of the past, and how important books are to preserving their lives:

> If noman write hou that it stode,
> The pris of hem that weren goode
> Scholde, as who seith, a gret partie
> Be lost: for so to magnifie
> The worthi princes that tho were,
> The bokes schewen hiere and there,
> Wherof the world ensampled is. (Prologue 41–6)

Gower sees his writing very much as a duty:

> yit wol I fonde
> To wryte and do my bisinesse,
> That in som part, so as I gesse,
> The wyse man mai ben avised (Prologue 62–4)

and more so than in Chaucer and the *Gawain*-poet, his poems generate a constant sense that we are being shown things from Gower's viewpoint, a viewpoint that stresses the importance of wisdom. Amans may be the name of the clerk

---

[6] Fisher 135.
[7] Siân Echard, 'Introduction: Gower's Reputation', in *A Companion to Gower*, ed. Siân Echard (Cambridge, 2004) 7.
[8] Robert Epstein, 'London, Southwark, Westminster: Gower's Urban Contexts', in *A Companion to Gower*, ed. Siân Echard (Cambridge, 2004) 59.
[9] Staley (2005) 27.

confessing to Genius, but Book VIII reveals that he is Gower himself. Where Chaucer jumps from one characterisation to another to portray the variety of humanity, Gower draws in his focus in order to reiterate, from what purports to be his own standpoint, the ideal behaviour for each individual, and from what sources this can be illustrated. An energetic determination visible in his disciplined poetry makes him a poet of convictions that are ultimately hard to dismiss, and one who deserves the approbation that C. S. Lewis offered for his ability to unify themes in a way that had not been accomplished before in medieval writing. Indeed, as Lewis says, the concern Gower shows for form and unity 'is rare at any time and ... in the fourteenth century in England, entitles him to all but the highest praise'.[10]

The *Confessio* uses the scheme of the seven deadly sins to analyse the different crimes against love, and the division into eight books and a prologue helps to secure this impression of control. Book VII is, however, an oddity. It is an interruption, a puzzle, a digression. Macaulay famously called this one of Gower's 'most serious faults [of] plan and execution' and judged it damningly as useful 'apparently for no reason except to show the author's learning'.[11] Not until one draws back from the text and views it in perspective can these criticisms be seen to be false. Kurt Olsson has pointed out that in one manuscript of the *Confessio* the page headings show the subject not by the number of the book, but by its topic, and that Book VII is entitled 'Sapientia'.[12] The heading may not be authorial but it is still appropriate: it rightly implies that Amans's love-quest is vitally, as we can see from the opening statements given in the Prologue and the choice of exempla in Book I, a quest for greater self-knowledge. Book VII therefore fulfils an anticipation that has been growing in intensity since the very beginning of the poem, and

> what used to puzzle critics – that this book has no direct bearing on the lover's complaint, or on the 'dedly vices' so far confessed – turns out to be a source of power in Gower's invention and *compilatio*. ... The power of Book 7, an excursus in its entirety, is that it refers back and begins to draw together *distinctiones* that have been emerging in the confession as a whole.[13]

Its emphasis on wisdom is linked inextricably to the ideas of governance and kingship that are prevalent in the *Confessio*: the three most influential sources, the *Secretum Secretorum*, Brunetto Latini's *Trésor* and Giles of Rome's *De Regimine Principum*,[14] underpin Gower's work to provide a foundation that makes it natural that the book should be preoccupied with the kind of advice

---

[10] C. S. Lewis, *The Allegory of Love* (Oxford, 1936) 198.
[11] Macaulay *Works* I xix.
[12] Kurt Olsson, *John Gower and the Structures of Conversion: A Reading of the* Confessio Amantis (Cambridge, 1992) 192. The manuscript referred to is Cambridge University Library, MS Mm.2.21, fol. 137v.
[13] Olsson 191.
[14] For sources to Book VII, see Macaulay *Works* II 522, and Elizabeth Porter, 'Gower's Ethical Microcosm and Political Macrocosm', in *Gower's* Confessio Amantis*: Responses and Reassessments*, ed. A. J. Minnis (Cambridge, 1983) 135.

to princes more commonly found in medieval works explicitly designed to be 'mirrors'.

These all influence Gower, and yet still leave room for him to include material that is entirely his own, and this section of the *Confessio* is particularly exciting in terms of how the poet manipulates the ideas at his disposal. This book, moreover, is the most helpful in our understanding of Gower's attitudes to kings, and to the ways this works as part of the larger concerns with love and personal governance that the whole poem examines. It is, as will be shown, 'the crucial link between king and subject, state and citizen, rule and self-rule, counsel and confession, the ethical and political and the erotic'.[15]

The start of the book emphasises its digression from the shriving of Amans; Genius does not apologise for this – although he does apologise for his own lack of proficiency in carrying out this task, saying he is 'destrauht' (VII 6) – but firmly states that

> wisdom is at every throwe
> Above alle other thing to knowe
> In loves cause and elleswhere (VII 16–18)

and that listening to how Alexander was educated may well help Amans to progress to a new level of understanding about himself. Not only this, but it will help to make Amans happier, and will also allow time to pass. There are several significances here: they fulfil the Boethian idea that wisdom and happiness tend to evoke each other, and they allow Amans a necessary release at this point in his journey from the constraints of time, which has bound him to his love-sick condition. Finally, they show that wisdom really is the answer to Amans's love-quest, for it is the only way that Amans will realise what the proper object of his affection is: 'instead of confession we now, at Amans' own request, get homily'.[16]

Genius sets out his teaching plan, which follows the Aristotelian pattern. First, he will deal with Theoretique, then Rhetorique, and finally Practique, which 'enformeth ek the reule / How that a worthi king schal reule / His Realme bothe in warre and pes' (VII 47–9). Theoretique is subdivided into three: Theology, Physics and Mathematics, and Genius explicates these aspects with clarity and confidence. In the section on Theology, Genius explains that there are three kinds of beings, subject to three kinds of time. There are humans, whose life span is fixed, who are 'thing which began and ende schal' (VII 93); there are souls, whose 'beinge is perpetuel' (VII 98), and most vitally, above all there is God 'the Sonne / Whos time nevere was begonne, / And endeles schal evere be' (VII 99–101). It is highly significant that this belief, with its simple but strict explication of the structure of all that is, seen and unseen, comes at the start of Genius' teaching. God is king and lord of all, and his existence outside the boundaries of time itself makes his rule absolute, the ultimate example of

---

[15] Diane Watt, *Amoral Gower: Language, Sex, and Politics* (Minneapolis, 2003) 119.
[16] Russell M. Peck, *Kingship and Common Profit in Gower's* Confessio Amantis, (Carbondale and Edwardsville, 1978) 140.

perfect kingship. Time, which constrains temporal beings, is a space through which, like Amans, we can journey towards a greater appreciation of the importance of governing our own selves. This will enable us to progress towards a closer harmony with God's rule and therefore make earth a better reflection of that example.

The idea of man as a microcosm within the macrocosm, or physical universe that he inhabits,[17] is one that is very relevant in Gower's work. It derives ultimately from classical thought, and was later discussed in the *Secretum Secretorum*, but Gower's version has been demonstrated to owe further interpretative aspects to the framework provided by Giles of Rome's *De Regimine Principum*.[18] This becomes in this latter work 'a political doctrine in which ethical self-rule is a basis for rule radiating outwards from the self to embrace rule within the family and finally rule within the state'.[19] In Book VII of the *Confessio* Gower is able to pull together ideas of love, rule, family and politics that he has busily thrown out in earlier parts of the poem; it is now that their function and purpose as part of a highly structured, tightly imagined scheme become evident. The reader is led, as Amans is, towards revelations in these final two books that will show the skill of the narrative as a whole. It is imperative that this is recognised, and that the sense of security in the direction of each part is felt as a result of the confidence we perceive in the control of the writer/narrator, because without that the whole work cannot hope to teach very much at all. Gower's imagined world is as ordered and as harmonious as he can make it; if it were not so, then discussing the structure of the microcosm and the macrocosm would hardly be much of a success.

Physique is defined in a mere ten lines, after which Mathematique is described. This science is divided by Gower into four: Arsmetique, Musique, Geometrie and Astronomie. The first three are dismissed quickly and efficiently, but the fourth, Astronomie, is accorded much greater space. This is not surprising, given the structural buttressing this gives to the investigation into the life and death of the nefarious Nectanabus of the previous book,[20] but nevertheless, what Genius has to say does emphasise some relevant points. Before he tells what Aristotle taught Alexander about the stars, Genius explains that he was taught how everything in the world was put together. First the earth was made, then the water, then air and finally fire. These elements have corresponding parts in the makeup of human beings, Melancholy being linked to the earth, Phlegm to the water, Blood to air and Choler to fire. All these aspects are associated with particular parts of the body, and which, in balance, create physical and mental well-being. The body itself is thus a little empire, with the heart 'above alle othre ... lord and Sire' (VII 485). The heart, for 'whom reson is special / Is yove as for the governance' (VII 488–9), must rule with the soul, which has a special place in Man's composition, being made by God in such ways as 'can noman

---

[17] See C. S. Lewis, *The Discarded Image* (Cambridge, 1964) 153.
[18] Porter 136.
[19] Porter 136.
[20] Macaulay, *Works* VI 1789–2366.

pleinli devise' (VII 494). Because the soul is that aspect of Man that has God's imprint upon it, it has the capacity for making him the noblest of creatures (VII 498), but its yoking to the body means there is a constant struggle between the physical and the spiritual.

It is rare, Genius says, that the soul has all the governing of the body, but if so, then Man will not be subject to the pains of physical desires ever again (VII 507–10). However, the relationship is unique, and one that sets up a system of service that shows clearly, though from another angle than that given earlier in the book, that everything is subject to, and ordered by, God:

> Al erthli thing which god began
> Was only mad to serve man;
> Bot he the Soule al only made
> Himselven forto serve and glade.
> Alle othre bestes that men finde
> Thei serve unto here oghne kinde,
> Bot to reson the Soule serveth;
> Wherof the man his thonk deserveth
> And get him with hise werkes goode
> The perdurable lyves foode. (VII 511–20)

The soul serves God, but, while bound to the earthly body, must also serve reason, whose function becomes invested with even more significance when this is explained. Reason is not only necessary to inspire ethical and moral decisions that will ensure good rule of personal and larger social and political concerns, but it must also be remembered that the soul depends upon its healthy management in order to serve God effectively, too. This subject returns more forcibly at the end of the book with Genius' discussion of chastity.

What follows is a long description of the division of the earth into continents, and then of the planets and their properties. Each planet is discussed in terms of what it governs, and the sun is even seen as a king, 'coroned / With brighte stones' (VII 817–18). The sun runs his course through 'Middelerthe' (VII 864) and is thus 'the chief Planete imperial' (VII 866). It may seem surprising to create a hierarchy where the sun's place at the centre, with three planets above him and three beneath, actually make him the superior planet. His influence is on geniality, liberality and skill in handling financial matters. The planets may appear to have a power that is all their own, but they are also subject to a greater influence: God is always master of them all. Genius elaborates upon the planetary positions by detailing the astrological signs that are associated with each one, and telling Amans that each planet, each sign also has certain stars that are bound to it, as well as distinct parts of the earth that it oversees. The emphasis here is on the universe as an ordered system of inter-reliant bodies that manoeuvre harmoniously within their fixed spheres; Genius is offering Amans a view of his world that gives a vertiginous perspective of his place in its workings. It is a view that makes an individual feel insignificant, and yet one that elucidates the important part that every small piece of that universe plays in its continued existence.

This section on astronomy finishes with a detailed analysis of the fifteen different stars that influence certain herbs and stones, and a list of the famous astronomers who Genius describes as 'gracious and wys' (VII 1447). The fifteen stars, identified as coming from a treatise called *Liber Hermetis de xv stellis et de xv lapidibus et de xv herbis, xv figuris*,[21] can be seen, according to Peck, as suggesting 'through number symbolism the conjoining of heaven and earth, eternity and temporality'.[22]

The study of Rhetoric that follows this exposition of the stars and the planets also insists upon the virtues of order that the successful mastery of this art can bestow. Rhetoric can be a great force for establishing peace, and a powerful tool in creating harmony, Gower's longed-for ambition. Genius attempts some elegant phrasing of his own to set out the benefits of using language positively:

> With word the hihe god is plesed,
> With word the wordes ben appesed,
> The softe word the loude stilleth;
> Wher lacketh good, the word fulfilleth,
> To make amendes for the wrong;
> Whan words medlen with the song,
> It doth plesance wel the more. (VII 1582–7)

There is, however, a reverse side to this art, which can cause as much damage when used for evil ends as it can foster good when exercised responsibly. In stressing this, Genius underlines the individual's duty to use the power implicit in this skill wisely. For kings, who are instrumental in constructing all kinds of political alliances, this is highly pertinent. Genius uses the examples of Ulysses and Julius Caesar to illustrate his points, implicitly strengthening his case. Words and their management are crucial to the rule of a king: how that king governs himself and his words shows whether he is a good king or not. Critics have seen this discussion of rhetoric as problematic for its brevity,[23] and suggested Gower never really defines the term adequately at all,[24] but, as Olsson points out, he was not trying to prove his technical knowledge of the art, rather 'to identify the relationship between words – the "matter" of the trivium – and the content of the other divisions of "philosophie", to the end of showing the special power or "vertu" of language'.[25]

Genius' own mastery of rhetoric has a persuasive logic of its own; the sequence of topics must build to confirm his teachings, and does so successfully here, where the third area of knowledge, Practique, smoothly takes up this call for careful discrimination and control in language. Practique is the science of human behaviour, so it is less academic than Theoretique and Rhetorique, and

---

[21] Macaulay, *Works* II 526.
[22] John Gower, *Confessio Amantis*, ed. Russell A. Peck (Toronto, 1980) 515. Peck links this to Hugh de St Victor's discussion of the number fifteen in *De Arca Noe Morali*, III.16.
[23] Olsson 201.
[24] James J. Murphy, 'John Gower's *Confessio Amantis* and the First Discussion of Rhetoric in the English Language', *Philological Quarterly* 41 (1962) 408.
[25] Olsson 202.

its boundaries encompass far more that is immediately relevant to the rule of kings. Genius divides the subject into three sub-sections: Etique, Inconomique and Policie. Each of these deals with a particular realm of governance: personal governance, household governance and governance of the realm. The pattern seems comprehensive and promisingly confident, and the reader may anticipate that such a tightly defined plan will be executed in a similarly balanced way, but that is not Gower's intention. Throughout the *Confessio* it has become increasingly obvious that Gower's structural ambitions sometimes take directions that are difficult to follow: the reader must allow himself to be taken along the road Gower lays before him, trusting that this journey of ideas will justify the experience. At this stage, as with so many stages before, we must, with Amans, allow the lines to unfold, remembering that the areas that are not given sustained attention are not to be dismissed, just held to one side to enable another to be foregrounded more successfully. What rapidly becomes clear is that it is Policie that particularly interests the poet, as the first two parts of Practique are disposed of in a rather summary way.

Etique is efficiently summed up as advice to kings to rule their 'moral condicion / With worthi disposicion' (VII 1655–6), and also more physical guidelines on how to live healthily: 'Hou that he schal his hele kepe / In mete, in drinke, in clothinge eke' (VII 1662–3). Briskly Genius deals with Inconomique 'which techeth thilke honestete / Thurgh which a king in his degre / His wif and child schal reule and guie' (VII 1671–2); in ten lines he tells Amans that these guidelines for ruling a king's household are important because they reflect a larger ability to govern the kingdom. With hardly a pause, Genius then turns to his main theme, Policie. This strand of Practique can, more than the other two, examine rule in its widest possible context of the whole kingdom, and concentrates entirely on kingly virtues. These virtues form five divisions in this section: Truth (1711–1984), Largesse (1985–2694), Justice (2695–3102), Pity (3103–4214) and Chastity (4215–5389). As can be seen from the lines allocated to each, these divisions are not evenly made: Russell Peck reminds us that the five points here mirror the five points of each sin addressed in the first three books of the *Confessio*, and that the reversal of negative to positive behaviour has an effect similar to that of the *Parson's Tale* in Chaucer's *Canterbury Tales*:

> Here in the *Confessio*, the five points of Policy stand as remedy for all vice: Sin and good kingship are antithetical concepts, and these five are the points of right rule.[26]

Gower's use of exemplary narratives to illustrate his choice of virtues, and the choice of these particular five, differ markedly from the techniques of his sources. This reflects a new way of approaching kingship not seen before in medieval literature. Gower was trying something wholly his own, and though the parallel with the *Canterbury Tales* shows that he was not the only poet attempting such originality, it also makes obvious that Gower's work complements Chaucer's but

---

[26] Peck (1978) 142.

rarely derives from it. Gower's ethical concerns are central to his writing in a way they were not to Chaucer. In this section of the *Confessio*,

> far more singlemindedly than even Giles of Rome, Gower maintains that the good king is a virtuous king, and his discussion on 'Policie' is wholly ethical and idealistic in its orientation.[27]

The first virtue to illustrate this total commitment to a morally non-negotiable path is perhaps the most powerful: Truth. It is the 'chief' (VII 1723) of virtues, and Genius pronounces heavily that 'it were an unsittende thing' (VII 1736) if a man should find it lacking within a king. Peck glosses 'unsittende' as not merely 'unfitting', as Macaulay does, but 'a thing without proper place, something alien, or something which might provoke revolution or displacement of right order';[28] the adjective suggests real danger, an active and provocative situation that could lead to a kingdom in crisis. What is of particular note is the direction of this speech: Genius seems to be talking now directly to a kingly audience, issuing warnings that are more relevant to the ears of a monarch than to the novice lover Amans. The lines develop into an address that emphasises the vital importance of Truth:

> The word is tokne of that withinne,
> Ther schal a worthi king beginne
> To kepe his tunge and to be trewe,
> So schal his pris ben evere newe.
> Avise him every man tofore,
> And be wel war, er he be swore,
> For afterward it is to late,
> If that he wole his word debate.
> For as a king in special
> Above all othre is principal
> Of his pouer, so scholde he be
> Most vertuous in his degre;
> And that mai wel be signefied
> By his corone and specified. (VII 1737–50)

In this passage the sense of audience changes again: Genius seems at times to be directly addressing the king himself, and at others his subjects, who must bear responsibility for the fate of their kingdom if they swear allegiance to a king whose word they do not wholly trust. Again Gower stresses the need for recognition that both subject and king have an obligation to rule themselves responsibly; these two states, founded on virtuous principles and practice, are the only hope for a kingdom that is governed for the common good.

The crown is a physical symbol of these truths, and Gower includes at this point an exposition of its different components to underline the sacred aspects of kingship. The gold is excellence, earning the king reverence; the stones suggest

---

[27] Porter 156.
[28] Peck (1978) 143.

constancy in their hardness, honesty in their innate virtue and good fame in their brightness. The circular shape represents the kingdom itself, 'that he it schal wel kepe and guye' (VII 1774). Gower's image seems deliberately placed, between this declamation of the virtues of Truth and the exemplary story of Darius, Sultan of Persia, to focus the reader's attention absolutely on kingship. The crown becomes a symbol of the truth of kingship, a truth that has the most solemn and binding of natures.

Darius was wise, esteeming the counsellors he kept around him. He kept three favourites closest to his side: Arpaghes, Manachaz and Zorobabel. One night, when he could not sleep, he asked these three a question: which is strongest, wine, women or a king? Arpaghes said that a king is the most powerful, as he rules over men, and man is the 'moste noble creature / Of alle tho that god hath wroght' (VII 1830–1). Manachaz, however, argued for wine, since wine can transform men into much better selves than they are when sober. Above all 'wyn makth ek the goode blod, / In which the Soule which is good / Hath chosen hire a resting place, / Whil that the lif hir wole embrace' (VII 1863–6). Zorobabel disagrees with both of them. Women give birth to kings and vintners, he points out, and can make men obedient to them through love. 'A womman is the mannes bote, / His lif, his deth, his wo, his wel' (VII 1912–13): a woman, according to Zorobabel's eulogy, is inspiration and salvation, making knights out of ordinary men, and bringing forth honour and courage in their hearts. They are 'next after the god above' mightiest in their grace, truth and love (VII 1945–8). However, Zorobabel's argument does not stop there; he goes on to say that greater than all these three things is Truth, without which man is nothing (VII 1957–69). The king, pleased with Zorobabel's answer, gives him a reward.

Truth's surprise appearance in the contest is a model for the whole progress of the *Confessio*. The unexpected is an essential element in Gower's narrative. This is indicative of the ending that is to come: Amans abandons his initial quest for love in favour of a quest for good governance and it follows that here, too 'Truth, the unannounced candidate, claims the field'.[29]

Truth is followed by Largesse, a quality that Genius clearly makes relevant to a king's ear. Whereas earlier in the *Confessio*,[30] liberality as a virtue has been more generally talked about, here the king's generous impulses are specifically considered. In following the teachings about truth, this section benefits from the narrator's earlier conclusions, for here the ability to see through flattering supporters who give praise only to prompt greater rewards for themselves is clearly linked to the careful judgement needed to ascertain truth from self-serving avarice, and to give only to those who truly deserve it.

Gower first stresses that there was a time in the past when this topic would not even have become an issue, as all men worked for the common good, but now that time has long gone:

---

[29] See Peck (1978) 143–4.
[30] See Book V.

>   Anon for singulier beyete
>   Drouh every man to his partie;
>   Whereof cam in the ferste envie
>   With gret debat and werres stronge,
>   And laste among the men so longe,
>   Til noman wiste who was who,
>   Ne which was frend ne which was fo. (VII 1996–2002)

As a result of this greed and uncertainty, kings were created to be arbiters of the arguments that broke out. In Gower's argument this role as wise legislator of the kingdom's good is central to the king's being, and thus

>   So sit it wel in alle wise
>   A king betwen the more and lesse
>   To sette his herte upon largesse
>   Toward himself and ek also
>   Toward his poeple ... (VII 2014–18)

This largesse must come from the king's own wealth, however, and not that of the people, for that will only engender discord with the subjects; a king must learn to manage his means wisely, so that he can give to the deserving, and especially to those whose job it is to defend the kingdom's borders from their enemies. In this way, Genius says, the king will be able to keep his good name, just as the Emperor Julius did when he ignored the furious outburst of an overlooked but loyal knight, deciding instead of punishing him to give him the reward he was requesting, because he did genuinely deserve it: 'For every service axeth mede' (VII 2110). The asking for mede is entirely justifiable if it is merited, but Genius goes on to warn that a king must also be aware that his discretion is a powerful tool that must always be used with a care to the regal nature of his state.

To give too much is as bad as to give too little; the example of King Antigonus, who refused Cinichus both an extravagantly large gift and a tiny one on the grounds that both were unworthy of a king, shows that liberality must be governed by measure. Genius points out that prodigality is of no use to a kingdom, if by that the kingdom is made bankrupt and put at risk of its enemies. However, Genius also insists that if the king requires it, all subjects owe both themselves and their land to help support the greater good of the kingdom. This dual responsibility is brought back into the foreground so that Amans's presence, and presumably also that of the reader, can be reminded that their part in this government is not entirely passive: they too have a part to play. Kingship is an active office that all members of the kingdom must contribute to, part of the pledge that 'every liege man conforte' (VII 2143) when 'thei se cause resonable' (VII 2145).

The perspective moves back towards the king, as Genius develops his arguments against flattery, which he claims a king must learn to be impervious to or commit grave errors of judgement. Its deadliness has a threefold potential for damage and is therefore severely dealt with by Genius. Flattery departs from truth, and sins against God, the king, and the other subjects of the realm. The exemplary story of Diogenes and Aristippus[31] shows how a different perspective can result in a different way of life: Diogenes chose a humble road, living quietly with little awareness of the riches the world could offer him, whereas Aristippus joined the king's court, and through constant flattery gained many riches. Diogenes had a freedom that Aristippus did not, and Genius emphasises that this is the way more harmonious with reason. Diogenes told Aristippus that if he would think reasonably, he would realise that flattering the king is against all the philosophy that they have been taught. Genius reflects sadly that most people follow Aristippus' path, rather than the enlightened one of Diogenes.

Kings would do well to remember the actions of the Romans, who preferred plain words to flattery. If an emperor was victorious in battle then he rode in a chariot drawn by four white horses, with his prisoners walking alongside him, and all the nobles of the land before and after. But riding in the chariot with him would be a fool, continuously telling him that he should remember well all that is happening, for it may all disappear tomorrow:

> Thogh thou victoire have nou on honde,
> Fortune mai noght stonde alway;
> The whiel per chance an other day
> Mai torne, and thou myht overthrowe;
> Ther lasteth nothing bot a throwe. (VII 2391–5)

Gower again reconnects with themes raised earlier in the poem, significantly in Book V, where the subject was avarice. The reappearance of the wheel of fate and its uncertain effect on the lives of everyone is a powerful reminder here of the necessity to make every day as positive and well-governed as possible.

This sobering reflection is further borne home by the anecdote about the Emperor's coronation; in the midst of the celebrations the stonemasons arrived to ask the Emperor about the design for his tomb. The Emperor was not fooled by the fulsome compliments of his followers: he knew that death would come to him as it would come to all men. Genius piles up these exempla to emphasise this point, also including a tale of Caesar and a man who revered him so that it 'as thogh the hihe god it were' (VII 2455). This man gets up from his obeisance and sits beside Caesar, saying that if the Emperor were a god, then he did right to worship him, but if he were but a man, then he had every right to sit next to him. Caesar's reply was wise and swift:

> Thou art a fol, it is wel sene
> Upon thiself: for if thou wene
> I be a god, thou dost amys
> To sitte wher thou sest god is;
> And if I be a man, also
> Thou hast a gret folie do,
> Whan thou to such on as schal deie

---

[31] Macaulay, *Works* VII 2217–2354.

> The worschipe of thi god aweie
> Hast yoven so unworthely. (VII 2471–9)

In this way, Genius says, all men who were subjects of Caesar learnt to bring him tales only of truth and reason.

Sycophants 'can noght love' (VII 2491); they are so busy engaging themselves in self-advancement that they do not base their words on anything other than a desire to provoke a reward from their king. They cannot be trusted, and the king who gives favours to such men 'harmeth with his oghne hond / Himself and ek his ogne lond' (VII 2503–4), like King Ahab.[32] This king ignored the advice of the wise prophet Micaiah (Micah) and listened only to the flattering words of his adviser, Sedechie, who told him to attack the army of Benedab. Ahab died on the field and all his people were scattered. So, Genius concludes, it is best for a king to 'loven hem that trouthe mene' (VII 2687), for this fidelity can be the only way to rule wisely.

That Gower connects in this passage the themes of love, truth and flattery represents a successful attempt to appeal to the different implied audiences of the text. Amans is seeking love, but Genius is steering him towards a realisation that love must not be sought for selfish fulfilment; as with the false flattery, the result will only be a hollow and discontented continual striving. Amans, like any king, must learn to love truth, whether that truth has hard lessons to teach him or not, and to respect the wisdom that informs the revelation of that truth. At this stage in the poem he 'misuses his eyes, ears, and thought to gratify his willful fancy' and 'is guilty of indiscrete judgment and willful manipulation of Truth'.[33] He must move forward and realise that the love of God, which transcends every earthly experience, is the most precious gift that he can have. In learning to appreciate this and more effectively govern himself (and if a king, therefore by extension his kingdom) he will become a more honourable and genuinely loving person. Only then will a lover be able to love or a king be able to rule well.

The third part of Policie is Justice, connecting strongly with the issues raised previously. Here Gower heightens the rhetorical tension with a series of questions, dramatically challenging the reader to think about the consequences of lack of truth in rulership:

> What is a lond wher men ben none?
> What ben the men whiche ar al one
> Withoute a kinges governance?
> What is a king in his lignance,
> Wher that ther is no lawe in londe?
> What is to take lawe on honde,
> Bot if the jugges weren trew? (VII 2695–2701)

These questions are urgent ones, fundamental to Gower's explorations of rule in the whole of the *Confessio*, as well as evident in his other works: what is a

---

[32] Cf. 1 Kings 22.
[33] Peck (1978) 147.

kingdom without people? And what are people who have not the guidance of a king? The relationship is never more clearly argued than it is here, for Gower explicitly draws attention to the fact that people and king rely upon each other for their very survival. There is no realm without people, and a king can only bring those people together as a realm if he rules wisely. Furthermore, if the land he rules is a lawless one, then the realm will not hold true either. Justice is an inseparable part of the search for truth, and the key defender of it.

No source is known for this passage, and it seems likely that Gower's own thoughts shaped it. The ideas are rigorously worked out, and presented with a conviction that has a more powerful effect than some of the earlier passages of exemplary material. Genius says that 'ech hath his propre duete' (VII 2711) in supporting the justice meted out by the king and his judges; this idea of fealty, owed to the king by subjects 'the lordes forth with the commune' (VII 2710) is argued with confident authority, which grows as Genius moves on to address the limits of the king's power. In this passage he targets his teachings directly at the king, and the substance is uncompromisingly direct. A king has a force that can transcend the law, but he should not abuse it, especially when it involves the forfeiting of a man's life. He must remain impartial, exercise self-control and act 'for love ne for hate also' (VII 2724). This is his duty, because his estate is above all other earthly ones, but below that of God, who Genius reminds us 'wol himself a king chastise, / Wher that non other mai suffise' (VII 2735–6).

The idea of balance, of harmony, intersects again with the role of the king and his people. Genius emphasises the even-handed nature of true justice, which copes with rich and poor alike, filtering down through the means of judges appointed by the king to ensure 'his poeple be governed / Be hem that trewe ben and wise' (VII 2751–2). Strict adherence to this principle will ensure that the people are 'glad and stant upriht' (VII 2760), but laxity will result in a people 'mistorned' (VII 2764) and discontented. The examples that Gower chooses illustrate various possible manifestations of this just rule: the Emperor Maximin first ascertaining the character of a man before he made him governor of one of his provinces, and Gaius Fabricius, consul of Rome, rejecting a bribe of gold from the Samnites, saying that it was a useless thing, which appealed to none of his five senses. Fabricius' conclusion was that it was better to rule men who possess gold than to have gold and be ruled by those who gave it (VII 2804–10). These first two examples are meant to show an integrity on the part of the law-givers, who maintain a system unfettered by greed and corruption, but Genius remarks 'Ther be nou fewe of suche, I gesse' (VII 2818) and goes on to mourn the passing of this golden age, when every judge was 'frend to comun riht' (VII 2821) and which 'nou, men sein, is al withdrawe' (VII 2826).

The addition of that 'nou' brings the fourteenth-century context into relief; Gower's pause at this point stresses the difference that he discerns between the great law-giving kings of the past and the contemporary situation. Genius can only recover and go on by reminding himself, and his audience, that nevertheless 'the lawe, which is mad for pes, / Is good to kepe for the beste, / For that set alle men in reste' (VII 2829–32). There seems a weariness about this in contrast to the prophetic urgency seen in earlier passages; indeed, the proliferation of further examples that follow seem to be there to shore up an argument that feels the pressure of reality bearing against it. If Gower was talking specifically here about Richard's reign, then it would have been difficult to have seen a way to reverse the tide of bad management that his contemporaries were talking about when he was writing the *Confessio*.[34] At this point he seems to be able to do no more than hope for peace and truth and justice to win through.

The kings in the passage under consideration are truly exemplary, superlative executors of these virtues Genius has been discussing so determinedly. The Praetorian Consul Carmidotirus killed himself when he realised he had inadvertently broken one of his own laws; coming into the council chambers straight from a hunt, he forgot that any man who entered that place wearing weapons would forfeit his life. Although the other lords were ready to excuse him, Carmidotirus would not make an exception and weaken the law. King Cambyses found one of his judges to be lawless, so slew him and made his skin into the covering for a bench. He then appointed the judge's son to advise him in his father's stead, and made him sit on this bench, so that he would be constantly reminded of what covetousness could do:

> Thus in defalte of other jugge
> The king mot otherwhile jugge,
> To holden up the rihte lawe. (VII 2905–7)

The king must be concerned to keep justice for his subjects at all times; he must be prepared to overrule his own judges if they should prove to be unreliable. This is his duty, and Gower shows it to be one that requires an awe-inspiring strength of character and sense of solemn responsibility. A king is guardian of all that is good and just and true; if he has created a kingdom where such virtues flourish then he will, like Lycurgus, be able to leave his throne and even his country in the hands of deputies wisely appointed to govern according to his decrees. Lycurgus was a king whose laws were 'so wel begon' that there was among his subjects 'no distance / Bot every man hath his encres' (VII 2925–6). His was a kingdom of harmony and idyllic plenty:

> Ther was withoute werre pes,
> Withoute envie love stod;
> Richesse upon the comun good
> And noght upon the singuler
> Ordeigned was, and the pouer
> Of hem that weren in astat
> Was sauf: whereof upon debat
> Ther stod nothing, so that in reste
> Mihte every man his herte reste. (VII 2928–36)

The lyrical fluency of this passage indicates a more confident position from the poet and his spokesman, Genius. They stress the idea of common good, directly

---

34 See Saul (1997) 435–40.

under the control of the king. The singular, the individual and the selfish must be subsumed by the workings of a system that strives for the best interests of all its members. Lycurgus has created an ideal state, and safeguarded that by acting in a way that itself fulfilled the selfless nature of his achievement. There is a further detail of note: Genius adds that he had God at the centre of all that he did: 'He, which for evere wolde plese / the hihe god, whos thonk he soghte' (VII 2940–1). The 'wonder thing thanne him bethoghte' (VII 2942) is thus associated with a divine intervention, a source of heavenly support and help even for a pagan king.

Lycurgus is the epitome of all the best aspirations of an earthly king: he brought his advisers together and told them that the laws of the country had been given to him by Mercury, and were therefore sacred. He made them swear that they would uphold these laws at whatever cost, even when he himself was not there. Then he left the country, knowing that in order to protect its continued success he must not return. All the while he stayed away, the people were bound to keep the oath they had taken, and common profit secured: 'and in this wise he hath it knet' (VII 3008). The king's truly selfless sacrifice preserved his country's peace.

Amans must learn this lesson of abdication of personal ambition as he progresses along his own path to greater self-knowledge, and though 'it is perhaps a paradox that one returns home from exile by exiling egotism ... that seems to be the only way to "knet" well the garment of happy estate'.[35] The tale of Lycurgus has a deeper spiritual purpose than the other stories told in this section; not only does it build on the idea of personal sacrifice for the greater good, which is to be taken up again in the succeeding part dealing with Pity, but it also reminds the reader that every Christian follows Lycurgus' example by holding on,to the laws handed down to them by God, the ultimate example of the physically absent king. Genius lists the first law-givers: Moses, Mercurius, Neuma Pompilius, Lycurgus, Foroneus and Romulus, who all gave their races templates for how to live. Genius prays that 'God lieve it mote wel ben holde, / As every king therto is holde' (VII 3069–70). Present-day kings must carry on what these men began, or forfeit the right to rule:

> What king of lawe takth no kepe,
> Be lawe he mai no regne kepe.
> Do lawe awey, what is a king?
> Wher is the riht of eny thing,
> If that ther be no lawe in londe? (VII 3074–8)

There are echoes here of the earlier lines in this section on justice asking what a kingdom is without any men, or without a king's rule (VII 2695–2701); the urgency of those lines is evident again, driving the investigation forward in a rhetorically controlled way that manages to regain the lost momentum sensed previously. Justice is fundamental, it is the framework without which society

[35] Peck (1978) 149.

cannot function; it is 'on the beste / Above alle other erthly thing, / To make a liege drede his king' (VII 3093–4). Genius moves seamlessly into his next point of Policie, Pity, by noting that Alexander took this advice from Aristotle, forming his laws first before then putting them into practice. This plan, successfully implemented, made his subjects 'drede' him, a term that had much wider meaning than it has today. Alexander's subjects respected him, both because they feared his power, and also because they knew that his justice was fair and swiftly administered.

This justice must be tempered by Pity, a quality that Genius acknowledges is the civilising partner of Justice. He begins with the unsurpassable example of this: Christ, God's physical manifestation of pity for humanity. If we owe our salvation to His supreme act of pity, then we should show that pity to our fellow men while we live on earth: 'Wel oghte a man Pite to have / And the vertu to sette in pris, / Whan he himself which is al wys / Hath schewed why it schal be preised' (VII 3114–17). Pity makes a king 'courteis' (VII 3119) in 'word and in his dede' (VII 3121) and this will prevent his rule from becoming a tyranny. Genius underlines that this courtesy inspires a reciprocal appreciation from king and subject; the subject will 'drede' his liege lord, and be obedient to his rule, while the king's pity-inspired governance will produce love and respect, which will further evoke loyal service from the subjects. It is a perfect model for successful kingship, and Genius further illustrates this by enumerating the story of Codrus, king of Athens, who, when faced with the choice to die in battle or see his people defeated, chose death. This unusual decision is celebrated by Gower, who interjects his own rhetorical appreciation of Codrus' self-sacrifice, asking 'Wher is nou such an other hed, / Which wolde for the lemes dye?' (VII 3200–1).

It is not so much one man's sacrifice for another that Gower emphasises, rather the wish of a king to fulfil his obligations to his liegemen, even to death. A king can do no greater deed for his subjects, and in doing so earns himself the 'worthi name' (VII 3214) that will guarantee him honour and fame in the world. As further illustration, Genius tells how Pompeius, emperor of Rome, captured the king of Armenia as a prisoner of war. So humbly and patiently did this king suffer the terms of his imprisonment that Pompeius was moved to make peace with his former enemy and reinstate his kingship. He said 'it was more goodly thing / To make than undon a king, / To him which pouer hadde of bothe' (VII 3237–9); mercy and justice will temper tendencies towards cruelty and violence, which a good king will not show to be his only means of rule.

Kings have power, and power means control. We have seen that Gower is everywhere concerned to stress that control must be first of self and only afterwards of one's subjects. The power to make and unmake kings, the extreme example of how far that power can reach, also makes clear the weight of responsibility that comes with supreme power. A king must be wise enough to realise that governing in harmony with neighbouring rulers will benefit all in a way constant fighting will not. In this section of the *Confessio*, Gower underlines this truth by juxtaposing the qualities of pity and cruelty. With some relish he retells the histories of some cruel tyrants, Siculus, Dionys[36] and Lichaon. These kings all come to very bad ends, and Gower draws an analogy with the behaviour of a lion to show how humility and pity can avert such a fate. He draws on Bruno Lattini's *Trésor* as evidence that the lion will only attack the man who will stand in front of him. If, however, the man would come before the lion 'in signe of mercy and of grace' (VII 3394), then the lion would 'Restreigne his ire in such mesure, / As thogh it were a beste tamed' (VII 3396–7). If, Genius argues, a beast can show such pity, then how much more so will a king?

The density of exempla in this section puts the argument under some strain by packing in stories to cover as many different views of kings as Gower can manage. Legendary kings are drawn upon as supporting evidence for the notions of kingship that Genius describes, drawn from an impressive number and variety of sources. However, this is a vital part of Gower's role as a *compilator* in the tradition of such writers as Vincent of Beauvais. The proliferation of tales is designed for a specific effect: the *Confessio*

> has all the trappings of a *compilatio*. The magnitude of the undertaking is encyclopedic, and there is, even within its superficially clear *ordinatio partium*, a seemingly random, often highly imaginative introduction of material, frequently generating conflict where we cannot anticipate it. Gower is, at one level, a *tumultuator*, one who causes debates. . . . Gower as *tumultuator* seeks to generate an uneasiness, to the end of giving edge to our critical faculty. He also does more: his method is not precisely that of the dialectician, but he works towards concord in a program that continually introduces new authors, new issues. He does not allow us a security at any single juncture of this exercise, and this is to his point of making us wise: out of the discord he generates, we might come to a greater, extra-textual understanding.[37]

Unsettling as this approach can be, and frustratingly difficult to see the purpose of each tale, we must, as readers, trust the *compilator*. There is method in the apparent randomness of detail that can only be appreciated when the whole poem has been read. Gower leads the reader back from this image of leonine mercy to that of a tyrant so crazed by cruel acts that he 'lived worse than a beste' (VII 3491): Spertachus, who shows no mercy to the queen of Marsagete's son, when they meet in battle. In this story, it is this queen, Thamaris, who defeats Spertachus, and metes out justice with an equanimity that is admirable both for its intelligent execution and its level-headed swiftness: Gower's portrait of the ideal way of rule is not limited to male exemplars.

It is notable that this portrayal of female rulership should be followed by a warning from Gower that Pity should be carefully monitored, so that it does not become a weakness; although there is no connection between this warning and the actions of Queen Thamaris that immediately precede it, the juxtaposition cannot be accidental. Gower's work, encyclopaedic in scope as it is, does not

---

[36] Macaulay says that this is a mistake, a confusion of Diomedes of Syracuse with the tyrant Dionysius (532).
[37] Olsson 14.

offer a randomness of composition that may excuse such a placing as chance. The structure of the argument benefits from the neat oppositions of expectation that the Queen's gender allows for. The effect is to deepen the awareness of how weakened a ruler would become if 'Pite mesure excede' (VII 3328); if queens can exhibit qualities of good kingship too, and rule with justice and strength of purpose, then a king, with all the manly attributes of courage and honour at his disposal, should be able to do the same. The lexis of lines 3528–52 consciously underlines the masculinity of the ruler Gower appears to be addressing: 'Prince', 'Kinghode', 'knyhthode', 'Leon', 'manhode' and 'champioun' create an image of a strong male leader, and one who must 'make a good visage' (VII 3545) whatever he may be feeling.

Gower urges kings to keep a steady head and to control fears that may cause them to behave rashly or with emotion, rather than with considered thought. He strengthens his call by using exempla from the Bible as support; this is a tactic seen throughout previous books in the *Confessio* to denote a particularly important strand.[38] Gideon's great victory and Saul's defeat both came as a result of their response to the word of God; Saul's refusal to obey Samuel's warning against showing mercy to Agag meant that he lost both his kingdom and his life. On the other hand, Solomon's fulfilment of King David's advice to have Joab slain meant that his own rule could prosper. Gower notes that though Solomon was held in more dread by his people as a result of Joab's death, he nevertheless 'kepte forth withal / Pite, so as a Prince shal, / That he no tirannie wroghte' (VII 3873–5). It was less Solomon's powerful acts of retribution than his great wisdom that the people 'dradde' (VII 3880); his reign of peace marked by the wise counsel, 'which is the substance / Of all a kinges governance' (VII 3889–90).

Here Gower celebrates Solomon's virtues: he details how the king asked God for wisdom, so that he could rule in a way that would reflect honourably on his Maker. Gower uses Solomon as a kingly example elsewhere, but in Book VII he becomes a vital indicator of 'what thing of most necessite / Unto a worthi king belongeth' (VII 3891–2). Solomon humbled himself before God – 'I am but a child, and know not how to go out and come in' (3 Kings 3.7)[39] – and it is this humility that prompts God's generous rewards:

> The god of that which he hath axed
> Was riht wel paid, and granteth sone
> Noght al only that he his bone
> Schal have of that, bot of richesse,
> Of hele, of pes, of hih noblesse,
> Forth with wisdom at his axinges,
> Which stant above alle othre thinges. (VII 3906–12)

---

[38] See, for example, Book I 2789ff.
[39] Although the reference from 3 Kings is not explicitly mentioned in this passage, the allusion to a child-king, or at least a king who acknowledges the need of youth for guidance, may be a reference to Richard II. Gower will develop this in later lines, as seen below (0).

The inglorious end of Solomon's reign is not mentioned by Gower until it suits his argument for chastity in kings a little later on. This selective referencing can be disorienting to the reader, yet Gower's narrative shows no sign of uncertainty. He can use Solomon as an example of both a supremely good and a supremely bad king without any sense of inconsistency, as if the two phases of his rule were unrelated.

The precedence of wisdom, seen throughout the *Confessio*, is allied here with Pity because of the importance of this virtue in preserving peace, that other ambition of Gower's that binds the whole poem together. Genius is given some further thirty lines or so to bring Solomon's example into the debate about kingship in general. A king must not only believe in God, but be surrounded by counsellors who also believe, 'fulfild of trouthe and rihtwisnesse' (VII 3917). He must, to be truly noble, be a symbol of balance 'betwen the reddour and pite' (VII 3919), so much so that both God and the people praise his name. If the king does not live righteously, however, Gower warns that it is likely, as the kings of the Old Testament found, that his sins will be visited upon his people: 'The poeple takth that he deserveth / Hier in this world' (VII 3934–5). There is a darker undertone in Gower's concluding comment that he does not know how 'it schal stonde' with the king in the heavenly world. Again, however, the answer is in the 'reule of his persone', which should 'ben of the betre conscience' (VII 3941–2).

Gower's treatise on kingship has so far ranged widely, looking point by point at different aspects of the king's role, but carefully distancing itself from kings from more recent history, or even kings whose stories would be clearly relevant to recent history. There may be a shift in the next section of this examination of Pity, however, as Gower turns to a Biblical king whose situation does have something in common with Richard II. There is a natural progression here from the examination of Solomon in the earlier lines, so that discussion of this wise king's son, Rehoboam, does not seem to be forcing his argument. There is a subtlety in the way that Gower's treatment of wisdom combines with this portrayal of a young king who inherits the legacy of his well-loved and renowned father, struggling to maintain the peace and create his own place in the annals of fame.

Rehoboam was advised by two sets of counsellors: those who had been advisers to his father, and younger, newly arrived courtiers eager to make a place for themselves in the new king's court. Rehoboam chose to listen to the advice of the younger men, and in so doing alienated his people, who revolted against him. Ten of the twelve tribes of Israel chose a new king to lead them, and God turned his back on Rehoboam. Gower states that:

> Lo, thus the yonge cause wente:
> For that the conseil was noght good,
> The regne fro the rihtfull blod
> Evere afterward divided was. (VII 4130–3)

It is not impossible to see in this a warning to the young King Richard, who was also said to listen too closely to young and foolish advisers; it was, as Nigel Saul says, 'a common complaint' about his reign.⁴⁰ Here there is a clear emphasis on the line of succession, and its inability to protect the king if his behaviour is dishonourable. Though Rehoboam had Solomon as his father, and was the undisputed heir to Israel, his actions and his lack of wisdom outweighed this right. Richard's own reliance upon and development of the theory of the divine right of kings would similarly see him unable to prevent his own deposition. Gower sagely concludes that a king must keep both young and old on his side, 'Be so the king hem bothe reule, / For elles al goth out of reule' (VII 4145–6). The duplication of the end-rhyme 'reule' (first verb, then noun) adds a weighty surety to this final judgement.

Gower goes even further in arguing for the importance of royal counsellors, saying that it was better for a country to have a foolish king and wise advisers than a wise king and foolish advisers. That is because it is easier for one man to change than for many, and therefore better for the country to have many good counsellors than a good king with none at all. This idea is supported by a story about the Emperor Antonius, a wise ruler who claimed he would rather save one of his liegemen than slay a thousand of his enemies, but it is also promoted by the distinctive note of personal conviction in the voice of the narrator. This idea itself may seem radical, and from Gower, usually so circumspect and uncontroversial, surprising, but it fits in with the ideals of truth and wisdom that Gower has been illustrating throughout the *Confessio*. Of all his subjects, the king should exercise pity most judiciously when dealing with his liegemen, 'For thei ben evere under his hond / After the goddes ordinaunce / To stonde upon his governance' (VII 4178–80). The value of these counsellors is therefore placed extremely high by Gower, and is underlined by the story of Tarquin and Arrons that follows, which suggests that bad counsel can be overturned by the 'comun conseil' (VII 5294) of the people.

However, Gower is not, as these comments may seem to indicate, advocating that the advisers rise up and overturn the king; in this book, though ostensibly narrated by Genius to Amans, it is clear, as stated earlier, that Gower's voice imitates that of Aristotle, advising the king directly. Gower is intent upon educating the king and it is to him that this book is addressed: the poem talks about the overthrowing of tyrants 'but not about a revolution, about deposition but not about republicanism'.⁴¹ There is further evidence of Gower's intentions in the lines that sum up the section on Pity that he has just completed; he reiterates that Pity must be combined with justice in order to make a king's reign secure: 'Is non so good to the plesance / Of god, as is good governance' (VII 4193–4). The *Confessio* reminds us time and again all action, all thought, all feeling, must be directed towards pleasing God. A king, by virtue of his special position of responsibility, has the greatest role to play in doing this. Myra Stokes argues that

---

⁴⁰ Saul (1997) 435.
⁴¹ Watt (2003) 125.

The secular political power was ordained by God for the maintenance of justice or righteousness. The king, as regent of God's majesty (*vicarus summi regis*), should do all in his power to imitate the equity of divine justice in giving like for like – ill for ill, and well for well. He undertook to do so in his coronation oath, in which he pledged himself to the reward of the righteous, and the punishment of the evil (*vindictam malefactorum*).[42]

The coronation oath itself can be taken as the source for this intertwining of pity and justice, for in 1377, just as in 1952 when Queen Elizabeth II was crowned, the monarch had to answer the question: 'Will you to your power cause Law and Justice, in Mercy, to be executed in all your judgements?' In the case of Richard II, who took the coronation oath again in 1388 in order to try and appease the Appellant lords after the Merciless Parliament 'violated Richard's very terms of kingship',[43] these words were to be ironically underlined by events that saw 'his policies reversed, his household taken over and purged, and his friends either exiled or sent to their deaths'.[44] The first version of the *Confessio* appeared in 1390, a short year after Richard began to rule on his own, having come into his majority in 1389. Gower's poem can be read as a reflective commentary on the king's efforts to maintain peace by trying to co-operate with his advisers at that time, set against the memory of the chaos of the preceding years of the decade.

Gower's source, Latini's *Trésor*, also stresses the need for clemency tempered with justice, quoting Seneca's advocation that he would not 'go in fury nor in cruelty but will go along the path of the law, by deeds, by wisdom without pride, by judgement without anger'.[45] The balance between justice and mercy was seen to be central to successful government in the Middle Ages, and part of the contract made with the king's subjects at the coronation: it was a clause that those subjects would often try and ensure their king remembered. Langland, as we will see in his exposition of the responsibilities of kings, also takes this duality very seriously. The king as God's representative must not forget his function as arbiter of 'vertu most vailable' that will 'make a kinges regne stable' (VII 4201–2). The layering of audiences is a sophisticated working of narratological voices: we have reader and writer, Genius and Amans, adviser and king, and (elusive but apparent) Gower and King Richard II.

The earlier version of the *Confessio*, addressed to Richard II, contains towards the end the lines of celebration that also pick up this theme:

> Richard by name the Secounde
> In whom hath evere yit be founde

---

[42] Myra Stokes, *Justice and Mercy in* Piers Plowman*: A Reading of the B Text Visio* (London, 1984) 2–3.
[43] Staley (2005) 3.
[44] Saul (1997) 195.
[45] Brunetto Latini, *The Book of Treasure*, trans. Kate Forhan, in *Medieval Political Theory: A Reader*, eds Cary J. Nederman and Kate Langdon Forhan (London, 1993). From Chapter 96, 'On the Argument about whether it is preferable to be feared or loved' 91.

> Justice medled with pite
> Largesce forth with Charite. (VIII 2987–90)

This theme has, then, become a motif of central importance to that of kingship; its relevance to Gower, writing during a time when the king was still struggling to control political events in England, is evident not only in its frequent appearance, but also in its disappearance from the later versions, which remove flattering references to Richard like these and replace them with a general denunciation of the state of the nation, and of those people in the higher estates who have caused the corruption. In Book VII, Gower prepares the way for these later developments, and it is no small indication of his skill that both continuations work well with his illustrative material.

The final area of Policie that Gower addresses is that of Chastity, which he presents as another aspect of the all-important royal requirement of self-control. Above all men, a king must practise chaste behaviour because 'his ordre as a prelat / Schal ben enoignt and seintified' (VII 4246–7). Aristotle told Alexander that he should seek out the company of good women, who would 'gladen his corage' (VII 4259), but that he should not let them beguile him. Gower says that it is natural for a man to love, but he must not lose his wits, like King Sadana Pallus of Asyrria did, so that he lost his kingdom. It is surely significant, as Russell Peck has observed, that Gower here qualifies the exhortation to Amans that loving is an innate part of being human; this is still true, but within this book, where the emphasis has shifted from the amorous court to the political one, he stresses that even loving must be tempered by control. A king cannot afford to luxuriate in the delights of love when he has wider responsibilities for his people.[46] He notes that King David also had many loves, but he managed to maintain his knighthood; not ever forgetting the 'luste of armes' (VII 4350) that kept his kingdom safe. David is contrasted a few lines later with Solomon, whose lusts led him into idolatrous practices. The kingdom was lost, as prophesied, and split between Jeroboam and Rehoboam, and 'thus was the wiseste overlad / With blinde lustes whiche he soghte' (VII 4513–14). Gower laments this fall from grace in such a mighty king, in all other respects the ideal ruler:

> It sit a king wel to be chaste,
> For elles he mai lihtly waste
> Himself and ek his regne bothe,
> And that oghte every king to lothe.
> O, which a Senne violent,
> Wherof so wys a king was schent,
> That the vengance in his persone
> Was noght ynough to take al one,
> Bot afterward, whan he was passed,
> It hath his heritage lassed,
> As I more openli tofore
> The tale tolde. (VII 4547–58)

---

[46] Peck (1978) 151–2.

That rhetorical 'O' introduces a personal note of anguish from the poet; the shame is that the wisdom of this king, so celebrated, so universally acknowledged, and filled with so much promise for the land of Israel, should not have been sufficient to warn him to guard against loss of self-control.

Gower's identification of corruption in rule with lack of sexual control can be seen in Book V of the *Confessio*, but it is here, in Book VII, that the analogy is more systematically worked out, with the ensuing tales of Lucrece and Virginia. In the Tale of Tarquin, Arrons and Lucrece, Genius shows Amans (and Gower shows Richard II) a desperate situation where tyranny and cruelty result in calamitous events. First comes the description of the fall of the Gabiens, who allow Arrons to enter their city, believing his lie that he had been turned out by his own family. Once in the city, Arrons decapitates the princes and the city is at the mercy of Tarquin, who proceeds to kill everyone 'withoute reson or pite' (VII 4699). The addition of the slaying of the citizens to the original Ovidian story reminds the reader that Gower connects the ability to use pity effectively with the ability to rule wisely; in this story he pulls together all the elements of Policie that he has highlighted in Book VII, and the contrasting elements of the story powerfully reinforce the main themes of his argument. On the one hand, the Gabiens' mistaken impulse of pity for Arrons shows that even a virtue as commendable as pity needs to be underpinned by wisdom, and on the other, Tarquin's lack of any mercy is held up for the audience's own wisdom to judge in the light of its outcome.

That the link between this prelude and the main tale may be seen as 'tenuous' and 'incidental'[47] is to miss the point that the tale is here precisely because it deals with the relationship between lust and chastity, which does not only confine itself to the rape of Lucrece. It is no accident that the juxtaposition 'renders the story of Lucrece's rape subservient to a larger narrative about the political community',[48] but the result of Gower's calculated skill in embellishing the story with details that make that larger narrative a reality.

Tarquin and his son prepare a sacrifice of thanks to Phoebus, but a serpent crawls out from under the altar and eats it. The meaning of this is clear: the king has angered the gods by his pride and 'unrihtwisnesse' (VII 4724), and the god warns that whoever shall be the first to kiss his mother will take revenge on the merciless pair.

A knight called Brutus, on hearing this prophecy, dropped to the ground and kissed it, realising that 'therthe of every mannes kinde / Is Moder' (VII 4743-4). His wisdom is lost on his fellow Romans, who think he has tripped over by accident. Their lack of perception, made comically obtuse by Gower, makes their rush to embrace their own mothers when they return home to Rome even more ridiculous. The Romans are not loyal to their king, and Gower's portrayal of an army where each individual is determined to be the one to bring down Tarquin shows the disunity that the king's actions have caused. That the knights respond individually to this prophecy, rather than being brought together in opposition

---

[47] Watt (2003) 120.
[48] Watt (2003) 120.

to the king, indicates the desperate state of affairs. There is a further irony in that though Gower has been promoting the need for everyone to achieve greater self-control, that very achievement is seen here to be dangerous: it can become wholly self-centred and cause a complete disintegration of community.

As Book VII progresses, this sense of community becomes more insistent, placing the individual's contribution within the framework of their society to illustrate the interdependence of ruler and people. There is a complex patterning of focuses here. The attention on the individual lover wanes as the didactic construct of Genius's lecture comes to its end: Amans is a silent presence for most of it, and his personal quest seems lost amidst Genius's lengthy speeches. However, the subject of chastity moves to become of extreme importance to Amans's situation, revealed in Book VIII, just as the waxing of the political and social issues surrounding kingship moves towards the background for a little while, before being joined with Amans/Gower and his intimate conclusions about love for a highly measured final piece. Book VII begins with a description of the strictly defined makeup of the universe, and ends with a discussion of the very particular part of that universe concerning the question of how earthly social and political harmony can be achieved. The personal and the impersonal are, as part of that imagined reality, one and the same, as shown in Book VIII.

The disruption from within the Romans continues its deadly progress when, at dinner one night, Arrons asks his men who has the best wife. Away from home, and holding siege to the town of Ardea, his men find such a debate very inflammatory, and eventually one of the knights, Collatin, suggests to the boastful Arrons that they ride secretly together back to Rome to see what their wives are doing in their absence. This is agreed upon, and the men arrive first at the palace, where, disguised, they find Arrons's wife 'al full of merthes and of bordes' (VII 4799). The convivial atmosphere generated by the Prince's lady does not, however, contain a single reference to her husband, and the two men leave to find out what Collatin's wife is doing. They find Lucrece surrounded by her women. As she works, she explains that the labour is for the good of the war that her husband is fighting in, and that she hopes that soon she shall hear 'Som good tidinge of his astat' (VII 4819). She is heartsore, she says, until she knows Collatin is safe, and as her tears begin to fall Collatin reveals himself to her. Their joy is witnessed by Arrons, who is smitten with love for the loyal Lucrece, and immediately starts to plot ways to possess her. Gower makes it very clear that Arrons's faults of tyranny make his honour 'remuable' (VII 4896), and that it is lust, and not love, that drives him to masquerade as a cousin of Collatin a few days later, and gain access to Lucrece's home. She courteously welcomes him, and offers him food and lodging for the night, unaware of his identity or his true intentions. When night falls, Arrons rapes Lucrece, and then he rides away. Lucrece is so distraught by what has happened that she takes her own life, and her kinsmen vow to get justice for the tragic crime. Among her kinsmen is Brutus, who is a real cousin to the family, and it is he who persuades Collatin and Lucrece's father to put her body on a bier and carry it out into the city so that the story can be told. He emerges as the opposite to Arrons, restoring unity and stability where Arrons brought division and chaos (first to Gabiens and then to Collatin's household) ... Brutus turns private grief into public oration (VII 4847–57). The rape and suicide of Lucrece become the catalysts for public action.[49]

The townspeople, hearing the sorry tale, are reminded of all the sins Arrons has committed, and those of his father, too. They rise up and force the pair of tyrants into exile, 'and taken betre governance' (VII 5123). Gower's storytelling does not show itself at its most skilful here, but there are details that clearly show the direction he wishes the tale to take. Tyrants may be kings, and may have power to control many events, but they cannot control everything, and so they cannot be entirely safe even in this life. They are not immune from the justice that is meted out on earth, and they must therefore behave well from motives of self-interest if they will not do so from the love of virtue.

The story of Virginia that follows reinforces this injunction; Virginia's father is so incensed by the governor of Rome's evil schemes to ruin his daughter that he kills her, and then takes his case before the powers of the city, saying

> That betre it were to redresce
> At hom the grete unrihtwisnesse,
> Than forto werre in strange place
> And lese at hom here oghne grace. (VII 5269–72)

Livius is described by Gower as a lion, 'which of no drede set accompte / And not what pite scholde amounte' (VII 5241–2), and also as a wild boar. His rage is desperate and ferocious and has a regality about its justification, shown by the symbolism of the beasts chosen in describing him, that contrasts with the baseness of Claudius' actions. His voice, demanding justice and pointing out that this situation makes all the people vulnerable to the same sort of treatment, is heard. Gower emphasises, by carefully pronounced repetition, the effect this appeal has:

> And that broghte in the comun feere,
> That every man the peril dradde
> Of him that so hem overladde.
> Forthi, er that it worse falle,
> Thurgh comun conseil of hem alle
> Thei have here wrongfull king deposed (VII 5290–5)

'Comun' is the key word; Gower shows the power that the people have, and the result of that power when used collectively, communally, against a corrupt ruler. Both kings in these two stories commit crimes that are 'both personal and political';[50] their failure in all aspects of life has a catastrophic effect on the people they are supposed to be governing, and these people therefore have

---

[49] Watt (2003) 121.
[50] Porter 160.

every right, Gower implies, to try and redress the balance. Indeed, it appears more than a right, but a moral and ethical necessity to take action.

The severity of this exemplary tale is followed by the final one of Book VII: the Biblical tale of Sara and Tobias.[51] Here the individual virtue of Tobias is shown as vital to a greater political good; it is the opposite viewpoint from that seen in the first two stories, but emphasises the link both between Amans and the wider world and kings as readers of this poem and their kingdoms. The relationships are parallel. This is the only tale of the last three in this book to take a positive male character as its central model, a fact that helps structurally to balance the negative examples.[52] Sara is so beautiful that she is sought after by many men, but each time she marries, a fiend comes and strangles the new husband on their wedding night. Eventually Tobias is taught how to school himself and his desires by the angel Raphael, and his control is rewarded with a successful consummation: 'For he his lust so goodly ladde, / That bothe lawe and kinde is served' (VII 5362–3). The choice of final tale shows a sophisticated adroitness; not only do its elements of self-control and wisdom reflect positively everything that has been said throughout this book and the rest of the poem, but the details of the story left unstressed make the point once more that God must be at the centre of all endeavours. Tobias listened to the angel's advice, and placed God at the heart of his new marriage by spending three days in prayer before he attempted to touch his wife, and for this abstinence and control he was rewarded.

Genius reminds Amans that though animals are only bound by the laws of nature, man is bound to reason as well. When these laws are in balance, all governance will be effective:

> Wherof a king himself mai taste,
> Hou trewe, how large, hou jouste, hou chaste
> Him oghte of reson forto be,
> Forth with the vertu of Pite,
> Thurgh which he mai gret thonk deserve
> Toward his godd, that he preserve
> Him and his poeple in alle welthe
> Of pes, richesse, honour and helthe
> Hier in this world and elles eke. (VII 5389–97)

These lines echo almost exactly those at the start of Book VII, when Genius discusses the relationship of man's soul to God and reason (VII 511–20). The difference here is the change from man to king as subject. Genius' reworking of Aristotle's tutelage of King Alexander successfully encompasses a treatment of both humanity in general and kings in especial, and the structure of this book, with the carefully engineered movement from one to the other, shows Gower's own scholarly and rational control of material. Gower takes this teaching provocatively further by showing that knowledge can be acquired

---

[51] Tobias 3–6.
[52] Olsson 212.

through natural observation, as well as from sacred texts, and that it is open for discussion by the laity, by poets such as himself. In the story of Lycurgus Gower showed that even pagan kings may receive help from God. It was a well-known point of speculative theology, and one important to both Langland and Chaucer, that God did not confine his grace to what He had promised to Christians in the New Testament.

This seventh book has taken Amans on a tour of virtues that can create an ideal world; there is a great deal of material that the lover can digest as relevant, even while a large proportion of it is aimed directly at a more royal listener in the hope that its exempla may foster the qualities that are necessary for good rule. The kings in the exempla are described in terms that would be familiar to medieval audiences, with references to knighthood and feats of arms. The poet

> has no respect for antiquity nor for the rich resonance of its allusiveness, and no hesitation at all in re-embodying its narratives in the social and moral contexts he understands.[53]

This makes Gower's stories of kings more relevant to his own age, and comparisons become more effective criticisms while still maintaining some security of distance. Gower's adaptations comment on current political situations, but 'only with considerable caution and some ambivalence'.[54]

Gower ends Book VII with a courteous but almost plaintive comment from Amans: he says that 'The tales sounen in myn Ere, / Bot yit my herte is elleswhere' (VII 5410–11). Love is the only topic Amans wants to hear about, and he reminds Genius of his role as confessor and counsellor: 'Lef al and speke of my matiere' (VII 5422). The natural stress on the 'my' of this line shows Gower's appreciation of comic effect, for the demand, be it never so politely arranged, is clear. Amans feels that there has been too much digression, and this ironically shows how far he still has to go before he can show himself to be in control of his desires, despite all Genius' efforts. There is a wry humour, too, in remembering the reasons Genius gave Amans for embarking on this programme of study at the beginning of this book. Far from being happier or wiser, Amans seems impatient and deaf to the value of Genius' lessons. Time has indeed passed, but Amans at this point thinks it is time wasted on topics, because he does not see their value. We remember that Book VII began with a exposition of time, and that it operates on three levels. Amans is still stuck in human time, but that of the soul, and beyond that the eternal timelessness of God, are working their effects. This book is a timely digression, necessary for Amans to grow in knowledge. This 'perdurable lyves foode' (VII 520) will aid him towards greater self-governance whether he knows it or not. Gower is, as creator of this poem, aware of this; his alter ego Amans represents man's limitations in learning how to live in a frustrating and unpredictable world.

Gower uses the framing device of the love-lorn man and his confessor to

---

[53] Derek Pearsall, 'Gower's Narrative Art', in *Gower's* Confessio Amantis: *A Critical Anthology*, ed. Peter Nicholson (Cambridge, 1991) 77.
[54] Watt (2003) 126.

show the strength of human desires, and there is a gentle self-mockery in his portrayal of Amans's wish to move on from all that has been said in this book. This distances the reader from the subject material, and carefully buffers the poet from any real kings who might pursue his work. Amans's presence in the poem allows the seriousness of the instructions to kings to stand strikingly alone in a way that they otherwise would not. James Simpson has noted this effective technique, too:

> Gower, it could be suggested, chooses a cunning model of the king in choosing Amans, since he can readily escape from any charge of criticising the king by claiming that Amans is a pathetically nugatory, comic figure, and is in any case John Gower, not the king at all. But I think this argument stops short of appreciating the subtlety of Gower's political position in the *Confessio*: for Gower the king's self is inextricably bound up with the selves of his subjects.[55]

He is a necessary cipher here: a cipher whose true identity can be revealed only in the final chapter of Gower's great poem.

The sense of possible audiences, both royal and not, is one Gower handles with circumspect dexterity: 'He, like Chaucer, was a poetic strategist.'[56] Just as Chaucer uses the dream narrative as a protective method in his work, Gower tailors his thoughts by using the love-quest of Amans as his cover. Gower's audiences must be linked, always, just as he argues a king and his subjects are always joined by their actions.

In learning together, readers will finally understand Gower's vision of the ideal state:

> The resolution will grow out of one last argument on learning to see well. By explaining the blindness of cupidity Genius hopes to open Amans' cupidinous eyes. Only then might there be hope of regaining his proper kingship and a passage home.[57]

King, reader, Amans, poet: they must all learn to 'see well' if the *Confessio* is to succeed.

It is fitting that chastity should form the final argument of the *Confessio*, because it binds lover and king into one receptive audience. Amans listens because he wishes to become a better lover, and win his lady, and being a better lover, understanding how this is backed by principles of truth, justice, generosity and chastity, will help a king to realise his potential to rule with wisdom and self-discipline. The love at the heart of Gower's work is far more than the conventional courtly love between a knight and his lady. The *Confesssio* 'employs the language of courtesy or of erotic petition in order to explore the much more dangerous subject of power – individual, communal, and regal'.[58]

---

[55] James Simpson, *Sciences and the Self in Medieval Poetry: Allan of Lille's* Anticlaudianus *and John Gower's* Confessio Amantis (Cambridge, 1995) 281.
[56] R. F. Yeager, *John Gower's Poetic: The Search for a New Arion* (Cambridge, 1990) 8.
[57] Peck (1978) 159.
[58] Staley (2005) 2.

Love, infused with and motivated by Christian teachings, urges a recognition and inclusion of the wider community in all actions. It is a socially responsible inspiration which, Gower believes, will produce a peaceful and secure kingdom. Book VIII aims to create a literary space where this idea can at last be fully realised.

Gower's achievement in the *Confessio* is to make the issue of kingship relevant to every estate; to bring the debate through discourses of courtly love and transform the Mirrors for Princes available to him into a poem whose huge scope encompasses every aspect of governance. Statistically, his concern with kingship can be proved by noting that of the 141 stories in the poem, ninety-eight of them are about kings.[59] His material is variously worked through literary vehicles such as the dream vision, the confession, the schema of the seven deadly sins, and the exempla provided by the compilatio. That, I hope, has earned Gower the right to appear first in this study. Of all four major Ricardian poets, his work is the most consistently concerned with the nature of kingship, and much the most outspoken about the need for reform of matters that kings are involved in.

---

[59] See Fisher 188 for a tabular breakdown of this fact.

2

Langland: *Piers Plowman*

Although very little is known about William Langland, the fifty-two manuscripts that survive of *Piers Plowman* suggest that it was one of the most widely read poems of its time. These manuscripts represent at least three, and arguably four, separate versions of the poem, each with its own identity, which have been respectively designated as the A, B, C and Z texts. The B text will be the one used here, as it is the most complete: it is also the base text of A. V. C. Schmidt's accessible edition of the poem.[1] The B text has been dated to between 1377 and 1379, which makes it perhaps the earliest of the works under discussion here, although the C text has been dated to the late 1380s, making it evident that Langland continued to revise his poem in the light of maturing years and changing experience.

Langland was probably a cleric, born in the Malvern area of Worcestershire circa 1330; he married and went to London, where he lived until returning to Malvern in later life. He may have died about 1387, based on evidence gained from the poem's contemporary references. The care with which the different manuscripts are copied suggests that they were reproduced in London. They also show a high regard for the integrity of Langland's text, a rare occurrence in the transmission of medieval works from this period, which in turn implies that the poet occupied a more mainstream place in Ricardian poetry than has previously been claimed, a place that justifies his status as a poet whose work has never disappeared from the literary scene.[2]

Piers Plowman is a dream-vision poem, a poetic vehicle used extensively by all four of the Ricardian poets, and as such it shares certain similarities with those other works. However, Langland differs from Gower in that kingship is not one of his main concerns, although his work does engage with issues relevant to it, as we shall see. The poem contains eight main visions divided into a prologue and twenty passus. The first two visions are called the 'Visio' and the others the 'Vita': the Visio describes the vision of Piers Plowman, while the Vita looks at the life of Do Well, Do Better and Do Best. I have used this division in order to examine the poem's references to kingship.

---

[1] William Langland, *The Vision of Piers Plowman*, ed. A. V. C. Schmidt, 2nd edn (London, 1995).
[2] See Simon Horobin, "'In London and in Opelond": The Dialect and Circulation of the C version of *Piers Plowman*', *Medium Aevum* 74 (2005) 248–69.

The Visio

Vision One: Passus I–IV

The Dreamer falls asleep and dreams of 'a fair feeld ful of folk' (Pro 17). This field is the antithesis of Chaucer's Tabard Inn, for Langland's depiction of the three basic orders of society emphasises the moralising potential that lies in the gathering that Chaucer seems rather, by his choice of place, to minimise.[3] The first reference to kingship occurs in line 92 of the Prologue, when Langland gives a description of the clergy, who make an improper profit out of working on the king's behalf: 'Somme serven the King and his silver tellen.' They chase up debts owed to the crown from guardianship cases, wardships, and from lost property and strayed beasts, and are permitted to act as stewards in manor houses. They are so concerned with serving mammon that their religious duties are 'doone undevoutliche' and the Dreamer comments 'drede is at the laste / Lest Christ in his consistorie acorse ful manye' (Pro 98–9).

This criticism of the clergy focuses on their obsession with worldly profit, a dangerous practice that undermines the vital nature of their true calling, to help keep the nation spiritually healthy. That Langland begins his satirical portrait of fourteenth-century society with the religious orders gives an early indication of where the centre of his thoughts lies; the clergy are not behaving as they should, because, as the instances of the verb 'to serve' in this passage shows, the clergy are serving the wrong master. The Dreamer explains that they have moved far away from the love that St Peter bequeathed through the four cardinal virtues of Prudence, Temperance, Justice and Fortitude; these form gates to the heavenly kingdom above: only those who possess and practise these virtues may pass through to their reward. However, temporal power now lies with the cardinals of Rome, who have forgotten what those virtues mean. These men have the power to elect the pope, God's representative on earth, and although there is a tension about the assertion that the Dreamer does not wish to find fault with the cardinals, the horror of the idea they might be corrupt makes him question the validity of everything else in society: 'For in love and lettrure the eleccion belongeth; / Forthy I kan and kan naught of court speke moore' (Pro 110–11). He must, in accordance with those virtues, speak out, and yet because the authority they are based on is suspect, that seems to be impossible. This self-deprecating, yet successfully derogatory treatment of a 'court' slides easily into the succeeding description and treatment of the king.

The Dreamer turns back to the secular court, looking to the king for reassurance. 'Thanne kam ther a Kyng: Knyghthod hym ladde; / Might of the communes made him to regne' (Pro 113–14). This is a more hopeful image, showing a ruler who is preceded by the representative positive associations of knightly or courtly conduct. There is no direct criticism of the king, either as an individual, Richard II, or as a representative monarch. It would be simplistic to

---

[3] James Simpson, *Piers Plowman: An Introduction to the B-text* (London, 1990) 21.

suggest that this silence was because of fear of retribution. The whole structure of Langland's poem proposes that political problems are symptoms of a deeper malaise that needs a cure at its own level. At this point in the poem, the solution seems to be very much centred on the moral and spiritual integrity necessary for successful government.

By switching the emphasis of leadership from the church to the monarch in this way, Langland's visionary illuminations gain a sharper edge. This brings out the qualities necessary to maintain a successful harmony within a kingdom; Kind Wit comes with the king, and is highlighted as vital 'For to counseillen the Kyng and the Commune save' (Pro 115). This figure, representing the power of individuals to establish a civilised way of life, teaches and encourages people to learn crafts and skills, which results in their being able to live and support each other, in a system of 'lawe and leaute – ech lif to knowe his owene' (Pro 122). There may be a reference here to Ecclesiastes 5. 8–9, which sets out this ordered hierarchical system quite clearly. This triumvirate balance of king, commons and Kind Wit would seem, then, to stand in the Prologue as a pattern for success, and yet the following passage immediately challenges this idea.

A lunatic kneels before the king praising his just rule, and praying that he will be rewarded in Heaven for being such a fair monarch. He is described as speaking 'clergially' (Pro 124) and this small adjectival addition indicates that appearances are not what they seem. A lunatic, a madman, who talks as a clerk should is an oddity, even a paradox. It may signal, too, that what he says may not be implicitly trusted:

> 'Crist kepe thee, sire Kyng, and thi kyngryche,
> And lene thee lede thi lond so leaute thee lovye,
> And for thi rightful rulyng be rewarded in hevene!' (Pro 125–8)

However, the 'clergially' could also indicate a rationality that is wrongly perceived as madness, for these words are a summary of St Thomas Aquinas' discussion of the proper rewards of kingship, and the fable that follows also concludes with the same ideas as the *De Regimine*, pointing to a measured parallel between them.[4] The licence allowed to the clergy to address the king as 'thou' could also be used here to emphasise the earnestness of the attempt to advise the monarch.[5] An angel descends, as if prompted by the lunatic's prayer, and addresses the king, in Latin this time, 'for lewed men ne koude / Jangle ne jugge that justifie hem sholde, / But suffren and serven' (Pro 129–31). The angel's words, which are anonymous verses from an early fourteenth-century sermon, warn the king that all things are mutable, and that he must look to tomorrow for the reward he deserves. The angel reminds the king that his rule must be fair and godly, too:

---

[4] See P. M. Kean, 'Love, Law and *Lewte* in *Piers Plowman*', *Review of English Studies* 15 (1964) 241–61.
[5] For further discussion on this point, see David Burnley, 'Langland's "Clergial" Lunatic', in *Langland, the Mystics and the Medieval English Religious Tradition: Essays in Honour of S. S. Hussey*, ed. Helen Phillips (Cambridge, 1990) 31–8, and Helen Barr, *Signs and Sothe: Language in the Piers Plowman Tradition* (Cambridge, 1994) 29.

'Iustus es, esto pius!' (Pro 134). The king is a divine instrument, and his rule must try to emulate God's. This emphatically spiritual aspect of kingship and its responsibilities is linked by the angel to Matt. 7.1–2, 'Qualia vis metere, talia grana sere' (Pro 136); there is a foreboding within the severity of the angel's tone that undercuts the warmth of the lunatic's earlier praise. This creates a bleak picture of the separateness of the king, of his weighty duty to God, and the necessity for scrupulous administration this demands.

The angel's lofty admonitions are interrupted by a rough 'goliardeis, a gloton of wordes' (Pro 139), who reacts angrily to the angel; he responds, in Latin, that as the verb 'to rule' comes from the word 'king', whoever scorns the law lacks rule and should be not be called a ruler. He seems to be saying that the king has no choice but to administer the law to the letter, or risk losing the respect of his kingdom for being illicit. The emphasis here is on the precedence of the civil laws, and their manipulation; the goliard becomes angry because the angel seems to dismiss the importance of civil law, concentrating only on the spiritual responsibilities the king has, not his earthly ones.

The commons then speak out, crying 'Percepta regis sunt nobis vincula legis!' (Pro 145). Their view is that everything the king says has for them the force of law behind it; their perspective allows only this, and they are bound by fear or the confines of their society to react to this belief. To attempt to challenge this would be futile and foolhardy. To illustrate this more succinctly, Langland then tells the fable of the cat and the rats to show a darker and more cynical view of the nature of kingship.

This exemplum, a traditional folk tale, was used in a sermon by Bishop Brinton in 1376, but although topical allusions are very tempting, it is more important to see it as concerned 'not merely (with) topical politics but the perennial issue of power in this world and the perennial need for a central authority to maintain social order'.[6] The fable tells how a group of mice and rats get together to complain about a cat who has been terrorising them. They form a plan to put a bell on it so they can be warned of its presence, but no one is brave enough to volunteer to put on the collar. One mouse speaks up and says that it would be better to leave the cat alone, because 'the while he caccheth conynges he coveiteth noght oure caroyne' (Pro 189).

The mouse wisely understands that all the while the cat has the freedom to do as it pleases, it is always going to hunt for something more satisfying than mere rodents' meat. In addition, if there were no cat, the mouse points out, the balance of order would be disrupted and the added independence that the mice and rats would have would mean trouble: 'For hadde ye rattes youre wille, ye kouthe noght rule yourselve' (Pro 201). The mouse also describes how the possibility of the cat being succeeded by a kitten would also mean life would take a turn for the worse: 'That witnesseth Holy Writ, whoso wole it rede: / Ve terre ubi puer est rex!' (Pro 195–6).

This reference to Ecclesiastes 10.16 is perhaps the clearest reference to politics

---

[6] Schmidt, introduction, *The Vision of Piers Plowman*, xxxix.

of the 1370s if the boy-king Richard II is seen as the kitten, who is manipulated by his advisers after the death of Edward III. It is an outspoken idea: sermons on the accession of Richard in 1377 chose Isaiah 11.6 ('and a little child shall lead them') as their Biblical text instead. Langland offers a more sobering reflection on the suitability of a young monarch for a nation. The dream allows the poet to avoid responsibility for any implied criticisms, however: he parenthetically steps back from the tale '(What this metels bymeneth, ye men that ben murye, / Devyne ye, for I ne dar, by deere God in hevene!)' (Pro 209–10). The wry tone belies the Dreamer's assertion that he 'dare not' try and work out the interpretations of his vision. This is a device that both Gower and Chaucer use as well, to even greater effect.

The lawyers are then described, paralleling the criticisms of the clergy earlier on: they 'noght for love of Oure Lord unlose hire lippes once' (Pro 214). Myra Stokes points out that

> the clergy are selling God's law, as the 'clerkis of mannes law' are selling that of the human King. When justice itself is for sale, divine and secular, what hope of a just society, spiritually or politically?[7]

The legalistic language consolidates the authority of these two kinds of power, and the material additional to the A Text, entered in the B Text (Pro 87–211) emphasises rather than obscures the significance of the two laws they represent.[8] The king is portrayed as a victim to such corrupt practices, which does not suggest a ruler in control of his subjects, but rather one whose clergy and lawyers exploit his power in his name; they become the focus, marginalising his authority as they appropriate it for themselves.

By the end of the Prologue, Langland has presented us with ideas of kingship that embrace the godly and the secular, the political and the sociologically practical. He realised that both orthodox men of affairs and reformers would find *Piers Plowman* a powerful idiom for thought about the contemporary community but deliberately avoided stability and closure to give it a 'wholly ad hoc authority' of its own.[9] This constant shifting, consistent with the dream vehicle of the poem's structure, is particularly effective at layering concepts. Langland's 'essential principle' is his

> application to spiritual matters of the rules he derives from his pre-occupation with law and justice in the secular world. He trusts his sense of justice and equity, and does not seek to transcend the kind of observance of it he realises to be essential in a well governed and equitable state on earth.[10]

He uses diverse threads to pull the debate together, and the powerful opinion that survives at the finish is that of the vital importance of order. Without structure,

---

[7] Stokes 62.
[8] Stokes 63.
[9] Anne Middleton, 'The Audience and Public of *Piers Plowman*', in *Middle English Alliterative Poetry and its Literary Background: Seven Essays*, ed. David Lawton (Cambridge, 1982) 123.
[10] Stokes 60.

without each person's clear sense of purpose within a well-ordered scheme, Langland warns of injustice and – by clear implication – misrule. The monarch's task is to exemplify and to maintain this order, and Langland's frequent references to kingship assert the fundamental importance of this role.

In Passus I, the ideas of kingship presented in the Prologue are explored through the theme of Truth. The Dreamer watches a Lady come down from the castle, and he challenges her to tell him the meaning of the things he has seen so far. Her answer unfolds a pattern for living that is to remain central to the poem from this point forwards. Above all, the Lady exhorts, 'rightfully Reson sholde rule your alle, / And Kynde Wit be wardeyn youre welthe to kepe' (i 54–5). She shows him the dungeon, where she says that Wrong lives, 'Fader of falshede' (i 64), who encouraged Judas to betray Christ, and Adam and Eve to sin. The Dreamer is struck with terror, and asks the Lady who she is. Her answer, that she is 'Holi Church' (i 75), fills the Dreamer with awe and a desire to know how he may better live his life. Holy Church maintains that Truth is the best way to live, as by it Man is most able to follow the example of Christ. The argument then turns back to the subject of kingship:

> Kynges and knythes sholde kepen it by reson –
> Riden and rappen doun in reaumes aboute,
> And taken *transgressores* and tyen hem faste
> Til treuthe ytermyned hire trespas to the ende. (i 94–7)

Truth's primary agents are stressed as being the monarchs and their knights. They are clearly essential earthly examples for the rest of the people to follow:

> For David in hise dayes dubbed knyghtes,
> And dide hem sweren on hir swerd to serven truthe ever.
> And that is the profession apertly that apendeth to knyghtes,
> And naught to fasten o Friday in fyve score wynter,
> But holden with hym and with here that wolden alle truthe,
> And never leve hem for love ne for laccynge of silver –
> And whoso passe(th) that point is apostata in the ordre. (i 98–104)

Leadership is not merely to be an example of pious perfection, fasting to show spiritual health and strength: no, Holy Church emphasises the duty of the knights to support and defend all those who choose to try the road of Truth. They are to be at the continual service of their charges, ensuring their way is as free as possible of impediments, and looking after their welfare, both physically and morally. This medieval idea of the duty of knights has its roots in much of the writings and thoughts of the period; Orderic Vitalis, for example, an historian from Saint-Evroul writing about 1123–37, shows an 'almost obsessive concern for order and the elusive goal of a more peaceful society'.[11] This manifests itself in an admiration of the skills of kings such as William I and Henry I as dukes of Normandy, who 'forbade disorders, murder and plunder, restraining

---

[11] Richard W. Kaeuper, *Chivalry and Violence in Medieval Europe* (Oxford, 1999) 13.

the people by arms and the arms by laws'.[12] Orderic is equally critical of rulers who were not able to demonstrate this strength, and states that 'a ruler at any level ... had to offer God the "fruit of justice" in order to escape the charge of barren governance'.[13]

The Middle Ages represent, to the historian, a time of change and struggle, when states fought to create and maintain stability. On a simple level, then, the idea of godly kings and knights is a crucial insight into how people of the time would have wanted to idealise their rulers. The role of knights was a vital one in the wider one of leadership and kingship:

> as they worried about the problem of the order in their developing civilisation, thoughtful medieval people argued that chivalry (reformed to their standards) was the great hope, even as they sensed that unreformed chivalry was somehow the great cause for fear.[14]

Chivalric biographies and handbooks, which were plentiful, formed the ideals of this chivalry, not surprisingly given the prestige that good knightly conduct offered.

Richard Barber draws attention to the thirteenth-century work of Raimon Llull, whose *Le libre del Orde de Cavelleria* details the way a knight can use his chivalry as 'part of the established pattern of Christian society'.[15] Llull's work emphasises the importance of the knight's religious life, stressing the vitality this gives to the relationship between God, the king and the people. The knight's example is a reflection both of his king's character and of the people's spirit; he should therefore aim always for nobility in his bearing and actions. In contrast to this, Geoffroi de Charny, writing in the 1350s, 'adopts an eminently practical approach to knighthood' in the *Livre de Chevalerie*.[16] He paints a realistic picture of the knightly life, and warns, for example, that a knight should be a proficient horseman before he try his hand in the tournaments. Barber puts Langland's portrayal of knights firmly in the idealistic camp; however, this may not be the whole truth. Langland's careful coupling of the king with the knight in their defence of Truth, his insistence that they fight actively for the very real social relief of the people, their stance active rather than passive, makes his portrayal of the knightly virtues tougher than that. Truth can also be seen as an important shield for Justice, that other pivotal ingredient in successful government discussed in the Prologue.

Langland's view is unequivocal: 'whoso passe(th) that point is apostata in the ordre' (i 104). As a king's instrument of just rule, a knight cannot afford to be tempted by either money or fondness for the wrongdoers, and his response must be both fair and effective. Then Holy Church reminds the Dreamer that Christ himself, 'kyngene kyng' (i 105) made ten orders of knights: cherubim and

---

[12] Kaeuper 14.
[13] Kaeuper 15.
[14] Kaeuper 29.
[15] Richard Barber, *The Knight and Chivalry* (London, 1970) 146.
[16] Barber 147.

seraphim, seven similar orders and one other, presumably the earthly one. The angel-knights were shown Truth and expected only 'to be buxom at his biddyng' (i 110). Lucifer and those angels that stood with him broke his bond of obedience, and for that were cast out 'into a deep derk helle to dwelle there for evere' (i 115). Holy Church warns that this fate, too, is reserved for all those who do wrong, 'And alle that werchen with wrong wende thei shulle' (i 128), linking this passage to the dungeon the Dreamer asked about earlier in the passus.

The rest of the passus, while not dealing directly with kingship, develops the debate about Truth, Holy Church urging that the Dreamer apply his energies into pursuing it so that he may learn more about God and his love. Indeed, Holy Church says, Truth is the lens through which God's love becomes visible, 'For Truthe telleth that love is triacle of hevene: / may no synne be on hym seene that that spice useth' (i 148–9). Love is the most precious and most valuable of the heavenly virtues, and

> Forthi is love ledere of the Lordes folk of hevene,
> And a meene, as the mair is, (inmiddes) the kyng and the commune;
> Right so is love a ledere and the lawe shapeth:
> Upon man for hise mysdedes the mercyment he taxeth. (i 159–62)

Without love, leadership is barren. Rulers who act with love act best with 'myghte', that is, the power of God, and can therefore strive more successfully for the harmonious workings of state. Christ is held up as the ultimate example: 'he was myghtful and meke, and mercy gan graunte / to hem that hengen hym heigh and his herte thirled' (i 174–5). This combination of power and humility is the template that earthly kings, as well as everyone else, should aspire to; Holy Church sternly reminds the Dreamer that he will be judged in Heaven as he has judged on earth, and refers him to St James's assertion that faith without works is dead (Jas 2.26). The allegorical figure of Holy Church, that 'lovely lady in leere in lynnen yclothed' (i 3) herself of authoritative status, leads the Dreamer from his pictorial landscape of tower (Truth) and dungeon (Wrong) to an image of Love as 'the graithe gate that goth into hevene' (i 205). Without knowledge of Truth, Love cannot be fully understood. The Dreamer is left dazzled by this teaching, and the compelling persuasions of Holy Church evoke awe and fear. She 'uses the homiletic, didactic style we might expect of the authority figure in an *oraculum*';[17] Langland's use of this allows the weighty arguments to convince with the strength of the formality of the address, and the final benediction 'now loke thee Oure Lord!' (i 207) reverberates as a fitting end to the piece.

In the first two sections of *Piers Plowman* there are contrasts which, it has been argued, fall between 'literal and allegorical statements, almost between a practical and an idealistic way of looking at the world'.[18] The issues of Justice and of Truth, bound under the enfolding 'plante of pees' (i 152), Love, seem to be anchored more securely in the allegorical world of Holy Church, who,

---

[17] Simpson (1990) 25.
[18] Priscilla Jenkins, 'Conscience: The Frustration of Allegory', in *Piers Plowman: Critical Approaches*, ed. S. S. Hussey (London, 1969) 127.

perhaps 'possessing the finest perception and the most informed judgement' appears to function to 'correct the literal'.[19] However, as the succeeding passus show, this is far from being an assured assumption.

When the Dreamer begs Holy Church to show him how he can recognise what is false, Holy Church tells him about Mede, a character who has many carefully developed associations. MED defines 'mede' as either (a) a gift; noble or royal endowment, (b) a material reward; compensation (for work or services); wages, earnings, salary, or (c) a fee; ransom; reparation; the payment of a fee, a bribe; also bribery, graft.[20] Holy Church's initial description of Mede, that she 'ylakked my leman that Leautee is hoten' (ii 21), sets the tone for the rest of her description:

> In the Popes paleis she is pryvee as myselve,
> But Soothnesse wolde noght so – for she is a bastard
> For Fals was hir fader that hath a fikel tonge
> And nevere sooth seide sithen he com to erthe;
> And Mede is manered after hym, right as kynde asketh:
> *Qualis pater, talis filius. Bona arbor bonum fructum facit.* (ii 23–8)

Mede is corrupt and a corrupting influence on those around her; as the daughter of False she has inherited his deceitfulness and mendacity. Holy Church scorns her, and warns the Dreamer that anyone tempted to accept Mede will 'lese for hire love a lappe of *Caritatis*' (ii 35). She quotes Psalm 14, reminding the Dreamer that the just man is praised and the man who commits usury and accepts bribes is condemned. Our first appreciation of Mede, then, is that she is dangerous, untrustworthy and full of guile. Of the three definitions given earlier, the third group of illicit rewards clearly fits her best.

The allegorical vision of Lady Mede and her followers provides a sensual contrast to the austere purity of the Lady Holy Church. Myra Stokes says that this alludes to 'the contrast in Revelation between the whore of Babylon [...] and the bride of the Lamb "arrayed in fine linen, clean and white" (Rev.17:4, 19:8)'.[21] Indeed, the richness of Mede's attire, 'The Kyng hath non bettre', fills the Dreamer with wonder as he looks at her, 'wonderliche yclothed – / Purfiled with pelure, the pureste on erthe, / Ycorouned with a coroune' (ii 8–10). Mede's attire is so rich and luxurious that it stuns the Dreamer's senses; she wears red rubies, gold wire, diamonds and blue sapphires set against a robe of scarlet. He learns that although Holy Church's father is God Himself, Mede still holds a higher place on earth than she does. Holy Church will be wed to Mercy, but Mede is to be married to False Fickle Tongue, a 'fendes biyete' (ii 41). Holy Church tells the Dreamer that he will discover all he needs to know about Mede

---

[19] Jenkins 127.
[20] A recent essay has stressed that Langland's Meed is not a depiction of mere pecuniary reward, but an image of all kinds of materials that can be used as incitements and bribes: J. A. Burrow, 'Lady Meed and the Power of Money', *Medium Aevum* 74 (2005) 113–18.
[21] Stokes 99.

at the wedding, and then, praying that he will not succumb to Mede's temptations, she leaves him.

The Dreamer then dreams about the wedding and the attendant guests that arrive to witness it. He notes that 'Symonie and Cyvylle and sisours of courtes / were moost pryvee with Mede of any men' (ii 63–4). The Seven Deadly Sins are bestowed upon the happy couple, in exchange for which they agree to sign their souls away to Satan after a year has passed.

Mede's marriage to False 'implies a fixed semantic relationship'.[22] However, this stability is soon to shift dramatically. Theology grows angry when he hears what has happened, and rebukes Civil Law, saying that Mede was intended for a more honourable match, to Truth. His argument is that far from being illegitimate, Mede is 'muliere, a maiden of goode' (ii 132) and her lineage is good enough for her to 'kisse the Kyng for cosyn and she wolde' (ii 133). False Fickle Tongue is faithless, and unworthy of her; Theology tells the deceivers to take her to London, where they must be careful of Truth and Conscience, who would be very angry if they found out what had taken place. Civil Law agrees to do this, but Simony will not consent until he receives money.

The money is found and distributed among the notaries, enough gold is given to False Fickle Tongue so that he can easily dominate Mede should the need arise, and the whole group of them set off for the capital. However, Truth overtakes them and reaches the king before they do. The king is outraged at the news and commands that the band be arrested and Mede brought to him, but Drede (Judgement) hears what the king said, and warns False Fickle Tongue to flee. They all disappear, apart from Mede, who 'ac trewely to telle, she trembled for fere, / And ek wepte and wrang whan she was attached' (ii 236–7).

Although this passus offers no substantial comment on kingship, it contains the beginnings of a scheme that has been described as 'the only complete dramatic sequence in *Piers Plowman* which centres on the theme of government'.[23] In the character of Mede, Langland creates a manifestation of many possible, and often confusing and conflicting ideas, which are to influence perceptions of principles as the rest of the poem progresses; she is

> not merely 'wealth'; not merely 'the power of the purse', and not, in fact, 'cupidity' though she must always call cupidity into being: she is the reward of a life directed to the wrong end.[24]

Mede is brought before the king, and is treated well; the law lords and the clergy offer her their support, and the learned men and a confessor also come forward with aid. Her reception indicates that whatever she is accused of, her status is that of a noblewoman of considerable influence. Her confession, however, shows that her rank and influence are deceptive: beneath them she is 'shamelees' (iii 44). Her bargain with the confessor to look leniently on lust as a sin in exchange for a new glass window for his church is parenthetically

---

[22] Simpson (1990) 44.
[23] Anna P. Baldwin, *The Theme of Government in Piers Plowman* (Cambridge, 1981) 24.
[24] Kean (1964) 250.

condemned by the narrator: 'Forthi I lere yow lordes, leveth swiche werkes – / To writen in wyndowes of youre wel dedes / Or to greden after Goddes men whan ye [gyve] doles, / On aventure ye have youre hire here and youre hevene alse' (iii 69–72).

The entrance of the mayors, whose execution of their office as intermediaries between the king and the common people in matters of law is exposed as corrupt, and their collusion with Mede's philosophy of accepting any bribes that come their way, allows for a comment on kingship that prepares the way for the king's treatment of Mede and Conscience. Solomon's warning that '*Ignis devorabit tabernacula eorum qui libenter accipiunt munera*' (iii 96), reinforced by the description of him as a wise ruler, is a reminder of the ideals that the king of the poem should try and uphold. It is soon clear that this king is no Solomon. Conscience initially does obeisance, but when the king asks him if he will marry Mede, he is outraged and refuses immediately. Indeed, so violent is his response that the energy of the language is in startling contrast with the preceding passages of reflection: '"Crist it me forbede! / Er I wedde swich a wif, wo me bitide!"' (iii 121).

In his denunciation, references to the historical events of the fourteenth century are woven in. For example, Conscience tells the king that it is Mede's fault that his father was brought down from his throne. This could fit with a portrayal of the fate of Edward II, who was murdered, or more likely, as has been suggested by scholars, the Black Prince, whose recovery of the throne for Peter of Castile backfired when the king would not pay him the money he had promised for his support.[25] As Edward III was the king when Langland wrote these lines, that seems to be the best explanation. Just as the fable of the belling of the cat illustrated earlier, Langland's possible contemporary references make the poem a carefully objective commentary on the perils and duties of leadership; this could be about any king, or a specific one.

Conscience damns Mede for many evils: she is responsible for corrupting popes and diminishing the work of the church, and she aids criminals to escape the law, while making innocent men suffer out of spite. She feels no guilt for what she does, because she can buy herself out of any opposition. She is a threat to the whole system of government, both spiritual and temporal: 'Ther she is wel with the kyng, wo is the reaume' (iii 153). On a literal level this indictment is plain, but it may have a more historical undertone too. It has been suggested that Langland is referring to Alice Perrers, mistress of Edward III, who has often been blamed for the weakness of Edward's rule.[26] Conscience also specifically refers to Mede's use of settlement days, a fourteenth-century form of administration that took place in the informal surroundings of the manor house, rather than in the courtroom. It bought with it obvious opportunities for the use of bribes and payoffs, which are condemned here because they harm the poor and honest, who cannot compete with such measures. Mede's hold on the rich is so

---

[25] Schmidt: notes in his edition of *The Vision of Piers Plowman*, 419.
[26] Anna P. Baldwin, 'The Historical Context', in *A Companion to Piers Plowman*, ed. John A. Alford (Berkeley, 1988) 80.

total, Conscience stresses, that the poor have no way even of protesting, and for that he curses her: 'now Lord yyve hire sorwe, / And alle that maynteneth hire men, meschaunce hem bitide!' (iii 166–7).

Mede's response is equally emotional. She cries out in protest to the king and demands to be allowed to defend herself, a right the king grants readily. However, his distancing from her at this point is clear: 'I kan namoore seggen' (iii 173), and he warns her that the charges of Conscience put her in danger of extremely severe punishment. Mede is not cowed by this and furiously counters Conscience's attack, arguing that she is indispensable to life in all its permutations. She accuses Conscience first of hypocrisy reminding him of his own redress to her services in the past. She points out defiantly that she never killed a king, or gave support to the murder of one, an allusion perhaps to the murder of Edward II following his forced abdication in 1327. Moreover, Mede says, 'In Normandie was he noght noyed for my sake – / Ac thow thiself, soothly, shamedest hym ofte' (iii 189–90). Edward III's campaign for the throne of France in Normandy in 1360 was abandoned at the Treaty of Brétigny for Aquitaine and three million crowns. Mede accuses Conscience of being too cowardly to sit out the severe weather of the time and the hardships of war, losing for England wealth that could have come back had Edward stuck to his claim. It was Conscience, Mede insists, who made robbers of the soldiers, while she remained loyally behind with the king and brought him cheer and courage: 'I batred hem on the bak and boldede hire hertes, / And dide hem hoppe for hope to have me at wille' (iii 199–200). She boasts that had she been commander of the army, then the king would have had the whole of France. Her argument is, in fact, that she is vital to good government:

> It bicometh to a kyng that kepeth a reaume
> To yeve [men mede] that mekely hym serveth –
> To alies and to alle men, to honouren hem with yiftes;
> Mede maketh hym biloved and for a man holden.
> Emperours and erles and ale manere lordes
> Thorugh yiftes han yomen to yerne and to ryde. (iii 209–14)

A king is not a king unless he is seen to be powerful and rich, she says; all men of consequence keep retainers, so how much more so should the monarch? Mede is the very basis on which society functions, she argues, for don't all men get paid for doing their jobs effectively?

The king seems swayed by Mede's eloquence, and turns to Conscience to say that 'Mede is worthi the maistrie to have' (iii 229), but Conscience is unimpressed. He points out that there are two forms of meed, as set out by God: one the kind that you receive from God for living a good and just life, and another, earthly variety that stems simply from greed. He punctures Mede's assertion that meed is just another name for a wage by emphasising the difference in the two terms, and likewise differentiates between ordinary buying and selling and the nefarious acts of bribery and coercion. Having undercut all that Mede had to say, Conscience then invokes Scripture to prophesy a future without corruption. By using the story of Saul, who forfeited his life because he could not resist the temptation of wealth, defying the Lord's instructions to burn all of King Agag's land, Conscience sternly corrects Mede's version of the events of Normandy. Without the strategic retreat and compromise, Edward would have suffered far greater losses. Conscience anticipates a time when 'Shal na moore Mede be maister as she is nouthe' (iii 290) and when all the virtues will rule together, 'And oon Cristene kyng kepen [us] echone' (iii 289).

In this time, Conscience asserts, there will be no authority: 'Shal neither kyng ne knyght, constable ne meire / Over[carke] the commune ne to the court sompne' (iii 315–16) and there will be one single court with one judge for all. This vision is a daring and radical one, even if it is couched in a Biblical framework. The implication seems to be that the people will not be ruled by anyone, but there will still be peace and justice. The path to this Utopian existence is not to be smooth, however. Before this can happen, there will be a series of apocalyptic events and omens, and 'Makometh and Mede myshappe shul that tyme' (iii 329).

This is more than the incensed Mede can bear: 'Also wroth as the wynd weex Mede in a while' (iii 331). She has another try at besting Conscience, by quoting the Bible back at him, but she quotes only part of her chosen verse from Proverbs, and thus leaves herself open to a swift riposte from her adversary, who concludes the passus by revealing that Mede's show of learning only proves how treacherous her practice is. Her ignorance and bluster are in the end easily dealt with by Conscience's calm convictions.

In terms of kingship, this passus does have much to offer: in the debate between Conscience and Mede we see a struggle to reconcile practices of weakened responsibility and thus lax rule, with those of a notion of leadership set out powerfully in the Bible. The king in this passus is more than just a notional one; Langland's use of allusion to historical events makes it also an insight into the ideas of the period. The king as Judge, as Mediator, as Commander, as Protector: these roles are presented through the arguments, embellished by anecdote and underlined by Scripture. For twenty-first-century readers, there is a great deal to unravel. The vision of the leaderless future is in some ways reminiscent of the fable of the mice and the cat in the Prologue: there the idea seemed to be that the people would be happiest if they could just remain out of reach of the ruler's unpredictable might, and here it appears to have been taken a step further, suggesting that the people would be better off with no ruler at all.

The first vision is completed with the king's exploration of how to settle the dispute. He calls for Reason to be brought to the court, and Conscience goes to find him. Reason is accompanied by Worldly Knowledge and Intelligence, who hope that they can pay him to help them extricate themselves from a legal predicament. Conscience warns Reason that they are only motivated by Greed, and urges him to leave them behind. On reaching the king, Reason is seated between the monarch and the Prince. His central position emphasises the importance of his role in the governing of the kingdom.

However, our expectations of seeing Mede brought in again are thwarted by the entrance of Peace, accusing Wrong of all sorts of misdeeds and complaining that he is too frightened of Wrong's thuggish henchmen to try and stop him.

The king realises that Peace speaks the truth, and Wrong, becoming uneasy at how black things look for him, turns to Worldly Knowledge and Intelligence for help. They advise him to keep a low profile and ask Mede to help smooth things over, because 'Whoso wercheth by wille, wrathe maketh ofte. / I seye it by thyself – thow shalt it wel fynde' (iv 70–1). The king's reactions are most under scrutiny, however. As Worldly Knowledge and Intelligence sue for a cash settlement, the king remains firm: 'The Kyng swor by Crist and by his crowne bothe / That Wrong for hise werkes sholde wo tholie' (iv 83–4). His integrity is tested further by the intervention of Mede herself, who goes to Peace and offers him gold as compensation for the actions of Wrong. Peace is prepared to accept this, and says so to the king, but the monarch is unmoved: Wrong must pay for what he has done, but in a way that will make him suffer. Still another tack is tried: Reason is approached to see if he will help soften the king's judgement, but he too is adamant that Wrong must be punished. In Reason's speech (iv 113–47) the tenets of the ideal state are set out. Reason will not have pity until all the corruption is swept away, until all the greed is expunged and the ways of Mede put aside forever:

> 'I seye it by myself,' quod he, 'and it so were
> That I were kyng with coroune to kepen a reaume,
> Sholde nevere Wrong in this world that I wite myghte
> Ben unpunysshed in my power, for peril of my soule,
> Ne gete my grace thorugh giftes, so me God save!
> For Nullum malum the man mette with inpunitum
> And bad Nullum bonum be irremuneratum.' (iv 137–43)

The authority with which he speaks, and the vehemence of the tone, make this a powerful indictment of the king's first steps to reject the influence of Mede. In strengthening the king's actions, Reason affirms the desirability of this tough but cleansing moral crusade.

In Langland, however, nothing is ever that sure for long. At the conclusion of this speech, we are offered a vignette of the lawyers shifting across to Mede's side, while Worldly Wise tells her that 'Madame, I am our man, what so my mouth jangleth; / I falle in florins ... and faile speche ofte' (iv 155–6). This clearly shows how unrealistic this vision is. It will be undermined by the nature of man, which Langland continually reminds us, is irredeemably flawed. There is hope; the honest people agree with Reason's words, and it is noteworthy that Langland's often surprisingly unbiased perception includes 'manye of the grete' (iv 159) in that description. Langland's ideas of leadership do not overlook the complexities of the society that they seek to reform; rather, in this poem, he constantly explores these problems, insisting that this labour is, perhaps, the best way of achieving the fairest means of government.

Mede looks wretched at this routing, and her power is obviously diminished, even if not entirely dissipated. The passus concludes with the king's anger at the Law, which he blames for accepting Mede's influence for so long, and his oath that he will not allow the absence of Justice to continue. Conscience warns the king of the difficulties that lie ahead: that without the wholehearted support of the commons, such a pure path will be 'ful hard' to keep to. Reason strongly commits his support to the king's plan, which enables the monarch to speak with energetic conviction that his oath will be kept, while Reason is on his side. Reason again pledges his complete allegiance, 'so Conscience be of oure counseil' (iv 192) and the king's hearty response, 'Goddes forbode he faile! / Als longe as oure lyf lasteth, lyve we togideres!' (iv 194–5) ends the passus with a positive sense of a new beginning.

This passus concerns itself with the way that the king reacts to the problem presented to him, and the way that he deals with Mede. In renouncing the actions of Wrong, and the manipulations of the Law that Mede can achieve so easily, the king has moved from being a character whose actions seem very much a reaction to influences around him to being a ruler who is beginning to form clear beliefs of his own, supported by advice from Reason and from Conscience. If these two qualities in a man come from impulses of selfless integrity, then his resultant actions are morally healthy and his judgements likely to benefit the common good. To a king, these qualities are especially vital, as Langland illustrates here.

Vision Two: Passus V–VII

At the end of the first Vision, there is a clear way pointing forward to the next; the Dreamer awakes, mourning that he did not stay asleep longer and see more, but soon he feels drowsy once more and is drawn back into sleep. Passus V is a long and challenging one: at the start, Reason is seen lecturing the crowd on the right way to behave, and of the changes that must be made for society to become more productive. Significantly, his sermon is conducted in front of the king, who he advises 'his commune to lovye' because 'It is thi tresor, if treson ne were, and tryacle at thy need' (v 49–50). Indeed, Langland's reiteration of the image of the field of folk, instigated earlier in the poem, is picked up again here with greater import. Having established the king's wish to change, we must now see how sage Conscience's warning was that this wish will not become a reality unless fundamental changes are made by everyone in the kingdom. The king is not an isolated figure, Langland seems to say: his subjects have responsibilities too, in the successful governing of the land that they cohabit; a view Gower also shares. Without co-operation the king's will is helpless.

Reason's sermon is thus an adjuration to the people to implement the changes by repenting of those sins that currently cause such distress. Langland alleviates the sternness of this lesson by vivid illustrations of the characters of the Seven Deadly Sins, a vehicle we have also seen Gower use. Their tales of woe are chaired by Repentance, who exhorts all of them to start again, praying for them at length. Christ's sacrifice is emphasised, and Repentance plants the image of the crucifixion firmly before them all. Throughout this, the king does not speak, nor do we see any reaction from him to what any of the characters say. It is the turn of the people to come under scrutiny, and Langland paints an unedifying portrait of their moral turpitude. The Dreamer's attention shifts to 'a thousand of men tho thrungen togideres' (v 510) who want to go and search for Truth, presumably inspired by what they had just seen. A pilgrim is approached for directions, but ironically, he cannot help anyone looking for Truth, as in his experience

> I seigh nevere palmere with pyk ne with scrippe
> Asketh after hym er now in this place. (v 535–6)

It falls to a ploughman, Piers, to declare that he will help the people on their way. He knows Truth, and has followed his ways for forty years. He is able to describe exactly how to find him, in an allegorical pilgrimage that many recoil from in horror. It seems too long and difficult for those hampered by earthly desires. Piers points out that it is only through rejecting payment for anything other than work he has honestly done that he feels himself to be a contented man. Truth is in effect his employer, and his avowal makes a stark contrast to the ways of Mede seen in the earlier passus.

All this shows that the end of Passus V, although not contributing as much as some of the previous passages to the debate on kingship, does illustrate that Langland also believes in the obligations of the people to reform. By implication, the king's relationship with his people is a symbiotic one. The integrity of the one relies upon and reflects the other.

In the sixth passus, Piers Plowman instructs the people so that they can prepare themselves for the journey to see Truth. It is the knight who gives his support with the clearest willingness: '"By Crist!" quod a knyght thoo, "he kenneth us the beste"' (vi 21); although he admits he knows nothing of ploughing, he is willing to learn, and for that Piers thanks him. Significantly, though, the offer is politely refused, for Piers points out that the knight has other duties that he would be better carrying out. There is an order of responsibility, a hierarchy that holds society together; Langland's vision strongly advocates the need for such a structure, stressing that successful government comes only when each person working within it does so efficiently. Piers must upbraid the lazy and punish the rebellious, like Waster, who swears violently that he will not work as the ploughman insists:

> 'Wiltow or neltow, we wol have oure wille,
> And of thi flou and of thi flesshe fecche whanne us liketh,
> And maken us murye thermyde, maugree thi chekes.' (vi 156–8)

This self-centredness puts Piers in a rage, and he calls on the knight to help him. Hunger is appealed to, and his summary treatment of Waster leaves the miscreant begging for mercy. In fact, the very presence of Hunger produces a sudden enthusiasm to work, and soon everyone is toiling to keep him from gaining a hold on them, too.

The fourteenth century suffered many bad harvest years, and with the ravages left by the Plague, hunger was a real and constant threat for many. In highlighting how motivating starvation can be, Langland makes a complex point about leadership. The idea that you should feed your workers enough to keep them healthy, but not enough so that they are satisfied and become complacent, is a cautionary one, born not only of the fear that supplies will run out before the next famine, but also of the acknowledgment that contented by some stock of provisions, workers become distracted from working to their full potential. It is the overseer's responsibility to look after his workers, but also to ensure their spiritual health: everything in moderation is the lesson that Hunger repeats to Piers. The Bible teaches that fair pay for fair work is blessed; Piers realises that the pains he and some of his workers have been complaining of are caused by the surfeit of food that they have been eating, and joyfully thanks Hunger for making him see his mistake.

Piers is a difficult character to analyse here. He is both a leader and a ploughman, and so his position of power is an equivocal one. Unlike the king, his convictions are strong, and his instincts morally sound, independent of support from advisers. He is tough but fair to the workers, and in his organisation of the people, with all their different talents, is shown to be an effective ruler. However, the passus ends with a grim warning, following the successful harvest produced by Piers's workers. They gorge themselves on the produce so much that they forget about their purpose and their quest; they become resentful of having to work at all, just as Hunger had predicted. The warning is given by a hard-to-determine 'I': 'Ac I warne yow werkmen – wynneth whil ye mowe, / For Hunger hiderward hasteth hym faste!' (vi 319–20). Famine will make desperate men, but replete with good food, men become more discontented with their place in society and start to want more. They begin to curse 'the Kyng and al his Counseil after / Swich lawes to loke, laborers to greve' (vi 315–16).

Social hierarchy, again, is shown to be vital to the stability of the realm, although Langland, or the Dreamer, or whoever the persona of the 'I' is, reminds us that natural forces and seasonal changes must be guarded against as much as possible, as they can be as destructive to successful government as corruption itself.

In this passus, the nature of the pardon that Truth sends for Piers Plowman is set out. He will be immune to all further punishments and from all guilt attached to sin. By association, so will anyone who follows the path set by Piers. It is noted that any king or knight who protect the church and who govern those beneath them fairly, will also be able to take their place directly in Heaven, after fast-tracking through Purgatory. In the margins of the document, the terms of pardon for the other professions are detailed: the content is based around the unworthiness of giving and receiving meed and clearly, therefore, relates back to the lessons of the preceding passus.

When a priest offers to translate the terms of Piers's pardon, however, the mood and the tone change abruptly: 'This pardon moste I rede; / for I shal construe ech clause and kenne it thee on Englissh' (vii 105–6). In his translation, explaining that it is as simple as doing well, and God will receive your soul, whereas doing evil will result in the Devil winning it, the priest angers Piers. He tears up the pardon and declares that he will stop working and rely on the teaching that God will provide for all the needs of His people instead. The priest is impressed with his learning, and challenges it; Piers debates the points with him, and the noise of the exchange wakes the Dreamer up.

The remainder of the passus is a reflection by the Dreamer on what he has seen; he wonders if the visions meant anything, like the Biblical ones of Nebuchadnezzar and Joseph. He concludes that Do-Well is the one person who will be assured of a welcome in Heaven, and resolves to try and find him so that he, too, can achieve such a reward.

At the end of the second vision, then, the Dreamer has given himself an active quest. No longer just a passive receiver, he takes what he has learnt and interpreted, and is determined to act upon it. In this he is echoing the path of the king, who also decides to change his direction and seek out a more resolute position as effective ruler of his people. Piers the Ploughman is an important intermediary in this; his social position, hierarchically low, is nonetheless shown in some ways to be above that of royalty. This implies that everyone, if they work hard and strive for moral goodness, can attain everlasting joy. Kings and knights, ploughmen and dreamers, all have to follow the same precepts if they are to reach their common goal of salvation.

The Vita

Vision Three: Passus VIII–XII

The Dreamer sets off to try and find Dowel, Dobet and Dobest, and meets various characters who teach him how to live a more virtuous life. Whereas the Visio suggested that the means to this life depended on a co-operative and just state, where the law helps to maintain boundaries of behaviour that will enable people to live righteously and in concord with each other, the Vita examines how the individual must interpret those laws, and deepens the investigation into how that individual effort must be made. There is therefore not as much that is relevant to earthly kingship as there was in the first part of *Piers Plowman*, but what there is does consolidate the Visio's prescription for good living and proclaims the divine kingship of Christ, for the poet concentrates on 'the kingship of Jesus, the Pantocrator, and on the transformation of society into the Kingdom of God'.[27] In this he is unusual, for fourteenth-century piety often chose to emphasise Christ's humanity, but here 'in the person of the incarnate Christ, which is to become Langland's main subject, the royal power and the Good Life are fused and inseparable'.[28] Langland sees the incarnate Christ as king while on earth, and it is this image that he stresses rather than Jesus the man.

The Dreamer's first task is to find Dowel, and the first people to help him are two Franciscan friars, who give him an explanation of the concept of sin. Our bodies are like boats, tossed about by waves (material possessions) on a sea

---

[27] Morton W. Bloomfield, *Piers Plowman as a Fourteenth-Century Apocalypse* (New Brunswick, 1961) 100.

[28] P. M. Kean, 'Justice, Kingship and the Good Life in the Second Part of *Piers Plowman*', in *Piers Plowman: Critical Approaches*, ed. S. S. Hussey (London, 1969) 104.

(the world). The Devil can therefore make us fall down several times a day, but because we are protected by Dowel, we have the energy to get back up again. God 'wol suffre wel thi sleuthe, if thiself liketh; / For he yaf thee to yeresyyve to yeme wel thiselve – / And that is wit and free will, to every wight a porcion' (viii 51–3); each of us has been give the power to govern ourselves by God, and it is up to us to learn how to do that successfully. This passage states very clearly the purpose of the second half of the poem, and the journey that the Dreamer must go on to discover the truth of this. At this point he does not understand: ' "I have no kynde knowyng," quod I, "to conceyve alle thi wordes, / Ac if I may lyve and loke, I shal go lerne bettre" ' (viii 57–8). Like Amans in the *Confessio*, he must be shown what the lesson of self-governance means, and he falls asleep again and dreams of meeting two tall men called Thought and Wit, who explain to him who the three figures of Dowel, Dobet and Dobest are, and where he can find them.

Dowel is characterised as an honest workman, Dobet as a humble cleric and Dobest as a bishop. They therefore represent three distinct layers of a spiritual hierarchy, and have 'crowned oon to be kyng to kepen hem alle / And rule the reme by hire thre wittes' (viii 105–6). This king is difficult to place, and his role is not developed further at this point; instead the Dreamer listens to Wit telling him that Dowel lives in the body, and giving an allegorical representation of the siege that this castle called Kind constantly undergoes by the 'proud prikere of Fraunce, *Princeps huius mundi*' (ix 8), or the Devil. That the Devil is also given royal status helps to make more potent the analogy of two fierce warring kings fighting for control of man's soul. The keeper of this castle is the knight Inwit, who works to guard Anima, or the soul, from being taken by the enemy at the command of Kynde, who is 'creatour of alle kynnes thynges, / Fader and formour of al that evere was maked' (ix 26–7). This presentation of God recalls Chaucer's characterisation of the First Mover in the *Knight's Tale*, which shows the reader an oblique portrait of God's all-powerful rule. This passus describes in detail how the governance of the body is arranged by Inwit, and that without Inwit's guiding vigilance, man would be easily won over by the Devil's attacks. God is ultimate King, and by giving us all our own free will, or Inwit, we are able to, and ought to, exercise the control that provides. Wit goes on to advocate marriage as another way of viewing the Dowel triad, claiming that this state, too, will aid discovery of those three virtues.

Dame Study, Wit's wife, takes exception to what her husband has just said, and speaks out against the misuse of reason by clerics and teachers. She stresses the importance of study and will promise to try and be obedient to it. The two, though in apparent conflict, nevertheless portray two sides of a complementary pattern for behaviour: both are necessary in the Dreamer's quest. Clergy, the next adviser that he sees, satirises incompetent priests, but prophesies that a king shall come to reform the church (x 264–327), which prompts the Dreamer to ask if this means Dowel is a secular lord. Scripture answers emphatically that this is not so, as the Bible teaches that it is very hard for a rich man to enter the kingdom of Heaven:

> 'Kynghod ne knyghthod, by noght I kan awayte,
> Helpeth noght to heveneward oone heeris ende,
> Ne richesse right noght, ne reautee of lordes.' (x 332–4)

He stresses that status has nothing to do with the ability to get to Heaven. All estates are equal before God, and it is how well they follow His command to love one another that is the only criterion:

> For ordinary man, royal power, both in the literal sense, and in the sense in which the king is added to the triad of the Good Life, cannot in itself ensure salvation, though both the political king and the kind of the triad are an important factor towards it.[29]

This thread is not pursued further, as the Dreamer interrupts to object to what he is being taught, saying that surely Scripture teaches that man's fate is predestined, whatever his learning or moral worth.

This provokes severe disapproval from Scripture, and Will falls asleep, to dream a dream within a dream about Fortune, who leads him on a tour of the world and its temptations. The material world, which he visits first, shows how Fortune will turn against him in old age, and that the friars, to whom he will appeal for help, will ignore his pleas. Lewtee confirms Will's feeling that it would be best to denounce these friars, for he says that all sin should be rejected. As in the parable of the wedding feast, many are called but few are chosen. Will is frightened by this analogy, and reflects that sinful Christians will be punished by God unless He shows mercy; a realisation that brings home to him the precarious state of his own salvation.

At this point the Emperor Trajan, a virtuous pagan, appears and stresses how important it is to love beyond the limits of the law, saying that the model for this can be found in the poor, and goes on to criticise the priests who are ignorant and thieving, and exemplify the opposite of those feelings of charity. In Trajan there is a portrayal of kingship that necessarily supports all the arguments that have come before, for it is part of the stress of Langland's argument that nothing is as important as living a good life: it is not the fact that Trajan is an emperor, a good ruler, or has been prayed for by the pope that is the focus here, but the fact that he could not have achieved his salvation unless he had love, too:

> Love and leautee is a leel science;
> For that is the book blissed of blisse and of joye: –
> God wroughte it and wroot it with his on fynger
> And took it Moises upon the mount, alle men to lere.
> 'Lawe withouten love,' quod Troianus, 'ley ther a bene'.
>
> (xi 166–70)

The medieval legend of Trajan described how the pagan emperor so impressed the sixth-century pope St Gregory with his sense of justice that he interceded

---

[29] Kean (1969) 104.

with God on the emperor's behalf, and his soul was saved. Langland's treatment of this seems to imply that Will now gains great hope from learning that a non-Christian can be saved by meeting the standards of God's justice. Trajan's outburst at the beginning of his appearance – 'baw for bokes' (xi 139) – seems to show that acting according to God's law does not necessarily mean that you need learned commentaries to guide you. The fact that Gregory interceded for him certainly has some bearing on the outcome: 'it is the immediate cause, but the final one, without which the prayer would never even have been uttered, is the fact that the pagan Emperor, by the light of Reason and Nature, lived the Good Life'.[30] Langland once more steers the emphasis away from status and towards the individual. Even Trajan is meant to be seen not as an exemplary ruler (although he was), but as an exemplary human being. His status is only useful in that it lends weight to the axiom that law without love is a worthless thing, not worth a bean.

Trajan goes on to praise poverty at length, and to stress that status has a function, because God, although he could have made everyone rich, did not:

> Ac for the beste ben som riche and some beggeres and povere.
> For alle are we Cristes creatures, and of his cofres riche,
> And brethren as of oo blood, as well beggeres as erles. (xi 197–9)

Related to each other as we are, we should work together so that our individual circumstances help to alleviate suffering where it exists, through giving alms or practical skills. God is King of Kings, but He does not use His law to display His royal power. When He pardons sinners,

> it is primarily because of the deep kinship He feels with fellow humans ... This king's subjects become His brothers. The fundamental tension in medieval society between ideals of hierarchy and community ... here meet and are reconciled in a moment of visionary redemption. The public becomes the personal and also the universal and the divine.[31]

This third vision works through issues of wealth, status and wisdom, concluding that though all three are not vital to receiving God's grace, they have their place, used in the context of love and adherence to God's law, in the living of a good life. They are therefore essential parts of the debate on Dowel, for each individual must learn to work for salvation through the means that God has given to him. Imaginatif, at the end of Passus XII, reiterates that wisdom and intellect are a kind of treasure that was once looked for in governing a kingdom. As Langland has illustrated, this wisdom need not come from books (a view that conflicts with that of Gower); it can be learnt by 'kynde' or with 'Kynd' who shows Will the natural world to make him realise that all living things conform

---

[30] Kean (1969) 102.
[31] C. David Benson, *Public Piers Plowman: Modern Scholarship and Late Medieval English Culture* (University Park, PA, 2004) 245.

to an order that relies on an innate wisdom about their place in that system. This kind of knowledge, based on a strong faith, is most worth obtaining:

> 'And wit and wisdom,' quod that wye, 'was som tyme tresor
> To kepe with a commune – no catel was holde bettre –
> And muche murthe and manhod' – and right myd that he
>   vanysshed. (xii 293–5)

Vision Four: Passus XIII–XIV

In the fourth vision, Will dreams that he is at a banquet with Conscience and Patience. There is also a theologian at the table, a gourmand who is taken to task by the Dreamer, demanding that he tell him about Dowel, Dobet and Dobest. The theologian stresses the relationship all three have to study and to teaching. Clergy's opinion is sought, and he professes no greater knowledge than that given by Piers Plowman, who said that teaching is worth nothing without love. Patience steps in and supports this view, elaborating on the strength of love, that can conquer anything or anyone, even kings and emperors. The theologian dismisses this as ridiculous, saying that the wisest men and the strongest have tried to make peace between nations and failed (xiii 174–8). This is as far as the criticism goes: Patience says abruptly that he is going to go on a pilgrimage with Conscience. Clergy will not go with them, and Conscience exclaims that 'Ther nys wo in this world that we ne sholde amende, / And conformen kynges to pees, and alle kynnes londes – / Sarsens and Surre, and so forth alle the Jewes – / Turne into the trewe feith and intil oon bileve' (xiii 208–10). However, this vision of concord is not yet to be, for Clergy insists that he will stay where he is and continue with his work of confirming people until Conscience has been brought nearer to a state of perfection.

The pilgrims meet a minstrel called Haukyn, dressed in multi-coloured clothes, who represents the active life. His garments are stained and torn with the temptations of the world, and he is a volatile creature, constantly fretting and boasting of his exploits. A narrator intervenes at this point to exhort the listeners, especially the nobles, to pay attention. This narrator specifically uses the minstrels of the king's household as an example of how the aristocrats warmly welcome someone who enjoys such a privileged position in the royal service. How much more so, the narrator argues, should the rich welcome the poor, who are the minstrels of the King of Kings, God? This inclusion seems to point to an audience who would appreciate the force of this suggestion, and the example certainly brings together associations from different levels of society, for a minstrel is both inside and outside the court circle, in some similar ways to a court poet like Chaucer.[32] He is not of noble birth, and yet has a unique access to the inner workings of the royal household. Haukyn, however, is a failed minstrel, working for both secular and ecclesiastical lords, but not earning

---

[32] See Green (1980) (105–7 and 110–12) for a wider definition of the differences between minstrels and court poets, which became more marked in the later fourteenth century.

enough with either to make a proper living. His presence on the pilgrimage gives Patience an opportunity to preach to him about renouncing his sins and living in charity with others: Haukyn does repent, and the Dreamer wakes up.

Vision Five: Passus XV–XVII

Will's fifth vision focuses on charity, expanding on the preaching of Patience in the passus before; kingship is not a prevalent theme, because at this stage the poem is concerned with expounding the way to find the way to grace, and the images are part of the structure of ideas that culminate in the succeeding passus. Among the historical examples of people who have shown the greatest charity, Anima offers the lives of King Edward the Confessor and King Edmund. Although the two kings are named, no other detail about them is given, so it would be dangerous to connect them to Richard II, although he had a special devotion to both of them. This vision has at its centre the strange dream-like image of the tree of mercy and compassion with the fruits of charity growing upon it, which is in the care of Piers Plowman himself. As he explains about the tree to the Dreamer, we become aware that Piers has been transformed into a Christ-like figure. Like the image of the boat that appeared at the beginning of the Vita, this tree reminds us of the fragility of our spiritual state, which needs constant attendance to prevent it from disintegrating. The images change faster and become more urgent with their teaching of charity and stress on the need for change and reform; the Dreamer sees Abraham and then Hope, who is Moses, who shows him a golden tablet with the commandment on to '*Dilige Deum et proximum tuum*' (xvii 12); the Dreamer is confused by what appears to be conflicting advice from each prophet: Abraham tells him to worship the Trinity, while Moses urges him to love the one God. The Dreamer asks which is right, and is told by the Samaritan that both are important. The parable of the Good Samaritan gives Biblical support to the teaching to act charitably, and the interaction that the Dreamer has with the Samaritan himself shows him that loving is not only the right course of action, but the only reasonable one, too: 'For unkyndenesse is the contrarie of alle kynnes reson' (xvii 346).

Visions Six, Seven and Eight: Passus XVIII–XX

These final three passus contain the Dreamer's last three visions. The Good Samaritan has provided the crux of the Vita, for in this the teachings of all the other allegorical figures combine with the earthly examples of exemplary men and the reactions we have seen from both the sinner Haukyn and the Christ-like Piers to illuminate the Biblical exemplum for this virtue of charity with powerful resonances. In Passus XVIII the Dreamer has a vision of the Crucifixion and the harrowing of hell, where he sees Christ going down to hell to release the souls trapped there. Everything that Langland has written so far has been preparing the Dreamer and the reader to this point, for the greatest love of all is that shown by Christ in suffering crucifixion to redeem mankind. The images of lordship connected with Christ can now blazon out in triumph: standing before the defiant Satan at the gates of hell, who demands to know who wants to enter, Christ answers:

> 'Rex glorie,
> The lord of myght and of mayn and alle manere vertues –
> Dominus virtutum.
> Dukes of this dymme place, anoon undo thise yates,
> That Crist may come in, the Kynges sone of Hevene!'
>
> (xviii 316–21)

He is both King of glory and the son of Heaven's King; the images of kingship pile up and create a sense of awe and wonder that prompts the Dreamer to awake praising God and calling to his wife and daughter to do honour to Christ's resurrection immediately. The Dreamer is profoundly moved by what he has seen, and starts to write it all down, when he falls asleep again and sees Piers Plowman covered in blood and carrying a cross.

This penultimate passus is extraordinarily complex and spiritually moving. The connection of Piers with Christ suddenly bursts upon Will, and he asks Conscience if they are one and the same. Conscience answers that they are different: that Christ is wearing Piers's arms, but that He is underneath. Will asks why Conscience calls Him Christ, rather than Jesus, and Conscience explains:

> 'Thou knowest wel,' quod Conscience, 'and thow konne reson,
> That knyght, kyng, conquerour may be o persone.
> To be called a knyght is fair, for men shul knele to hym;
> To be called a kyng is fairer, for he may knyghtes make;
> Ac to be conquerour called, that cometh of special grace,
> And of hardynesse of herte and of hendenesse –
> To make lordes of laddes, of lond that he wynneth,
> And fre men foule thralles, that folwen noght hise lawes.'
>
> (xix 26–33)

It is because Jesus came and died upon the cross, gaining victory over death and the forces of evil, that He is called conqueror, and deserves the title of Christ. That Langland links the dominion of God to earthly titles so carefully, describing in detail in this passus what each distinction means, shows an awareness of their power and their usefulness in helping to understand the mystery that is God.

Then Will sees Piers again, accompanied by the Spirit of God, who Conscience says is called Grace. Terrified, Will kneels with the others, and prays for Grace to help him. Grace explains that the time will come when the Antichrist will attack, and He therefore leaves each of them with powers that will help them to combat this. To Piers He gives the four gospels, comparing them to a team of oxen, and four horses who turn out to be Augustine, Ambrose, Gregory and Jerome. These great authorities of the church support the teaching that the gospel-writers give, and the seeds of cardinal virtue that Piers is also given will, when planted and grown, give people the chance to eat them and become stronger in the pursuit of the Good Life. To the rest he gives skills according to their estate and calling;

this passage illustrates the earlier conviction of the fundamentally God-given shape of the hierarchical society, and how important it is to maintaining God's law throughout the land:

> 'Thynketh [that alle craftes,' quod Grace], 'cometh of my yifte;
> Loke that noon lakke oother, but loveth alle as bretheren.
> And who that moost maistries kan, be myldest of berynge;
> And crouneth Conscience kyng, and maketh Craft youre stiward,
> And after Craftes conseil clotheth yow and fede.' (xix 255–9)

God, as the Holy Spirit, decrees our position in life; He has also decreed that we should appoint Conscience as our personal king, so that our vices can be regulated and our craft carried out with integrity. Conscience joyfully exhorts everyone to eat, for they have earned the right to do so, provided they have fulfilled the dictates of Piers's pardon to pay what they owe. This call to share in the Mass, the fundamental sacred act for all Catholic Christians, is met with horror by many of the people. Dissent immediately appears among those who do not see why they should give up their pleasures and vices while they can still enjoy them. This is hardly the reaction that Conscience, or the reader, was expecting, and creates an intense sense of disappointment after the joy of the preceding details of the gifts of spiritual grace.

The passus ends with a description of an earthly king and a lord, who try to explain the virtues of Prudence, Fortitude and Justice, but from their own selfish and cynical perspectives: the lord says that his reeve is perfectly within his rights to take what he can from his workers, because he is just acting on advice from the steward and the accountant. In the same vein, the king argues that he must defend the land and the church against unlawful men, and so it is his right to take what he needs from his subjects in order to protect them properly. Conscience warns him that though this is true, he must still ensure that he only does so if it is really needed. At this point Will wakes, and the passus ends.

The final passus, and the Dreamer's final vision, create a picture of a world doomed to eternal struggle, for here a battle commences between the forces of Kind and the forces of the Antichrist. The apocalyptic war looses death and destruction on the people of the earth, and Will, extremely frightened, appeals to Kind to save him. Kind advises him to learn to love, telling him that it is the only way to live, and so Will finds his way through Contrition and Confession to Conscience, who stands defending a place called Unity. Unity comes under attack from all kinds of charlatans, until eventually an exhausted Conscience declares that he is going to try and find Piers Plowman, the only one 'that Pryde myghte destruye' (xx 383). The last thing that Will hears before he wakes up is Conscience's plea for Grace to help him.

The insecurity of the poem's ending shows Langland to be very much a poet of his age, for there is no happy resolution to the Dreamer's visions. The poem ends with unease and a sense that in confronting difficulties Langland has created

a direct facing, an immersion in the problematic character of the times, to the
point where the poem with the poet, having together been submitted to the
crisis itself, seem to have become in part its victims.[33]

In this final analysis of the state of the world, Langland moves back towards
the real problems of the troubled society of his times. He shows the corruption
within the church, which he stresses throughout the poem is the most insidious
danger to authority, and goes to great pains to show the majesty and joy that can
come from serving God. *Piers Plowman* exposes rottenness in all estates, but in
the Dreamer's eight visions develops a progressive sermon of hope that becomes
an argument pointing back to its own beginning with the 'feeld ful of folke' all
going about their business, most of them concerned only with self-serving ends.
Hope is still possible, but only if people will listen and change. *Piers Plowman*
shows a poet who is constantly aware of the importance of applying spiritual
lessons to everyday life:

> in contrast to more idealistic treatments by other Ricardian poets such as
> Chaucer and the *Gawain*-poet, truth in *Piers Plowman* never abandons the
> everyday social world.[34]

That social world is not the courtly one of Chaucer, nor the more distantly
focused one of the *Gawain*-poet, but it shares the same concerns, and like Gower
the poet possesses an absolute conviction that is necessary for the individual to
take responsibility for his spiritual life and learn how to govern his actions and
emotions. This must have felt particularly important at a time when little seemed
stable and sure. *Piers Plowman*

> is made up of perplexities created in Langland's world and time by opposi-
> tions: between perfection intellectually conceived and the imperfect actuality;
> knowledge of right conduct and failure in those who possess that knowledge
> to act righteously; the *imago dei* and man's tendency to besmirch it with sin;
> the God of Justice and the God of Love; divine and worldly wisdom.[35]

Like Gower, Langland is directly critical of some aspects of his society; unlike
Gower, he is not concerned especially with the role of the king. In his exploration of the meaning of Christ's kingship, and in his inclusion of examples of
rulers such as the king in the Visio and Trajan, he shows, as all the Ricardians do, an acknowledgment of the impact the governance of kings has on the
spiritual health of the whole country. It is an acknowledgment, however, that is
subordinate to the responsibility of each individual to reform, for the law of God
applies equally to everyone.

---

[33] Charles Muscatine, *Poetry and Crisis in the Age of Chaucer* (Notre Dame, IN, 1972) 109.
[34] Benson (2004) 238.
[35] George Kane, *Chaucer and Langland: Historical and Textual Approaches* (London, 1989) 119.

3

The *Gawain*-poet

Our third poet is the presumed author of the four poems in British Library Manuscript Cotton Nero A.x. He is usually called the *Gawain*-poet, and his poems demonstrate clear similarities of language, style and theme: among these, the poet's treatment of the ideas of courts and kingship are consistent enough on many points to bear detailed examination and to contribute to a wider perspective of fourteenth-century literary representations of this topic. The manuscript has been dated to around 1400, and MED dates the poet's work to about 1390, which would mean that he was writing at the same time as Chaucer, Langland and Gower. The *Gawain*-poet works in the cultural contexts of his period; like Langland, Chaucer and Gower, he shares 'a recognition of the hierarchical nature of social bodies'.[1] His portrayal of society in each of his poems is based on the belief that without the secure underpinning of true values, these systems would collapse into chaos. He is a commentator who 'prescribes individual penance for national ills',[2] perhaps deducing from the swiftly changing reigns of the kings of his century that the only hope for the future was through internal spiritual strength.

The *Gawain*-poet's work, unlike Langland's, cannot be read as being primarily informed by a satirical or political impetus, but this does not necessarily mean that he is untouched by political events or social change, or that his work, as has been suggested, 'would seem to argue a kind of escapism or reaction'.[3] That idea relies on a narrow view of the reality of the world in which the poet lived, and which, incidentally, he shows himself capable of describing in very detailed ways. He is always aware, however, of the higher-order reality of God's universe, and sees that as giving meaning to the world of sense perception at all levels.

Abstraction is not necessarily an indication of a repudiation of circumstance, or a refusal to connect with it. In his treatment of ideas such as truth, faith, loyalty and patience, the poet reveals himself to be sharply aware of the world around him and the thought that moulded it. He not only shows a full appreciation of his English roots, but is also able to integrate with that an understanding of European influences,[4] and this understanding makes his work rich in reflections of a very diverse nature. Though he does not deal with the function of different

---

[1] Lynn Staley Johnson, *The Voice of the Gawain-Poet* (Madison, 1984) xii.
[2] Johnson (1984) xii.
[3] Charles Muscatine, *Medieval Literature, Style and Culture* (Columbia, SC, 1999) 88–90.
[4] Derek Brewer and Jonathan Gibson, eds, *A Companion to the Gawain-Poet* (Cambridge, 1997) 7.

contemporary professions or estates, he does, through his concentration on the individual's place in the moral and spiritual hierarchies, present energetic and provocative engagements with the world as he experiences it; his poems

> suggest a poet who was conversant with the contemporary languages of power and more than capable of employing those languages to question the very powers that no doubt employed him.[5]

Pearl

Pearl, the first poem in the manuscript, concentrates on describing the realm of Heaven, showing its sublimity through what seems to be the vision of a grieving father.[6] The father's obvious deep feelings of sorrow at losing his Pearl, and his frequent use of endearments and expressions of love when addressing her, make the nature of the relationship a personal and very poignant part of the poem. In accepting the vitality of this, as will be seen later, the poem reveals a deep overall emphasis on the individual's struggle to comprehend the spiritual mysteries of grace in a way that a strictly allegorical interpretation would not.

The Dreamer's central difficulty is in understanding the position of his Pearl in Heaven, a difficulty that is so crucial to his acceptance of her departure from the temporal world that it dominates the majority of the poem. The Dreamer's grief, expressed so movingly in the first stanzas, is allayed by the visual manifestation of Pearl as a 'mayden of menske, ful debonere' (162), dressed in attire that signals her to be royal. His own social status is elusive, but when Pearl compares him to a jeweller it may imply that he was someone beneath the highest echelons of society but above the lowest orders. In this respect, his social identity, as Felicity Riddy has remarked, is very different from those adopted by Chaucer and Langland: while Chaucer's dream visions have as their narrators a learned, lover-like figure who reads himself to sleep, *Piers Plowman* uses a 'dissatisfied vagrant, half hermit, half layabout, who falls asleep wherever he happens to be'.[7] Gower, as we have seen, reveals his narrator to be none other than himself.

The awed descriptions the Dreamer gives of Pearl's regality and the emphasis throughout on her royal status confirm the distance he feels from such a position. Even the very first line marks the liking for Pearl as a characteristic of royalty: 'Perle, plesaunte to pryncez paye.' This sense of distance and of impossible attainment underlines the poem's concerns with spiritual reward and how it is obtained; it is vital that the Dreamer feel that chasm of expectation in order for the poem's tension of debate to hold. This tension is felt through the examination of order.

---

[5] Johnson (1984) 197.
[6] There are many contending theories about the precise nature of the relationship between the Pearl and the Dreamer, but the argument for the father/daughter tie has been accepted here. For a useful summary of some of these ideas, see A. C. Spearing, *The Gawain-Poet: A Critical Study* (Cambridge, 1970) 128–33.
[7] Felicity Riddy, 'Jewels in *Pearl*', in *A Companion to the Gawain-Poet*, ed. Derek Brewer and Jonathan Gibson (Cambridge, 1997) 149.

The purity and orderliness of Heaven show a transcending reverence for hierarchy that inevitably implies a comparison with social organisation on earth. However, the construction of that hierarchy presents many paradoxical images. The key concept of a king and his court challenges ideas of the ruler and the ruled, of strength and vulnerability. The *Gawain*-poet's description of the court of Heaven, his emphasis on the supremacy of the world beyond the earthly one, and his choice and treatment of the father–daughter relationship all demonstrate how this interrogation of established beliefs and interpretations produces very provocative revaluations.

Pearl presents a version of the established tradition in medieval religious writing that shows God as a

> powerful and knightly king, full of *deboneirté* ... possessing in himself all the qualities that would be the most desirable in an aristocratic husband – wealth, *largesce*, power, beauty.[8]

God is represented both as a prince and as Pearl's husband. Significantly, despite the centrality of that concept to Christianity from New Testament times on, God is not presented as father; that role is only exemplified in the Dreamer himself. This adds force to the idea that the poem's focus is on the courtly, kingly aspects of God's relationship with mankind, that the fatherly aspects of His love are specifically related to the unfathomable grace that He grants to his subjects, or children. Though evidence from the text makes it very probable that the relationship between the Dreamer and Pearl is that of father and daughter, it is never unequivocally stated, and this lack of definition itself pushes attention away from that position and towards the bonds of other, spiritual obligations.

To begin with, the father fails to understand what has happened to his 'privy perle wythouten spotte' (24), but is brought to see the wonder of her transfiguration. His grief, initially overwhelming, becomes tempered by what he learns from Pearl's experience. His privileged vision of Heaven invokes a yearning to act in a manner that will earn him a place there too, and his faith is strengthened by it. Though on earth a daughter is subject to her father's wishes, in Heaven she is part of a ruling power that does not regard such bonds. It is true, then, that

> there seems to be a special significance in the situation where the doctrinal lesson given by the celestial maiden comes from one of no earthly wisdom to her proper teacher and instructor in the natural order.[9]

The Dreamer's almost comical disbelief at her new status is wonderfully drawn: 'Wer fayr in heuen to halde asstate, / Oþer elleʒ a lady of lasse aray; / Bot a quene! Hit is to dere a date' (489–91). That the social hierarchy of fourteenth-century England is an important part of the poem is illustrated by the Dreamer's 'naively blasphemous'[10] comic outrage at the idea of Pearl's fast-

---

[8] Spearing (1970) 155.
[9] *Pearl*, ed. E. V. Gordon (Oxford, 1953) xiii.
[10] A. C. Spearing, *Medieval Dream Poetry* (Cambridge, 1976) 123.

track promotion in Heaven: 'I may not traw, so God me spede, / þat God wolde wryþe so wrange away' (487–8). It is easy to sympathise with the idea of God's grace being so extraordinarily unfathomable to a medieval reader immersed in a society where the ladder of preferment was strictly delineated. Where opportunity for such preferment existed, it was usually reserved for the high-born. The number of social conventions that needed to have been violated in order for a child of relatively low birth to succeed to a regal position would have been too many to contemplate. The idea is so absurd that the Dreamer's response is involuntarily, instinctively induced. His expletive, underlining his vehement disbelief that God could work such an awry system, reveals the extent of his inability to comprehend this unnatural order of things. Pearl tries to explain to her father that the hierarchy of Heaven does not need to acknowledge earthly relationships. Everyone is equal, everyone is crowned:

> The court of the kyngdom of God alyve
> Has a property in hytself beyng.
> Alle that may therine aryve
> Of alle the reme is quen other kyng. (446–9)

Mary is queen over them all. The difference is subtly marked: she is 'quen of cortayse' (432), whilst the others are queens 'by cortaysye' (468), that is, by the good grace of God's kindness.[11] By using the same terms of description, the sense of harmony is maintained, and yet the change of preposition indicates that Mary's state is superior in ways that church doctrine would have expounded for the first audience of the poem. 'Cortaysye' is a vital element of the poet's argument: here it 'refers to God's liberality, which rewards, as the poet goes on to show in the parable, not according to merit, but according to its own dictates'.[12]

The idea of courtesy and how it functions in poems of the *Gawain*-poet has been a fruitful source in further illuminating ideas of nobility: Derek Brewer, for example, draws attention to the various shades of meaning in the term, and how it is used to effect in the poet's different works. His assertion that 'courtly culture was a notably oral culture, though it had a manuscript base'[13] stresses the necessary tensions in the speeches both the Dreamer and Pearl make in the poem. The Dreamer admires Pearl's eloquence, 'Þaȝ cortaysly ȝe carp con / I am bot mol and manereȝ mysse' (381–2), marking the social gulf between them. She has become convincingly a queen because she converses with the assurance and 'courtesy', or elegantly phrased speech, of the ruling elite. Courtesy in this form is thus a vital part of definition in the poem, as indeed it will be found to be in the other three poems of Cotton Nero A.x, and the ability to control and craft words in this way a clear sign of superior inner grace. Mary's supremacy over all the other queens points to her superlative possession of the qualities of courtesy;

---

[11] Ad Putter, *An Introduction to the Gawain-Poet* (London, 1996) 167.
[12] W. O. Evans, '"Cortaysye" in Middle English', *Medieval Studies* 29 (1967) 153.
[13] Derek Brewer, 'Courtesy and the *Gawain*-poet', in *Patterns of Love and Courtesy: Essays in Memory of C. S. Lewis*, ed. J. Lawlor (Evanston, 1966) 62.

she can raise up queens who exhibit those same courteous standards, who are all equal, sublimely so, yet also paradoxically beneath Mary's own transcendent presence as ultimate definition of those qualities. She is 'the equivalent of the theologians' *Regina gratiae*'.[14] Pearl reflects and is part of Mary's sublimity, and such a representation could be read as a flattering comparison to an earthly court, where the nobles would reflect in a similar way the ultimate ideals held and embodied by the royals who led them.

The relationships in the heavenly court of *Pearl* are difficult to define. There is a strict structure, but so harmonious is its formation that all seem equal. The use of the Parable of the Vineyard to illustrate this makes it clear that, though the principle may seem unjust to the Dreamer, everyone who enters with a pure heart, no matter how hard or how little they have struggled, will receive the same reward at God's court. This parable can be interpreted as a comment on the ascent of Richard II to the throne. He was still young when he was crowned, not quite the infant that Pearl was, but still young enough to be termed a child; following the Augustinian tradition of grace evidenced in the parable, any sense of earning that position by length of service is irrelevant, but therefore of particular note to a monarch whose experience of rule began so early in his life. It affirms his right to rule, and his inviolability to criticism. This part of *Pearl* could also show that the *Gawain*-poet was aware of contemporary political issues such as the attempts by the Cambridge Parliament of 1388 to renew the labour statutes and protect the rural economy. In its presentation of the grumbling workers, unhappy at their equal pay with those who did not start their labour until late in the day, 'seems to catch the authentic note of the fourteenth-century equivalent of the trade-unionist'.[15]

The Pearl explains that as the concepts of time, of date, have no relevance in God's transcendent universe, so arguments about age or length of service are essentially irrelevant. In God's court, unlike a medieval king's court, there is no sliding scale of meed for loyalty to the crown. Pearl's own position as 'maskelleȝ bryd þat bryȝt con flambe' (769) is clarified. Though it seems a mark of particular favour, Pearl is 'maskelles' but not 'makeleȝ'. She is both spiritually special, and yet one of 144,000 other brides of Christ. The dichotomy of the hierarchy is here exemplified. Pearl's rank does not separate her from the rest of her world; rather she becomes more integrally a part of it. Interestingly, it has been noted that the procession of virgins of the New Jerusalem in *Pearl* all wear identical clothes to Pearl, and each wears on her breast 'Þe blysful perle wyth gret delyt' (1104).[16] This can be seen as a livery badge, in the same way that all the angels in the Wilton Diptych wear the badge of the white hart, Richard II's motif. In this painting, the king, portrayed as a boy, kneels before Mary, who holds the infant Jesus towards him. Flanking Richard are the figures of Edward

---

[14] Gordon, *Pearl*, note to line 432, 61.
[15] Spearing (1970) 102.
[16] The identical clothes conform to descriptions of courtly ladies in conventional romances; Chaucer's *Legend of Good Women*, for example, and later works such as *The Floure and the Leafe* have similar resonances, although here the *Gawain*-poet uses the convention to transform them into something spiritual, rather than secular.

the Confessor, John the Baptist and Saint Edmund, while Mary is surrounded by the eleven angels previously mentioned. Visually, it is a powerful endorsement of Richard's holiness, of his already accepted place in the hierarchy of Heaven. Just as *Pearl* stresses the glory, the richness, the magnificence of Heaven, so does the Wilton Diptych. Strong colours, detailed robes, jewels and careful beautiful composition make a work of art whose sumptuous realisation of skill and craftsmanship reflects the priceless nature of what is being portrayed. The magnificence is absolutely necessary. It shows, as the extravagant imagery of *Pearl* does, a persuasive rhetorical power 'of the spirituality of its attitudes to wealth and status, for which jewels are a metonym'.[17] The connection of heavenly and earthly courts is in this way translated by the imagery of the poem into a fluid relationship that endows each realm with mystery, for

> *Pearl*, if it seeks to make heaven legible through the familiar clothing of royalty, nevertheless also makes the royal strange in the process, transfiguring royal trappings and the attendant values that perhaps (who knows?) were close to the poet's actual historical acquaintance.[18]

The comparison emphasises a belonging, a part of an 'order' of heavenly being whose partisanship is visually obvious.[19] In the Book of Revelation the virgins have God's name written on their foreheads (Rev 14.1), but no other mark is mentioned; this shows how the *Gawain*-poet manipulates the material to make it more contemporary. These virgins are meant to be seen in fourteenth-century terms, as retainers of the Lamb, and as such the poet invites comparisons with an earthly court. It is a reminder of obligations in both worlds: that belonging brings with it ideas of ownership. In Heaven all are subject to God's grace; the livery badge reminds also that on earth all are subject to the king.[20]

In using such costly items in order to underline the unimaginable but overwhelmingly lavish surroundings of the Heavenly City, the *Gawain*-poet makes by association a comment on the earthly king's possession and usage of precious stones and treasures. In contrast to Langland, whose portrayal of the Lady Mede, dripping with signs of her wealth, is clearly satirical, the *Gawain*-poet's treatment throughout *Pearl* is starkly different. Not only does the *Gawain*-poet use expensive objects as signs of beauty, but it is a beauty of purity, or spiritual power, that they represent.[21] Far from being symbols of corrupt avarice, they resonate with holiness, their perfection a fitting reflection of the superlative glory of God. The *Gawain*-poet constructs a vision of Heaven so full of marvels that the Dreamer is 'rauyste wyth glymme pure' (1088). His senses

---

[17] Riddy 152.
[18] Alan J. Fletcher, '*Pearl* and the Limits of History', in *Studies in Late Medieval and Early Renaissance Texts in Honour of John Scattergood*, eds Anne Marie D'Arcy and Alan J. Fletcher (Dublin, 2005) 169–70.
[19] Riddy 153.
[20] For an explanation of why these badges have particular relevance to Richard II, see John M. Bowers, '*Pearl* in its Royal Setting: Ricardian Poetry Revisited', *Studies in the Age of Chaucer* 17 (1995) 136–8.
[21] Riddy (152–3) develops this idea.

are overloaded with the wonders he sees, and the awe he feels is correspondingly complete. The poet uses the language of the commonplace to emphasise the gulf between what the Dreamer sees, and what he is: he stands 'as stylle as dased quayle' (1085), the incongruity of the homely image also making his experience the more sympathetic to the observer. Historians, significantly, have often credited Richard's reign with the beginning of this deification of earthly kingship: it has been argued that Richard relied on ostentatious shows of wealth to maintain England's image as a powerful state, that he was 'the first English king to cultivate magnificence in the style of his court, self-consciously and on principle'.[22]

Yet there are no comments on the moral shortcomings of English courts in *Pearl*, or yet hints or suggestions that the Heavenly City is anything other than the ideal version of parallels on earth. What creates the tension is the reflective element already stressed. The *Gawain*-poet uses the court to provoke contemplation and inner change; a secular image for spiritual ends. The structure, the artistic features, the very form of the poem show it to be more firmly rooted in the courtly life of the period than any of the other poems by this poet. The rhymed stanzas of octosyllabic lines, the noticeable use of French-derived vocabulary, and the use of the courtly love-vision made popular by French poets all unequivocally indicate this to be a product of courtly influences. Richard II, who had been tutored by a Frenchman, Guichard d'Angle, had a reputation as a connoisseur of all things French. Therefore the inclusion of these elements stresses that though the central figure of the Dreamer may appear to come from relatively lowly origins, the poem itself is aimed at readers who would appreciate the cultivated, elegant manoeuvres of the *Gawain*-poet's stylistic patternings.

The sources that the *Gawain*-poet might have used for *Pearl* have been much debated by scholars. The Vulgate Bible is undoubtedly one, and the poet was probably influenced by the *Roman de la Rose*. Suggestions of similarities with Boccaccio's *Olympia* and Dante's *Divina Commedia* have also been made. *Olympia*, in particular, is a text of interest because it, too, is an elegiac piece dealing with the death of a young girl, where the father is consoled by his daughter, who tells of the joys of Heaven. In its similarity of theme to *Pearl*, there is scope for speculation that the *Gawain*-poet knew Boccaccio's work, although no evidence has yet been found to confirm this. Clearly the *Gawain*-poet was well-read and his readers, whether they were of a provincial court of the Midlands or the sophisticated court of London that was Chaucer's milieu, would have appreciated that.

The audience seems to have been one that would have known court life very familiarly, for

---

[22] Patricia J. Eberle, 'The Politics of Courtly Style at the Court of Richard II', in *The Spirit of the Court*, eds Glyn S. Burgess and Robert A. Taylor (Cambridge, 1985) 168.

even when the scene of action is nowhere near a court, the *Gawain*-poet cannot actually get away from it: if it is not the place where the action is, it is still the vantage point which the poet looks out from.[23]

The courtly perspective, which can be seen most obviously in *Sir Gawain and the Green Knight*, is a vital part of the narrative vehicle in *Pearl*. It is true that the poem can be seen as 'a romantic adventure of the spirit',[24] with a 'hero' whose quest the audience can follow, but when the various possible underlying influences are brought to the surface (the dream-vision, the elegy, the courtly romance, the Bible, devotional treatises, lapidaries) it can be seen how truly complex a narrative this 'adventure' advances. The court is the centre for everything and harmonises all.

When, for example, references to the landscape of the *Roman de la Rose* are found in *Pearl*,[25] the secular allusions only emphasise 'the transformation – from rose to pearl, from God of Love to Lamb of God'.[26] The familiar nuances, combined with the divine context, make the poem more approachable, more palatable in its appeal. While the immediacy of the tone is achieved by using the Dreamer as the narrator, the blending of familiar sources increases that accessibility to the literate audience generally accepted to have been the *Gawain*-poet's target.[27] It is entertaining, aesthetically rich in description, contains touches of humour, and deals with a situation of emotional interest; it would seem that the *Gawain*-poet, like Langland, knew the most effective ways to make an impact. Unlike Langland, however, the *Gawain*-poet's targets are the individual inhabitants of the confines of his courtly surroundings. This poem speaks directly to them; the first-person narrator is a reminder that this is a poem set in a particular time, a particular world: like Gower and Chaucer, this poet uses the narrative voice to stress the relevance to the individual listener. The voice is perhaps more intimate in tone than in the other works; overtly Christian in a way that Chaucer's elegy for the duchess of Lancaster is not, more directly and succinctly appealing than Gower's mammoth *Confessio* can be, it nevertheless shares with these works a sense of a persona searching for order in a world that is bound by mysteries.

The heavenly court sends questioning glances at its worldly counterpart, trying to reconcile the differences and find patterns and analogies. One way of explaining the otherwise incongruous insertion of John 1.28–29 in lines 817–24 of *Pearl* is that Richard II was well known to have venerated John the Baptist, and that this reference by the *Gawain*-poet acknowledges that.[28] God is King of Heaven and Earth. This is not the only representation that the poet offers. God is more often described as the Lamb, a metaphor of such meekness that it makes

---

[23] Putter 18.
[24] W. A. Davenport, *The Art of the Gawain-Poet* (London, 1978) 51.
[25] See Gordon, *Pearl* xxxii; P. M. Kean, *The Pearl: An Interpretation* (London, 1967) 94.
[26] Spearing (1970) 120.
[27] Spearing (1970) 5.
[28] John M. Bowers, *The Politics of Pearl: Court Poetry in the Age of Richard II* (Cambridge, 2001) 84.

a paradox of His omnipotence. In using both images, the *Gawain*-poet achieves something quite remarkable; the poem's language moves from the definable real world to the indefinable heavenly one, 'moving simultaneously outward and upward, away from self and the world and mutability and the senses and toward "unknowing"'.[29] The intersections of these realms of expression are held in a tension of structural beauty; the whole poem is an intricate pattern of linguistic virtuosity that itself complements this theme of complex simplicity. God's relationship with humanity can be condensed into one word, love. Yet the nature of that love constantly escapes complete human comprehension. The poet uses images from both secular and religious writings to try and grasp that elusiveness.

The Lamb of God is an image taken from the Book of Revelations, where He is also enigmatically the Lion. The description of the Heavenly City in *Pearl* is steeped in references to this text, evident through the description of gems and priceless treasures that precisely echo those of the Biblical original.[30] The lapidary imagery has been shown to have a great influence on emphasising the differences between the earthly and spiritual kingdoms, for the *Gawain*-poet uses it prolifically in his depiction of the Dreamer's vision of earthly paradise, as well as underlining the direct borrowings from Revelations in his description of the Heavenly City. That lapidaries, like *Pearl*, place precious gems in the ownership of a worldly prince or king, may give some pause for reflection. Pearl is 'plesaunte to prynces paye' in the first line of the poem; a jewel, valuable and precious to royal owners. The pearl was also a popular jewel in the Middle Ages in courtly fashions, so prolific that it was called the 'pearl age'.[31] This was almost literally, then, an image embedded in the heart of the court. As such it might almost be said to convey gentle satire on the court members, or at least to exhibit that 'magnificently tender didacticism'[32] for which the poem is known. The contrast between the purity of Pearl in the poem, her garments decorated with 'perleȝ pyȝte of ryal prys' (193), a crown of 'mariorys and non oþer ston' (206) on her head, and the ladies of an aristocratic court, whose dresses would have been adorned for vanity, is very strong. The style of Pearl's gown, with its long sleeves, kirtle and mantle, is very precisely that of a medieval woman of high birth. But Pearl's attire is representative of her inner purity, whereas the gowns of earthly women would often merely represent material wealth and show. Her garments are white and made of linen, just as the Bride's are in Rev 20.8. The colour signifies that they have been washed in the blood of Christ, another reference to Revelations and to the unblemished state of Pearl's soul.

As a representation of a pure soul she is transfigured by the end of the poem into a jewel that God possesses. The movement from one kingdom, one king,

---

[29] J. Stephen Russell, *The English Dream Vision: Anatomy of a Form* (Columbus, 1988) 161.
[30] See, for example, Robert J. Blanch, 'Precious Metal and Gem Symbolism in *Pearl*', in *Sir Gawain and Pearl: Critical Essays*, ed. Robert J. Blanch (Bloomington, 1966) 86–97; Spearing (1970) 96–170; idem (1976) 111–27; Putter 159–98.
[31] Gordon xxxiv, and see below for discussion of references of pearls and Queen Anne (0).
[32] David Lawton, 'Middle English Alliterative Poetry: An Introduction', in *Middle English Alliterative Poetry and Its Literary Background: Seven Essays* 9.

to another, is emphatic. However, unlike the apocalyptic assimilation of earth with the divine world, where the two realms mingle, the Dreamer's vision distinguishes the separateness of both, letting Pearl's absorption into the Heavenly City be the climax of his revelatory experience.

Perhaps this is because the stress of the *Gawain*-poet's narrative is on the individual's state of spiritual grace, not that of the whole world. The 'precios perle wythouten spotte' is a symbolic image of an inner purity that works triumphantly both in this world and the next. At the end of the poem, when the Dreamer is catapulted back into his own world, he has learnt to defer to God's will: 'Now al be to þat Prynceȝ paye' (1176). He concludes that 'To pay þe Prince oþer sete saȝte / Hit is ful eþe to þe god Krystyin' (1201–2). Just as Jonah in *Patience* and Gawain in *Sir Gawain and the Green Knight* have to learn patient acceptance, the Dreamer has learnt to accept God's unfathomable ways, and to trust in Him: 'A God, a Lorde, a frende ful fyin' (1204). This triad shows the *Gawain*-poet's efforts to translate the spiritual world into something that humans can begin to relate to; God is at once ineffable, a Lord who deserves service in the same ways an earthly lord requires obedience, and, more intimately, a friend who sees each individual for what they are.

In this way *Pearl* differs from the other poems of the poet; *Patience* and *Cleanness* are, indeed, 'concerned chiefly with the kingdom of men, and with how God intervenes in it in order to enforce his hatred of certain vices' while *Pearl*, in contrast, 'is concerned with the kingdom of Heaven, which is the promised reward for the corresponding virtues'.[33] This intimate, localised concentration succeeds in highlighting the fundamental relationship between mankind and God, between the subjects and the king. The portrayal of God in the other three poems of the manuscript emphasises the strength and power of His reign, using anthropomorphic symbols to illustrate this, but in *Pearl* the poet is interested in the more difficult concept of a king who is the epitome of both meekness and strength. The image of the sacrificial Lamb who is also the Lion may not be a direct comment on an ideal earthly king's love for his subjects, yet the very nature of its deliberate choice as an analogy means it cannot help but raise issues about the way one might rule.

In this divine paradox, the two seemingly opposite distinctions of meekness and might are also inherent in the medieval ideals of the attributes of the perfect knight: one that would have the qualities necessary to be both a masterful *auxilium* (warrior) and an able and wise *consilium* (counsellor).[34] In utilising this code, the *Gawain*-poet shows himself part of a tradition that can be traced back to Beowulf, who is eulogised not only for his heroic and courageous acts (3173) but also because he was 'wyruldcyning[a] / manna mildust ond mon(ow)ærust' (3180–1).[35] In the fifteenth century Malory is still combining these virtues in his work; Ector's threnody on Launcelot, for example, celebrates him as having

---

[33] Spearing (1970) 100.
[34] For a discussion of this, see David Burnley, *Courtliness and Literature in Medieval England* (London, 1998) 23–36.
[35] Fr Klaeber, ed., *Beowulf* (Lexington, KY, 1950) 119–20.

been 'the mekest man and the jentyllest that ever ete in halle emonge ladyes' and also the 'sternest knyght to thy mortal foo that ever put spere in the reeste'.[36] Chaucer's Knight, perhaps most famously, is admired because he is both 'ful worthy ... in his lordes were' (*GP* 47) and yet 'wys ... of his port as meeke as is a mayde' (*GP* 69). He loves 'chivalrie, / Trouthe and honour, fredom and curteisie' (*GP* 45–6).[37] Langland, too, describes a knight who is approved by Piers Plowman because he is prepared to fight and yet let meekness be his master in the endeavour to find Truth.[38]

Just as *Pearl* emphasises the Lion/Lamb image that is God's awesome, ineffable mystery, reminding us how impenetrable His metaphors are, so the two extremes of earthly knighthood represent the highest ideals that a man could hope to attain in the Middle Ages.

The *Gawain*-poet is drawn to the romance tradition, and writes confidently within it, as we see in *Sir Gawain and the Green Knight*. I would argue that here, in *Pearl*, he uses the setting of the courtly Heaven to make more accessible this point about the kinship between the roles of the divine King and His earthly followers, of whatever status. Though imagery directly drawn from the Book of Revelations is often specifically used by the *Gawain*-poet, there is still plenty of differentiation that gives scope for commentary. The aspects of an essentially feudal town that the *Gawain*-poet uses in his depiction of the Heavenly City make the link with situations on earth a firm one; the manuscript itself has an illustration that 'medievalises the City even more completely'.[39] Ultimately unattainable as this pure combination of Lamb and Lion is in human terms, the striving to attain both meekness and forcefulness is nevertheless essential to medieval knighthood. It may be the Dreamer whose experience shapes the contents of the narrative, rather than a knight or a king, but what Pearl teaches him is very sophisticated indeed. He may not be able to comprehend it, but 'the figurative meaning of the maiden's talk of "courts," "queens," or heavenly "marriages" is not a matter of fact ... but a matter of faith'.[40] Though there are no explicit references to lords, or kings, the fact that any mention of courts and courtesy in writings of that period would automatically carry associations of those roles makes it difficult to argue that the poem does not have assertions to make by implication. The text itself uses many feudal terms; for example, 'bayly', 'empress', 'realm', 'kingdom', 'court' all make appearances in one short passage (441–8), and critical appraisal has highlighted the legal terminology embedded within the poem, which reflects its origins as part of a society governed by a system of law.[41]

---

[36] Sir Thomas Malory, *The Works of Sir Thomas Malory*, ed. Eugène Vinaver, rev. P. J. C. Field, 3rd edn, 3 vols (Oxford, 1990) 1259.18–21.
[37] References to Chaucer are from *The Riverside Chaucer*, ed. Larry D. Benson (Boston, MA, 1987). Field has argued that the 'lordes' of *GP* 47 refers to Christ and not to the king: P. J. C. Field, 'The Ending of Chaucer's *Nun's Priest's Tale*', *Medium Aevum* 71 (2002) 304–5.
[38] *Piers Plowman* vi 34–40.
[39] Gordon, note to line 917: 77.
[40] Putter 175.
[41] Kean (1967) 185–96.

Pearl is not just a rather poignant tale of grief, it is 'a presentation of a human discourse the purpose of which is to demonstrate the complete inefficacy of that discourse'.[42] As such it contains layers of meaning that twist away from clarity as the poem itself moves around the Dreamer's attempts to grasp understanding from his vision: 'connections between the various aspects of the matter are not made explicit through the formal design; the true connections are made obliquely, through imagery and association'.[43]

Cleanness

In *Cleanness*, the second of the poems in the manuscript, the treatment of kingship becomes vitally integrated with the poem's theme of purity, particularly in the third section, where the story of Belshazzar's feast is retold to illustrate how the anger of God will be visited on rulers who do not respect His word. The hubris of the king is shown to be the direct cause of the downfall and suffering of the people he rules: 'And thus was that londe lost for the lordes synne' (1797). Daniel reminds King Belshazzar of the example of his father, Nebuchadnezzar, and the lesson he was forced to learn after his pride, too, overreached itself. While Nebuchadnezzar believed that God was the source of his success, all was well: 'And whyle that was cleght clos in his hert / There was no mon upon molde of myght as hymselven' (1656–7). The king's fortunes changed when he began to convince himself that the continued success of his reign was really owing to his own talents, and, in a move more audacious than this, he gave himself god-like status:

> 'I am god of the grounde, to gye as me lykes,
> As he that hyghe is heven, his aungeles that weldes.
> If he has formed the folde and folk thrupone,
> I haf bigged Babiloyne, burgh alther-rychest,
> Stabled therinne uche a ston in strenkthe of myn armes;
> Moght never myght bot myn make such another.' (1663–8)

His punishment was total humiliation: he had to live like a beast of the field, and relearn God's complete supremacy before becoming able to resume his duties as king. Daniel's reminder of Nebuchadnezzar's fate highlights the enormity of Belshazzar's sin. By using the sacred goblets as drinking vessels for his feast, he has forgotten the respect and reverence due to God, and has sullied the honour of the position that he has been allowed to hold.

It is significant that the *Gawain*-poet uses the term 'Soverayn' in line 1670 to denote God. The linking of the earthly and heavenly rulers is thus firmly emphasised. Nebuchadnezzar does not follow the pattern of sovereignty set by God, where firm, fair, careful leadership creates a strong, profitable kingdom. But he learns. However, Belshazzar does not get the same chance. He is left

---

[42] Russell 160.
[43] Davenport (1978) 51.

to die in an ignominious way: 'Now is a dogge also dere that in a dych lygges' (1793). In these Biblical portraits, highlighted by the *Gawain*-poet, it is possible to perceive a comment on kingship in England at the time he was writing. These viewpoints are made evident through a discussion on the organisation and representation of the court: '*Cleanness* relates the decorum and purity of the ideal earthly court to that of God's heavenly one, and to the order and natural law of his Creation.'[44]

Right at the beginning of the poem, the poet describes God as being part of a court: 'He is so clene in his courte, the kyng that al weldes' (17). This imagery can be a highly significant illuminator of the *Gawain*-poet's views on kingship, if looked at across all of the poems. Here, in *Cleanness*, as Derek Brewer has observed, 'God is felt ... very much as a noble, just, warm-hearted, but therefore also passionate and indeed hot-tempered, feudal lord.'[45] The portrayals of courts and kings in all the works of the poet use the court itself as a reflection of the king's ruling 'health', especially in *Sir Gawain and the Green Knight*, which will be dealt with later. The character of God in the three other works is mostly consistent with this notion of a feudal lord; the idealised setting of Heaven in *Pearl* has already been mentioned. Here, in *Cleanness*, God is a deity with quickly invoked reactions. In *Patience*, too, He exhibits clear traits of a compassionate king who looks after subjects whom He sees very much as His responsibility and concern. Although the *Gawain*-poet's God is the true God of the Old Testament in this, showing a range of emotions from a desire for revenge to a sorrowful and deeply forgiving love, the anthropomorphic features make the portrayals go further: 'the *Gawain*-poet is exceptional among medieval writers in portraying God as someone who is occasionally overcome with nausea and bouts of ill temper'.[46] This makes for a God who is very different from the perfect, untouchable, unknowable deity more commonly portrayed in medieval times.

During the fourteenth century, England was ruled by kings who at times could be seen to parallel the lives of the Old Testament monarchs. Corruption and ineffectual government caused many of the crises the country faced during this period, and it should not therefore be surprising that the poet took the importance of purity for his text in much of his work.

In *Cleanness*, in contrast to the more mysterious and awe-inspiring images of *Pearl*, the world of God is detailed with domestic insights that make the humanity, and therefore the relevance, of the Old Testament characters more powerfully incisive. When Abraham sits outside in the sun 'even byfore his hous dore, under an oke grene' (602), when Lot's wife decides to add salt to the visitors' food, when the rich man of Matthew's gospel lists the appetising dishes that he has gathered for his feast, all peculiarly English delicacies, the effectiveness of this approach is very clear. The kings behave badly, and are punished, as

---

[44] D. J. Williams, 'Alliterative Poetry in the Fourteenth and Fifteenth Centuries', *The Middle Ages*, ed. W. F. Bolton (London, 1980) 158.
[45] Brewer (1966) 59.
[46] Putter 212.

quickly and as forcibly as the less noble characters. The kings, however, suffer greater wrath from God because they have so much more responsibility to maintain the 'cleanness' of their lands. In this detailed telling of such disparate tales from the Old Testament, told with such skill, the *Gawain*-poet essentially shows how a king should rule in order to gain the respect of his people. To abandon God's ways and live sinfully will bring down disaster, as exemplified by the fate of Sodom and Gomorrah.

The courts that are portrayed in *Cleanness*, then, are intriguing. They can be idealised places of harmony, showing God's court, or they can be more localised descriptions of a place that more closely resembles that of a fourteenth-century nobleman's feudal hall, complete with stocks and dungeons. The description of a king's court, the home of Belshazzar, uses both kinds of imagery to emphasise the extent of the corruption. It is certainly a court full of splendour and riches:

> When alle segges were ther set, then servyse bygynnes;
> Sturne trumpen strake, steven in halle;
> Aywhere by the wowes wrasten krakkes,
> And brode baneres therbi, blusnande of gold.
>
> Burnes berande the bredes upon brode skeles,
> That were of sylveren sygh, and seves therwyth;
> Lyfte logges therover and on lofte corven,
> Pared out of paper and poynted of golde. (1400–8)

The extravagances are not criticised, however. This is not what the poet feels is inappropriate; on the contrary, the courtly scene, the generosity of the king in inviting all his guests to participate so freely of his largesse, shows an image of a successful and praiseworthy leader. The sounds of the music are carefully detailed, as are the exquisite ingredients of the different courses served; it is a sensory exploration of a perfect courtly banquet. The elaborate feasting arrangements are to appear again, with as much significance, in *Sir Gawain and the Green Knight*. Belshazzar is the resplendent benefactor to all his subjects:

> So was served fele sythe the sale alle aboute,
> With solace at the sere course, bifore the self lorde. (1417–18)

Whether the rest of the tale is remembered or not, it is an effective contrast to be subsequently plunged into the description of Belshazzar's sacrilege towards the temple vessels. The long passages detailing the beauty of these artifacts far outweigh the passages about the feast that have already been encountered; the gap between the spiritual and the temporal is thus made abundantly clear. Purity, or cleanness, is not necessarily equated with poverty and austerity of living. The temple cups are so extravagantly decorated, so pricelessly forged, that their value is above monetary calculation (1542–98). Perhaps that is the point. The *Gawain*-poet shows that items so precious reflect what they are, reflect the sacred nature of their association. King Belshazzar's desire to use these vessels has nothing to do with celebrating God's power and goodness, and everything to do with selfish ostentation. This is his uncleanness, his sin. He pollutes the purity of their purpose by bringing them out of the temple, and his pride makes him defiant of any power greater than his own.

Patience

Patience, concentrating on the story of Jonah, may seem to have less concern with kingship even than these other poems, but it, too, shows some illuminating insights into the hierarchy of power. At the beginning of the poem, the narrator muses on the wisdom of learning to accept direction from his superiors with patient resignation:

> Other yif my lege lorde lyst on lyve me to bidde
> Other to ryde other to renne to Rome in his ernde,
>
> What graythed me the grychchyng bot grame more seche?
> Much yif he me ne made, maugref my chekes,
> And thenne thrat moste I thole and unthonk to mede,
> The had bowed to his bode bongré my hyure. (51–6)

It would do no good to complain, or to feel ill-used by the instruction that he receives; that is the way that the world is, and the best way to live contentedly within it is to learn acceptance of one's place. The narrator's liege lord, even if he were to listen to any attempt to disagree with his commands, would still be angered by his servant's complaints, and therefore life would not be pleasant either way. Misery will be the result, unless the narrator can teach himself to carry out his orders with composure. Patience, the quality at the centre of the poem, is thus specifically concerned with the ability needed to submit graciously to the rule of those in authority.

As the poem progresses, this focus is developed to embrace the portrayal of God, the ultimate ruler. Jonah becomes angry with God: he sees the relief of the Ninevites as a direct betrayal. His mission was to warn Nineveh of its imminent destruction, but having completed this task, God forgives them, moved by their repentance. In this way, the narrator's earlier explanation of the tightly bound nature of the relationship between lord and servant becomes sharply relevant. Jonah's anger stems from his initial inability to understand and accept God's ultimate authority; that, just as an earthly lord has overall sovereignty over his subjects, can direct them as his whim falls, God's actions are unquestionable, part of a higher design that mortals cannot, and should not, try and comprehend. Jonah's defiance, then, is dramatic. He challenges God's decisions not once but twice, learning little from his own salvation when he is rescued by the whale. His audacity in confronting God even after he has himself benefited from His capacity for forgiveness seems all the more daring. A God who threatens a whole city with retribution is surely not going to tolerate this? Jonah must be taught a lesson. Yet this is a lord who takes vengeance only when it is absolutely necessary. The *Gawain*-poet's subject is Patience, and in God's restraint, this aspect of the Biblical tale is emphasised. He gives Jonah a gourd under which he may hide from the sun, and then blasts it so that Jonah is left unprotected from the bright glare. Using this as an exemplum, God points out to Jonah that his complaint at the gourd's fate is no different than God's feelings for the Ninevites, except that as God has real responsibility for the growth and well-being of the people, His action in saving them was the more justifiable.

Just as in the Bible's telling of the tale, the reaction of Jonah is not shown. This silence, in the poem, is postscripted with a comment by the narrator, who reminds us that patience is 'a nobel poynt, thagh hit displese ofte' (531). This small observation implies a bigger realisation: that though God's commands are, and requests by earthly rulers may be, part of a plan that we should not question, the likelihood is that, at least sometimes, both will be difficult to accept. Acceptance is a skill that has already been championed in *Pearl*; the narrator seems to be advising quiet acquiescence as the most desirable state to be in; kings of whatever kind, by virtue of their position, must be obeyed. This may appear to be a very unheroic attitude compared with the active seeking and questioning of the Dreamer in *Piers Plowman*, but the poem gives no sense that this is an easy option. The acknowledgment that this may often cause displeasure is an honest awareness that such patience is a quality to be striven for. Moreover, the fact that the *Gawain*-poet describes it with the courtly adjective of 'noble' implies the honour attached to the successful following of such an inner discipline.

Sir Gawain and the Green Knight

This idea of a tightly interwoven relationship between the ruler and the subject, couched in terms familiar to readers of courtly romances, finds its most complete realisation in *Sir Gawain and the Green Knight*.[47] The *Gawain*-poet takes as his theme the 'trawþe' of Arthur and his court. Though there are many different possible interpretations of this Middle English word, the *Gawain*-poet seems to use it primarily to reflect the integrity of the righteous aims of the king's rule.[48] The defining settings of the poem are the courts of Arthur and Bertilak; in the detailed representation of each the poet provides scope for comment on the inhabitants, building up comparisons that may suggest and challenge ideals of courtly life. The opening scenes take place between Christmas and January, a period that may have had political significance for contemporary readers of the poem, as well as being a romance convention for a period when strange events could take place.[49] Arthur's Christmas feast shows the liberal hospitality of the king, who allows his knights to feast 'with rych revel oryght and rechles merthes' (58–9). The generosity of the arrangements, which include enough food for everyone to be served more than double helpings, and to have both

---

[47] *Sir Gawain and the Green Knight*, eds J. R. R. Tolkien and E. V. Gordon, rev. Norman Davis, 2nd edn (Oxford, 1967).
[48] See the alternative interpretations discussed in W. R. J. Barron, *Trawthe and Treason: The Sin of Gawain Reconsidered* (Manchester, 1980) and summarised by J. A. Burrow in *A Reading of Sir Gawain and the Green Knight* (London, 1965) 42–50.
[49] See Staley (2005) 211.

beer and wine, stresses the wealth and power of the king. In a time when real poverty was so near a threat, such plenty established the greatness of the ruler beyond a doubt.

Evidence of the importance attached to the proper way to behave at a feast can be found in the wealth of 'courtesy books' written in the fourteenth century; good manners, or courtesy, was one of the defining features of a good courtier or knight.[50] In *Sir Gawain and the Green Knight*, therefore, there is a long description of the behaviour of Arthur's knights at table: 'most kyd ... under Krystes selven' (51), they wash their hands and are seated in a strict hierarchy. The atmosphere is, above all, one of harmony: 'al was hap upon heghe in halles and chambres/ With lordes and ladies, as levest him thoght' (49–50). This portrait is a vital one: at the end of the poem this harmony will be called into play again, and its successful illustration here makes the homecoming of Gawain more warm and 'true' at the conclusion.

In the portrayal of Arthur, too, there are points of interest. He is described as being 'sumquat childgered' (86): which could imply that the king is irresponsible in his outlook, or that he is simply full of high spirits. However, it does not seem to be a criticism:

> ... he lovied the lasse
> Auther to lenge lye or to longe sitte,
> So bisied him his yonge blod and his brayn wylde. (87–9)

Rather, in the context of the feast that the *Gawain*-poet details, his attitude fits with an impression of a court that is stable and secure in its fashioning. The king's happiness stems from this confidence in his surroundings; the arrival of the Green Knight, huge and bizarrely coloured, is therefore all the more startling. The disruption breaks the atmosphere and the changes it to one of menace and uncertainty. The Green Knight appears as a lord without acknowledged superiors; he is therefore a kind of king who can be compared against Arthur, making his contrast the more effective. Later this comparison will prove to be relevant to the poem's structure. The *Gawain*-poet's long and precise description of the physical appearance of the Green Knight allows the moment of suspense to be maintained. The disclosure that many of the knights mistook the apparition 'for fantoum and fayryye' (240) therefore is not difficult to imagine; the court in its entirety is rendered powerless to act, not because they are discourteous, but because of the sheer scale and outrageous looks of the intruder. There may even be parallels with the tale of the unwelcome wedding guest, related by the *Gawain*-poet in *Cleanness*. The story, combining Matthew 22 and Luke 14, tells of the rich nobleman who prepared a feast for all his friends and neighbours. As the host moves round the room, greeting his guests, he notes that one man has not bothered to dress with any sense of the occasion, and has him thrown out; his attire is an insult to the courteous hospitality of the lord. The Green Knight's

---

[50] For a discussion of the importance of this material, see Jonathan Nicholls, *The Matter of Courtesy: Medieval Courtesy Books and the Gawain-Poet* (Woodbridge, 1985).

clothes, too, are unconventional enough to cause people to pause: the insult, if one was intended, set against the adventurous nature of his appearance. The poet stresses that this lack of immediate reaction has little to do with the innately courteous nature of the court. 'As al were slypped upon slepe so slaked hor lotes in hyye' (243); the magical aspects of the strange knight's arrival have the effect of an enchantment on the observers. In this way, they cannot be fully culpable for their hesitation in welcoming him, although the ambiguity is present: 'I deme hit not al for doute, / Bot sum for cortaysye' (246–7).

Arthur's own reaction to the Green Knight is also full of contrasting impulses; he is outclassed in social subtlety but remains courteous in very difficult circumstances. We are shown the 'wit and elegance, the *self-possession*' he can portray while at the same time 'we are not allowed to take his self-possession for granted, as though it cost him an effort to achieve'.[51] Arthur's very human attempts to maintain self-control make the impenetrability of the Green Knight the more unnerving: the world of romance does not seem to be as easily accepted by the members of his court as it does in most other Arthurian romances. Indeed, 'the effort that goes into pretending, for the benefit of all, that nothing out of the ordinary has actually occurred shows how uneasily they adjust from watching a romance-marvel to resuming the festive business of the day'.[52]

Arthur's speech towards the end of the first fitt, regaining calm in the court, shows how the 'combination of narratorial penetration and the *Gawain*-poet's usual gift for imitating tones of voice catches and crystallizes a whole range of varied motives as they stream past':[53]

> Thagh Arther the hende kyng at hert hade wonder,
> He let no semblaunt be sene, bot sayde ful hyghe
> To the comlych quene wyth cortays speche,
> 'Dere dame, today demay yow never;
> Wel bycommes such craft upon Christmasse,
> Laykyng of enterludez, to laghe and to syng,
> Among thise kynde caroles of knyghtez and ladyez.
> Never the lece to my mete I may me wel dres,
> For I haf sen a selly, I may not forsake.'
> He glent upon Sir Gawen, and gaynly he sayde,
> 'Now sir, henge up thyn ax, that hatz innogh hewen.' (467–77)

Arthur's first task is to reassure his queen, which he does by laughing the whole episode off as part of the Christmas entertainments; then, in a quiet but authoritative command contained in a joke to Gawain, he tells him to put away his axe, which still calls attention to what has happened. 'Hang up your axe' could mean 'have done with this business' as well as the literal interpretation; in this case both readings are appropriate, and the king is witty enough to exploit this

---

[51] Burrow (1965) 29.
[52] Putter 61–2.
[53] Spearing (1970) 176.

to try and 'absorb the abnormal into the normal'.[54] The portrayal of kingship in this opening scene is of a man aware of his responsibilities as a ruler, but full of human responses that show the effort that duty costs. The *Gawain*-poet's portrait of Arthur is therefore a shrewd and a sympathetic one, showing that kings, whether in the world of romance or reality, must constantly uphold the standards of courteous behaviour that they owe to their subjects.

Although the beheading game and the Lady's temptation of Gawain, the two major elements of the plot, have antecedents in older stories, the *Gawain*-poet makes a causal connection between them: Gawain's fate at the hands of the Green Knight depends directly on his ability to resist the temptation of Bertilak's wife.[55] In this story, using the vehicle of romance conventions, the poet is able to discuss the idea that a ruler affects the spirit and temperament of the court he controls, that he does in effect hold the key to the moral health of his subjects.

Gawain's quest is therefore not only about his personal spiritual integrity, as many critics have argued.[56] He is the most exemplary of the knights, and moreover, as Arthur's own nephew, is the ideal choice to illustrate how indomitable the king's leadership is:

> alle prys and prowes and pured þewes
> Apendes to hys persoun, and praysed is euer;
> Byfore alle men vpon molde his mensk is þe most. (912–14)

The Green Knight is openly delighted that Gawain accepts the challenge, saying that he was 'ferly fayn' (388) that this should be so. As kin to Arthur, Gawain's actions cast a sharper light on his uncle's attributes, bound as he is to him both by ties of knightly loyalty and blood. Later, when the Green Knight is revealed as Bertilak de Hautdesert, under the direction of Morgan le Fay, the importance of the family relationship is made evident. Morgan planned the whole escapade,

> For to assay þe surquidré, yif hit soth were
> Þat rennes of þe grete renoun of þe Rounde Table.
> Ho wayned me þis wonder your wyttez to reue,
> For to haf greued Gaynour and gart hir to dyye
> With glopyng of þat ilke gome þat gostlych speked
> With his hede in his honde bifore þe hyghe table. (2456–62)

She wanted to test her brother's reputation, to try and puncture the pride and arrogance that she saw as characteristic of his court. In setting up her own rival court at Hautdesert, and in testing Gawain's honesty and courtesy so ruthlessly, she had hoped to find fatal flaws in the Round Table and its ideals. Gawain's action in volunteering to be the challenger, rather than any of the other knights,

---

[54] Spearing (1970) 176.
[55] Norris Lacy, ed., *The New Arthurian Encyclopedia* (New York, 1996) 420.
[56] See, for example, Burrow (1965) 160–70; Spearing (1970) 219–36; P. J. C. Field, 'A Rereading of *Sir Gawain and the Green Knight*', *Studies in Philology* 68 (1971) 255–69; Davenport 180–94.

was to have made her victory all the greater. By resisting the temptations that she makes for him, however, Gawain ultimately brings shame on to Arthur and his court only insofar as he does not reveal possession of the girdle. This fall from grace, this venial sin,[57] causes him to feel great shame. He did not reveal possession of the gift at confession, before he meets the Green Knight; nor does he reveal his intention to break his promise to exchange winnings. In this he is at fault, but not so much that the confrontation is seen, or portrayed by the *Gawain*-poet as being, a sign of ingrained depravity. Arthur's rule is not, as Morgan le Fay wished to prove, rotten at the core. When Gawain returns to Arthur's court, everyone welcomes him with praise, and their humility is shown in the agreement that all will wear a green belt in recognition of their kinship with Gawain's ability to commit an act of weakness. In this simple gesture, the innate stability and moral healthiness of the court is affirmed with striking force; Morgan le Fay has managed only to prove the opposite of what she had hoped. The court as a whole has learnt something from Gawain's escapade; even the best of knights are not invulnerable to temptation. Their unity in response is a triumphant final image to the poem, showing how firmly they are all in accord, how affected they are by the actions of even one of their company.

Although acknowledging this harmony of attire, some critics have suggested that far from asserting a positive conclusion, it shows that the court does not grow, as Gawain does, through his journey.[58] This relies on a reading of Gawain's final speeches as bitter and sarcastic in tone, the belt as a badge of shame, rather than the badge of honour that the court view it as, and the poem's culminative structure as mysterious and unfathomable. This reading seems to imply Morgan le Fay's supremacy; Spearing remarks, as Larry Benson does, that because she is related to both Gawain and Arthur, this inherent evil will reveal itself, does reveal itself, in their actions.[59] Gawain's quest has therefore ended in disaster. This theory implies that he has proved the latent corruption of Camelot. This seems to be so only if a determined effort to see defeat is adopted at every point of the story. The unified court can only be an ironic image if Gawain can truly be seen to be a rather deflated anti-hero: but there are no signs at any point in the poem that Arthur or his court are in any way infected by a malaise of immorality. The ecstatic welcome accorded to Gawain parallels more the return of the Prodigal Son than any portrayal of a decadent and wilfully self-deceived company who have no sympathy with the true feelings or motivations of one of their most well-loved knights. Gawain's confession to everyone, a very public affair, illustrates this familial rapport with the court. As Spearing earlier acknowledges, 'Arthur is no Renaissance tyrant but a medieval prince, ruling by counsel of his nobles.'[60] This may politicise the king a little too far, but it rightly

---

[57] For a discussion of this precision of terms, see Field (1971).
[58] Spearing (1970) 222–36.
[59] Spearing (1970) 229; L. D. Benson, *Art and Tradition in Sir Gawain and the Green Knight* (New Brunswick, 1965) 32.
[60] Spearing (1970) 183.

discerns a sense of a tacit working together, albeit with the sovereign still very much in a position of ultimate authority.

Gawain's silence at the judgement can be read as a supreme example of the virtue of patience, of acceptance, that runs so strongly through the other poems of the *Gawain*-poet. Gawain is the best knight that Arthur has, and the poet makes clear how difficult it is for him to accept the forgiveness of his king, whom he feels he has failed. If the lines at the beginning of *Patience* are remembered, this virtue brings a healing property that will also ultimately help the knight to recover:

> When hevy hertтes ben hurt wyth hethyng other elles,
> Suffraunce may aswagen hem and the swelme lethe,
> For ho quelles uche a qued and quenches malyce. (*Patience* 2–4)

It takes the judgement of Arthur, combined with the benevolent behaviour of Bertilak, to show the strength of the ruling authority. Gawain will acquiesce, because he is a fundamentally a knight who reflects the king's wise and just rule. To dispute his sentence would be not only discourteous, in the courtly sense, it would imply a lack of faith. It would weaken the realm. It is by the king's ability to hold everyone and everything in a harmonious stronghold, not by force, but by a conscious effort of will and commitment by all his subjects, particularly the example of the nobles, that makes him so vital a leader. It is difficult to reconcile an ironic reading of the narration with the readiness with which he is forgiven by all. Rather than emphasising a gulf of misunderstanding, the courteous language in which the poem is couched, the emphasis on the joy felt and the warmth with which the welcome is offered, seem to stress this harmony:

> Þer wakned wele in þat wone when wyst þe grete
> Þat gode Gawayn watz commen; gayn hit hym þoght.
> Þe kyng kyssez þe knyght, and þe whene alce,
> And syþen mony syker knyght þat soght hym to haylce,
> Of his fare þat hym frayned. (2490–4)

The *Gawain*-poet's ideas of kingship are as strong as those of Langland, although they seem to be so different. In their exploration of the courtly life, stressing the need for honourable, patient subjugation, the poems reveal a tough but responsible commitment to a disciplined way of life. Kings, both earthly and heavenly, require obedience, because obedience is loyalty. And loyalty is one of the primary attributes of the ideal knight.[61] Just as the Anglo-Saxons believed in following their leaders towards death, unquestioning, to achieve certain glory, so the *Gawain*-poet tries to make plain the importance of upholding the 'trawþe' of the king's judgements. Only by achieving this can the kingdom be effectively ruled. Although he does not engage directly with contemporary events, this is

---

[61] See Gervase Matthews, 'Ideals of Knighthood in Late Fourteenth-Century England', in *Studies in Medieval History Presented to Frederick Maurice Powicke*, eds R. W. Hunt, W. A. Pantin and R. W. Southern (Oxford, 1948) 354–62.

because his poems assimilate the reign of Richard II by emphasising its place in an essentially hierarchical and securely bound universal kingdom ruled by God:

> Indeed, the richness of the poems combined with their artistic purity, the self-containment of their meaning, the sublime control and assurance with which they are composed, the total poetic energy they absorb, suggest a man for whom the perfection of his art has become a kind of defense against crisis.[62]

There are clear indications that the poet was aware of those moments of crisis, but that he chose to create in-built resistances to these situations based on the order that faith and obedience, reflected in the structured patterns of his alliterative lines, could restore. In this he cannot be said to be 'steadily and specifically royalist, revealing a concern for the precise practice of kingship by his obsessive recourse to regalian images'.[63] Instead, the *Gawain*-poet teaches us an important principle: that through attending to the resistances in his poems we learn 'a matching delicacy in how a historicist holds the view that a text both speaks to and is spoken by its history'.[64]

---

[62] Muscatine (1999) 111.
[63] Bowers (2001) 16.
[64] Fletcher 170.

4

Chaucer

This final chapter is concerned with the work of the best-known of all the Ricardian poets, Geoffrey Chaucer: 'the most receptive as well as the most inventive English poet of the Middle Ages'.[1] Chaucer's work has been consistently celebrated for its breadth of scope and range of styles; writing while in the service of different members of the royal family through the reigns of three different monarchs, he was in an excellent position to comment on the political and social events of his time. He travelled widely, carrying out royal business on the continent, and knew the courts of France and Italy well. Yet, as we shall see, he rarely comments on those kings whose lives he had the opportunity to observe from close quarters, or engages directly with ideas of kingship.[2] Indeed, to 'turn to Chaucer and ask that he sum up a conversation about the definition of regal authority is to ask the master of indirection for an answer he can only give obliquely'.[3] He is 'involved, yet objective, detached yet sympathetically moved'[4] by events around him, and this constant shifting of attitudes makes it difficult to assess with any final accuracy his relationship with the idea of kingship. It is only in a few of the shorter poems, written at the end of his life, that we see more or less overt attempts to engage with a royal audience.

In the ballad 'Lak of Stedfastnesse', apparently written between 1397 and 1399, there is an envoy to King Richard, in which Chaucer sets out his thoughts on the duties of the monarch.[5] Though it is short, and though the ideas are conventional, any such definition is so rare in the corpus of Chaucer's work that it is worth noting:

> O prince, desyre to be honourable,
> Cherish thy folk and hate extorcioun.
> Suffre nothing that may be reprevable
> To thyn estat don in thy regioun.
> Shew forth thy swerd of castigacioun,
> Dred God, do law, love trouthe and worthinesse,
> And wed thy folk agein to stedfastnesse.

---

[1] Dieter Mehl, *English Literature in the Age of Chaucer* (London, 2001) 8.
[2] For a discussion on Chaucer's affinities to the Ricardian and Lancastrian factions, see Strohm (1989) 24–46.
[3] Lynn Staley, 'Translating "Communitas"', in *Imagining a Medieval Nation*, ed. Kathy Lavezzo (Minneapolis, 2004) 292.
[4] Muscatine (1972) 145.
[5] Parallels to the Prologue of Gower's *Confessio Amantis* have been noted: Fisher 247–50.

84 *Chaucer*

Paul Strohm has argued strongly that the poem is linked to a specific occasion in Richard's reign – that of the Petition of Commons in September 1388 – when the king interposed to calm a dispute about livery badges, used to practise extortion in the countryside. Richard offered to set an example by abandoning his own insignia. The intervention was a strategic success, and for once the public voice was in accord in approving the king's actions. Strohm argues that Chaucer's poem may show a sympathy with this event, and with Richard's role as princely mediator.[6]

Whether Strohm is right about the occasion or not, this poem can clearly be read as an ideological creation in which Richard becomes the beneficiary, its lines 'bound over and delivered to the magnification of his regality and the service of his rule'.[7]

In the 'Ballad to Fortune', there is an appeal to princes in the envoy, and it has been suggested that this refers to the royal dukes of Lancaster, York and Gloucester, with the 'beste frend' of line 78 referring to King Richard.[8] This poem has also been assigned to Chaucer's later years.

Finally, in an apostrophe added to the 'Complaint of Chaucer to his Purse', written specifically to Henry IV, Chaucer appeals to the king for financial aid. The poem begins by wittily personifying his purse as a lady, and the poet's tone is that of a courtly lover, asking for favours from his mistress. Although the first line intimates privacy – 'to noon other wight / Complayne I' – the ending belies this. Henry is 'verray king', 'conqueror of Brutes Albyon', and his power to 'alle oure harmes amende' is clearly the real focus of this supplication. The conventional language covers subtle questions, which wryly, but gracefully, show awareness of the tensions under the new king's rule.[9]

Where Gower used rhetoric to give his exempla force, Chaucer uses language in ways less straightforwardly identifiable, more intricate in narrative focus. The examples of these three poems all show that when he wished to, Chaucer clearly could, and at times did, draw on his knowledge of and connection with kings. Even though 'the situation of address in Chaucer's poetry is ... complex and constantly shifting',[10] the material that he creates is rich in relevant insights.

Indeed, what is striking, set against the work of the other three poets, is how Chaucer's major poetic achievements push attention away from kingship and absorb it into the stories and themes he chooses to focus on. I hope to demonstrate in the rest of this chapter how this approach exemplifies itself in his longer works. They have been divided into three sections for ease of analysis: the first part deals with the dream poems, the second with *Troilus and Criseyde*, and the third pursues the treatment of kings in the *Canterbury Tales*.

---

[6] Strohm (1992) 69.
[7] Strohm (1992) 74.
[8] See Benson's note in *The Riverside Chaucer*, 1084.
[9] Staley (2005) 354.
[10] Strohm (1989) 46.

The Dream Poems

The Book of the Duchess

Chaucer's poem was written to commemorate the death of Blanche, first wife of John of Gaunt, duke of Lancaster, and is the only one of his works securely identifiable as composed for a specific royal occasion. In its concentration upon a contemporary situation and a contemporary person of high status, this work of Chaucer's is unique. As such it is closely connected to history:

> The *Book of the Duchess* is a surprising exception to the characteristic universality of Chaucer's poems. Though his poetry usually frees itself of the fourteenth century and requires for its appreciation only a deep knowledge of human nature, the *Duchess* seems to demand an understanding of its own time, like a language that has ceased to be current and needs a glossary to bring it to life.[11]

Gaunt was to have a claim to the throne of Castile after his second marriage to Constance of Castile in 1371, but he was not a king in any sense when the *Book of the Duchess* was written. Later he came unusually close to being one: he stood by the steps of two thrones but could not mount to either.[12] His court was 'as close to a royal court as a man not quite a king could ever hope to achieve',[13] and Chaucer, at that time 'a young pipsqueak of an esquire',[14] would have had frequent access to it through his role as diplomatic assistant.

At the time when the poem was written, Gaunt's position of power was still on the rise; as son of Edward III he was proving himself to be a capable leader and a skilful diplomat, and though still in the shadow of his popular elder brother, Edward the Black Prince, was nevertheless a magnate of considerable charm and force. After the death of his brother, he was 'arguably the most powerful man in England', and 'in some ways overshadowed the aged and infirm ruler'.[15] He was, as Thomas Hoccleve said in the 'Regiment of Princes', a 'noble prince'.[16]

Froissart, too, thought highly of the duke, calling him 'such a valiant knight, and so well respected'[17] and although chroniclers of the period, led most notably by the monk Thomas of Walsingham, often fiercely denounced him as immoral and ambitious, this may stem more from dislike of Gaunt's sympathies with

---

[11] Edward I. Condren, 'The Historical Context of the *Book of the Duchess*: A New Hypothesis', *Chaucer Review* 5.3 (1971) 195–212.
[12] Sydney Armitage-Smith, *John of Gaunt: King of Castile and Leon, Duke of Aquitaine and Lancaster, Earl of Derby, Lincoln and Leicester, Seneschal of England* (London, 1964) xxviii.
[13] Staley (2005) 182.
[14] Derek Pearsall, *The Life of Geoffrey Chaucer* (Oxford, 1992) 84.
[15] Strohm (1989) 53.
[16] *Thomas Hoccleve The Regiment of Princes*, ed. Charles R. Blyth (Kalamazoo, 1999) <http://www.lib.rochester.edu/camelot/teams/hoccfrm.htm> (5 April 2004).
[17] *Froissart's Chronicles*, ed. and trans. John Jolliffe (London, 2001) 16.

Wycliffe than from a detached and objective evaluation.[18] Significantly, Gaunt's modern biographer describes him as a vitally important champion of the ideas of kingship of the time. Anthony Goodman praises the work that Gaunt did to 'advance the embryonic authority of the state, as embodied in the sovereign dignity of the king', and concludes that he was 'the later medieval noble who most notably upheld royal authority, an example likely to have been more influential if it had not been undercut by his son's usurpation'.[19] With all this evidence, there would seem to be plenty of material for a young poet keen to make his way to use in developing flattering images of lordship; yet Chaucer's poem refers to Gaunt's status only in oblique ways. The interest in the dream poems lies as much in what Chaucer chooses to ignore as in what he includes about kingship; he maintains the boundaries of respect due to royalty, but engages with ideas of human interest, not opportunities for political commentary, as his contemporary Gower does in the *Confessio*.

The poem was probably written in 1368, or soon afterwards.[20] That was the year in which Blanche died of the Plague, and none of the arguments for later dates have been able to outweigh that fact. The *Book of the Duchess* is a courtly poem, in a courtly setting, and reveals a great deal of the inner workings of court life; the communication of characters portrayed shows some of the nuances of relationships between those of differing status, and the choice of material included in the dream shows how the life of the late fourteenth-century English nobility maintained its perception of itself as a place of highly mannered, cultured style. Though the poem does not show kingship directly, it does indirectly focus on its role, and engages with how grief and the management of that grief are handled by royalty and by their courtiers. The fact that the duke of Lancaster was seen as the most powerful representative of the king's role at this time poses a problem in how to represent that ambivalent position without offence to king or duke. The elegiac form, which is also a consolation and a celebration of Blanche's life, gives an opportunity for reflection on these concerns, providing contrasts to investigations from other poets.

The social dynamics provide tension within the poem; Chaucer the poet and the character of the Dreamer are both firmly lower on the social scale than the royal duke of Lancaster or the Black Knight of the poem. How, then, can Chaucer touch on an intimate subject without transgressing those boundaries, a subject that even without such social complexities would challenge the sympathiser's powers of tact and courtesy? John Burrow has recently suggested that Chaucer's solution, in utilising the dream poem framework, allows him to distance

---

[18] See A. Gransden, *Historical Writing in England*, Vol. 2 (London, 1982) 129–30, 138–9. She points out that after Gaunt's repentance in 1381 Walsingham changes his tone and becomes far less hostile to Gaunt.

[19] Anthony Goodman, *John of Gaunt: the Exercise of Princely Power in Fourteenth-Century Europe* (Harlow, 1992) 374–5.

[20] See J. J. N. Palmer, 'The Historical Context of the *Book of the Duchess*: A Revision', *Chaucer Review* 8.4 (1974) 253–61; Sumner Ferris, 'John Stow and the Tomb of Blanche the Duchess', *Chaucer Review* 18.1 (1983) 92–3; Howard Schless, 'A Dating for the *Book of the Duchess*: line 1314', *Chaucer Review* 19.4 (1985) 273–6.

himself successfully from those he writes about: 'the problem is one of "san et corteisie", of politeness, and in the face of it Chaucer employs one of the chief strategies of courtesy, that is, indirectness'.[21] This stress on the issue of courtesy occurs when the poet/Dreamer 'is in the act of intruding into a very private space, both metaphorically and literally'.[22] Indeed, as another critic has noted,

> Chaucer ... uses the device of the dream, conventionally and functionally, to exclude those reminders of common life, of business, war, and politics, that would cling to a realistic representation of his subject and thus smudge the purity of the feeling proper to the occasion.[23]

Bereavement is a tricky state to mark with any true success; Chaucer's poem is that rare achievement of communication that celebrates the duchess through her apotheosis into the figure of 'White', a woman who combines all the virtues and best attributes of the Lady of courtly romance. The graceful and dignified mourning for her many wonderful qualities turns into an acknowledgment, or consolation, of the experience of knowing her: 'we are presented with the impression of her immediate joyous presence – against the darkness of her absence'.[24]

Chaucer, as a member of the court, was yet on the margins of it; the son of a vintner, he was a useful and capable servant of the royal family, but his status could never be that of intimate friend with the duke or the king. The poem emphasises this, without rancour or ambition. Like Chaucer himself, his Dreamer is familiar enough with the inner workings of the court and how people lived to describe his surroundings with confidence, and little awe and wonder. There is acceptance and ease with roles that are delineated with a naturalness of long familiarity. Yet throughout, though the poem is deeply personal, 'all our intimacy is with Chaucer',[25] and the persona that he creates in the Dreamer. Clearly, to Chaucer, the royal status of the duke must be protected from intense scrutiny, though acknowledgment can be made that he is a man who grieves just as any other, and so

> he creates a dream fiction in which all three parties are represented by surrogates. These both are and are not the real persons for whom they stand ... the figures are all distanced from their real-life originals, unlike as well as like. Within this parallel world of dream, furthermore, Chaucer has relieved his own surrogate from the burden of speaking directly to the purpose.[26]

At the beginning of the poem, the Dreamer describes his sickness, that has lasted eight years, and which only one physician can cure (37–40). He

---

[21] J. A. Burrow, 'Politeness and Privacy: Chaucer's *Book of the Duchess*', in *Studies in Late Medieval and Early Renaissance Texts in Honour of John Scattergood*, eds Anne Marie D'Arcy and Alan J. Fletcher (Dublin, 2005) 74.
[22] Burrow (2005) 68.
[23] Charles Muscatine, *Chaucer and the French Tradition* (Berkeley, 1957) 102.
[24] John Speirs, *Chaucer the Maker* (London, 1951) 42.
[25] Pearsall (1992) 90.
[26] Burrow (2005) 74.

is so exhausted by his sufferings that he believes Death is the only end to his symptoms, and lack of sleep is making his waking fantasies hard to understand. Unlike the speaker in the source for this passage, Froissart's *Paradys d'amours*, the speaker here does not define his sickness as a love-sickness, but rather professes to be unable to say what is causing his distress.[27] Thus even so early in the poem, Chaucer's changes show awareness of the importance of observing the social decencies. The Dreamer's sickness in its undefined state becomes a yearning and a searching that later on will be complimentary to the Black Knight's grief-stricken mourning. Because of their difference in status, it would not be fitting to compare the desire that the Dreamer might be feeling to that of the Black Knight. Yet the Dreamer must be able to bring some understanding to the Black Knight, because Chaucer means to convey a sense of genuine sympathy with the duke's loss, and the 'mased' condition of his mind is a good way to achieve this.

To distract himself from his complaints, the Dreamer decides to read a book, rejecting chess and tables in favour of a French romance. This is full of stories of kings and queens, which, however, the Dreamer finds to be trivial in the light of his own situation. It is only when he comes to the story of Seys and Alcyone that his interest is kindled. This is another example of Chaucer's courtly tact. To assume a kinship with these kings and queens in the tales would be presumptuous. Chaucer must, however, find a bridge of sorts between the higher and lower estates, and the story of the grief-stricken Alcyone neatly provides the answer. Queen Alcyone, distraught at the loss of her husband, swears never to eat again until she has heard from him. Juno hears her and sends Morpheus to bring the body of Seys to Alcyone in a dream. Seys tells Alcyone to forgo her sorrow and live again, but she does not heed him, and dies three days later.

In Ovid's story, it is the queenly wife who is left bereft. Like the Dreamer at this stage in the poem, she is also so affected by her grief that she sees no way out but death, a path that the Dreamer immediately empathises with. He 'ferde the worse al the morwe' for what will happen to him. The implication, then, is perhaps that his pain is caused by the same distress as Alcyone's; that he suffers from grief, too. Several points begin their journey here. The royal characters in the story establish a link of sympathy that can be shown to transcend social status; grief is an emotion that all can feel. This, though delicately brought in, makes Chaucer's poem credible and yet non-invasive. The story itself, with its female lead, puts a little gender distance between the outside situations of the Black Knight and the duke and the courtiers reading or hearing the poem. Alcyone is, after all, an example of how not to cope with grief. She could only see her husband's death as a personal tragedy, and lost all sense of reason as a result.

The Book of the Duchess is a consolatio; that is, it is written to illuminate the spiritual truths behind the event that inspired it, and thus console the listener. The duchess's death was a tragic occurrence, and time would inevitably be taken

---

[27] Bernard F. Huppé and D. W. Robertson, *Fruyt and Chaf: Studies in Chaucer's Allegories* (Princeton, 1963) 32.

to mourn her passing. The Dreamer in Chaucer's poem has to learn how to come to terms with her death; only by reflecting deeply on the story of Alcyone and Ceys can this process take place. So he falls asleep, praying before he does so that he will find relief in his dreams. In this the poem is very unlike the *Gawain*-poet's *Pearl*, where the setting and literary references are all Biblical; Chaucer, despite the consolatio form, chooses to set his knight in a recognisably earthly wood, and many of his references are to classical and courtly works, rather than spiritual ones.

Despite this, the dream removes the substance of the poem a step from the reality of the courtly audience, who were after all Chaucer's aristocratic employers. This dream vehicle expresses ideas that might overstep the lines of acceptance by cleverly smudging those distinctions. Chaucer is able to shroud the rawness of emotion and the directness of the message of consolation behind the elements of courtly romance that he includes in the Dreamer's vision. By also utilising recognisable pieces from other poems of the period, the poet further protects himself by subtle use of familiar and unthreatening images from literature that firmly define his poem as part of that courtly culture.

As the Dreamer begins to recount his dream he reflects, with an early flash of that seeming naivety that he was to use in more complex ways in his later poems, that 'no man had the wyt' (279) to interpret what happened. Even Joseph and Macrobius, who both interpreted dreams for the Pharaoh and King Scipio, would not, he asserts, be able to explain what followed. More modest demurring, perhaps; Chaucer, the creator of this poem, is not attempting to solve anything, or, if this careful covering of implication is to be believed, even to suggest anything useful. He is only recounting a dream, and a dream so strange that unravelling it would be beyond him. The imagined audience is therefore lulled into listening, concentrating on the descriptions the Dreamer gives, rather than actively searching for metaphors and allegorical references. Though these are forcefully there, the result of this tactic is to lessen the stress of intensity on the search for understanding, and allow the audience, the reader, to lose themselves in the dream being spread before them.

It is May and the Dreamer finds himself in a bedchamber filled with the sound of many birds, singing so sweetly that he exclaims it was like a part of heaven. The harmony of both the high and low notes, where each sung 'in hys wyse' (301) and with great effort: 'ther was noon of hem that feyned / to synge, for ech of hem hym peyned / To fynde out mery crafty notes' (317–19), could also be said to subtly excuse Chaucer's art. He, like the birds, is using all his skill, and wherever he may be on the human social scale, his poetic tenor can blend with other higher poetic influences to make something very beautiful. This whole first passage, describing the season and the rich and intricate decoration of the room, displays this with aplomb; when the sources are examined, Chaucer's adaptation of the material evidences how the English poet measured his words to suit his own location and context. Machaut's *Le Jugement dou roy de Behaingne*, *le Dit dou Lyon* and Froissart's *Le Paradys d'amours* all talk of the spring and of the birdsong, but none stress the effort of the birds, or say, as Chaucer does, that 'they ne spared not her throtes' (320) in their singing.

Both Machaut and Froissart were attached to royal courts, and like Chaucer, worked from within that structure without belonging to the courtier-circle by right. Chaucer takes the work of these French poets, however, careful always to maintain the distance of clerk from royalty, and achieves an honest directness that is more personal than his counterparts. He presents the borrowings with awareness of the potential for humour in some of the classical references. Hence in the story of Seys and Alcyone, told by Machaut, Juno sends Iris as messenger to the god of sleep. She is described as delivering her message irreproachably well; in Chaucer's version, the messenger is not named, but is far from graceful and calm. He 'blew his horn ryght in here eere' (182) and seems more like a very realistically perplexed and humble messenger when faced with a god who will not wake up.

Chaucer is bolder than his French counterparts;[28] there is a wry observation of situation that captures the English humour, a sense which, properly judged and delivered, can cut through protocol, ease difficult situations and relax boundaries. Chaucer is daring enough to use these powers even in this sombre occasional piece. His sources are love poems, not elegies; they adorn the emotion with elegance and stylised passages of great control and rich description. Chaucer holds this, admires and imitates it, but pierces it with a wit that makes it a far more personal poetry than attempted before.

As the Dreamer listens to the birds, and marvels at the splendour of his room, which comes straight from the pages of the *Roman de la Rose*, he hears a hunting horn, and gets up, takes his horse, which has suddenly appeared as things do in dreams, and goes to join the proceedings. The hunt is a departure for Chaucer from his sources; in one, two beautiful women come and berate the Dreamer for his treacherous love complaints,[29] in another he finds a beautiful boat and is taken in it to a wonderful garden.[30] Though there is a hunt later on in Froissart's poem, it has nothing like the importance of Chaucer's. In the *Book of the Duchess*, hunting is significant not only because it is the sport of the nobility, but also because it was one of John of Gaunt's favourite pastimes. Like his father before him, his enthusiasm for the chase can be proved by the numerous surviving records of provision for taking care of hunting lands and the custodians of those lands. The duke was a prince of action, of vigorous energy; while the French poets were keen to show royalty against a backdrop of exquisite rooms and cultivated gardens. Chaucer intuitively places his Black Knight in a wood, with a hunt going on around them. It is a particular hunt: a hunt 'with strengthe' (351), the noblest form of the sport. That Chaucer chose to categorise it so precisely roots this work among royalty, and shows a perception of that royalty that by contrast with its French parallels, forces a recognition that English rulers were to be considered in a different way from their cousins across the Channel.

The Emperor Octavian is said to be the master of this hunt; he was a ruler

---

[28] See Barry Windeatt, ed., *Chaucer's Dream Poetry: Sources and Analogues* (Cambridge, 1982) xvi.
[29] Jean Froissart, *Le Paradys d'amours*, in Windeatt (1982) 44.
[30] Guillaume de Machaut, *Le Dit dou Lyon*, in Windeatt (1982) 66.

noted for his warrior strength and success in battle, as well as for his great wealth. Association with and allusion to such a powerful figure is complimentary to the duke, as Octavian was a figure much admired by the king, his father. That the duke was so close to the king at this time might make this figure of Octavian in the poem so paradoxically precise in its vagueness. They are, they can be, both different and the same in this classical representation. The setting of the hunt, favourite pastime of both father and son, is perhaps another signal of their juxtaposed situation. Machaut mentions Octavian in *Le Jugement dou Roy de Behaingne*, when his love-struck knight is describing how he would give up all the wisdom of Galen, and all the possessions of Octavian, if he could see his beloved every day. This may be where Chaucer picked up the name, using it in his own poem as an expression of this tremendous richness.[31] If this Octavian is the Black Knight, who is certainly in some sense John of Gaunt, he has both wealth and power, and had the love of his Lady, too. Gaunt's active movements, travelling and fighting almost constantly during his married life with Blanche, may well find a foreshadowing in Octavian.

Gaunt was, if records are correct, abroad when Blanche died. This depiction of Octavian may refer to this, making the obtuseness of the identification of the Black Knight and the Emperor with Gaunt a possible way to show the disparate facets of a magnate's life: the necessary royal duties and the private emotional landscape of his intimate relationship with his wife. He was, like Octavian, in control of the hunt, and in the forest somewhere close by, even if not seen, carrying on, following the chase, fighting his cause, while also still and alone in the middle of all that went on, coming to terms with a personal tragedy. Though medieval people did not have the range of explicit psychological explanations that are inescapable today, this very familiar English setting for this part of the poem may have been a deliberate choice, not only for reasons of flattery, but also because its familiarity would be in some sense comforting to the listeners. Chaucer's poem to the duchess moves because it unites; it still affects the reader, even from a distance of so many centuries, when any hope of fully understanding the context against which it was written must be vain, because the design and cut of the entire work is so sympathetically made.

Chaucer's ease with the technical language of the hunt, and the precision of the description given in lines 371–86 has been demonstrated to show command of the way in which these terms could metaphorically convey the situation of the duke;[32] as a Dreamer in this noble landscape, he is as much a part of the action as the other noble participants. He is distracted by a whelp, a dog, who insinuates himself in a very recognisably canine manner – 'Hyt com and crepte to me as lowe / Ryght as hyt hadde me yknowe, / Helde doun hys hed and joyned

---

[31] Helen Cooper suggests that the choice of Octavian arises from his position as the patron of Virgil, the greatest poet of imperial Rome, and that Chaucer was perhaps hinting to John of Gaunt that he might occupy a similar status: Cooper, 'Chaucer's Self-Fashioning', *Poetica* 55 (2001) 63.

[32] David Scott-MacNab gives a detailed examination and explanation of the hunting scene in the poem in 'A Re-examination of Octovyen's Hunt in the *Book of the Duchess*', *Medium Aevum* 56 (1987) 183–99.

hys eres, / And leyde al smothe doun hys heres' (391–4) – before leading him to where the Black Knight sits brooding under a huge oak tree.

Chaucer's description of the forest is worth considering; similarities with the *Roman de la Rose* have been noted by academics,[33] but the reality is that the two are very different. In the *Roman*, the trees are mostly domestic fruit-bearing varieties, but with other species planted carefully to a pattern to ensure good shade and aesthetically pleasing design. They grow in a cultivated garden, where the noble courtiers rest, taking pleasure from its artfully constructed beauty. The trees, unsurprisingly, are continental varieties rather than English. This portrait of the beautiful garden, a *locus amoenus* typical of French poetry, sets the courtier and the king within a natural landscape that has been designed to reflect the best that Nature can offer. Like the sophisticated French kings and their court, Nature itself has been transformed into something exquisite by the application of a little French style and manners.

Chaucer created a setting that establishes an equally appealing, but recognisably English, concept of Nature. In *The Book of the Duchess*, the forest exemplifies the triumphant achievement of this; it is 'litel used' (401) and its magnificence is 'as thogh th'erthe envye wolde / To be gayer than the heven' (406–7). The size and sheer green virility of the trees are credited to the dew, not the unseen but nevertheless incipiently felt army of gardeners that lurk behind the flowerbeds of the *Romaunt*. The forest is the preserve of kings, and it is an English forest, full of mighty oak trees that are 'huge of strengthe, / Of fourty, fifty, fedme lengthe' (422–3). England, strong, vigorously growing, yet attaining supremacy over all enemies with natural ease, can adopt the forest as a fitting sign of security, endurance, and power.[34] The forest and the hunt that takes place within it show the measure of the English royal princes. It is a bold statement for the poet to make, but it is a vital one. The poem draws identity in from many directions in order to consolidate the consolatory aspects of its approach.

In the *Romaunt*, the Dreamer finds a tall pine tree, beneath which there is a stream and an inscription that records that here was the spot that Narcissus died. In Machaut's *Fonteinne Amoureuse*, the young lord leads the Dreamer to a fountain, set up by Venus and Jupiter; the story of Narcissus is written around a pillar of ivory next to it. In Froissart's *Le Paradys d'amours*, however, the Dreamer sits down by a stream underneath some hawthorn bushes before being taken to the King of Love by Plaisance and Esperance. In *The Book of the Duchess*, there is no stream, but there is an oak tree, a huge one that stands out in a forest full of imposing trees, and beneath it sits the Black Knight. The oak has always symbolised Englishness; its image was engraved upon coins, and its stature became synonymous with all that was great about England. It was often also called the king of the trees, because of its imposing size and longevity. Its religious significance points to links with faith and Christian endurance; indeed,

---

[33] See Benson's notes to lines 402–33 in *The Riverside Chaucer*, 970.
[34] Compare, for an account of the way in which several post-medieval Western nations imagined their identities through a variety of forests: Simon Schama, *Landscape and Memory* (London, 1995) 23–242.

it is a symbol of Christ and has been claimed to be the tree that the Cross was made from.[35]

There is a notable shift here in the move from Narcissus, the Greek noble who according to legend fell in love with his own reflection and pined away to death, to John of Gaunt, represented by the Black Knight, grieving for the loss of his love, the fair White. This loss through death involves reciprocated feeling and as such breaks the mould of the lover's complaint from which it takes elements of its form. The Black Knight's suffering, his complaint, has the edge of pathos because of the awareness of the reader of the circumstances inspiring the poem; the love-sickness of the French poets, however beautifully framed and figured, cannot match its resonance. The oak must remind Gaunt of the natural cycle that should bring him through this bereavement; the forest binds past and present, duty and pleasure, king and commoner. Loss is an experience everyone can empathise with, but if royalty is weak, then the country will be too. The images Chaucer uses are those of masculine strength, combined with irresistible progress and growth; the oak, supporting the Knight, symbolic of endurance and kingship, shows the solidity of the resources he could draw on.

This sense of permanence and stability is important because Chaucer's initial introduction of the Black Knight shows the young lord to be in an over-wrought, emotional state. Though it is immediately obvious to the Dreamer that he is seeing a man of noble birth, 'a wonder wel-farynge knyght' (452), it is also plain that the knight is weak from grief and full of self-pity. 'He ferde thus evel' (501), and the Dreamer is moved by this sorry sight to approach him and make his presence known. The youthfulness of the knight has caused concern to those critics determined to see the Black Knight as John of Gaunt, for his age, twenty-four, is given precisely and does not correspond to Gaunt's age at Blanche's death: Gaunt was twenty-eight in 1368.[36] However, this does not necessarily mean that the Knight is not Gaunt, or that Chaucer got his dates wrong, or that the age was supposed to be a compliment to the duke. The fact that the poem is set in a dream, where nothing can be absolutely pinned down, makes it unnecessary to try to make the characters perfectly consistent.

The poem relies on the way the poet shades the allusions in the poem. What should be explored is the range of possibilities that Chaucer makes available, and how these enrich readings of the poem with their ambiguities rather than frustrate them. The poem confronts the tensions of distance and closeness, boundaries and common ground; the intimacy of love, which also carries with it the desperate grief of separation, whether through unfulfilment or death, and the changing points of courtesy within a relationship of different status. Chaucer cannot confront his audience with a grieving John of Gaunt, but he can show them an obliquely veiled yet nevertheless recognisable portrait of him.

There is no conflict between accepting this view and recognising the references to Gaunt's lands and name in the final lines of the poem; the 'long castel

---

[35] See George Ferguson, *Signs and Symbols in Christian Art* (New York, 1966) 35.
[36] See Benson's summary of the critical ideas on this point in *The Riverside Chaucer*: note to line 445, 970.

with walles white' (1319) set 'on a ryche hil' (1318) tie the portrait to the duke with puns on his titles. Their appearance as details of the landscape that belongs to the Black Knight allows for a little interpolation of distance, which maintains the fiction that this is simply a world of courtly romance. The duchess herself is thinly veiled behind the conventional persona of 'goode faire White' (948); the careful copying of descriptions from other French poems provides another gap of discretion needed to avoid jarring intrusive assertions about the real Blanche. The Black Knight's references to chess can be seen as another form of distancing, since the limitations of the game require him to describe his lady White as a 'fers' or queen, an image complicated by the narrator when he later refers to the Knight as 'this kyng' (1314): a duke and duchess are almost a king and queen, but not quite.[37] Gaunt's later efforts to become a king in Spain will have sharpened up that dichotomy for audiences as time went on.

The Knight does not at first know that the Dreamer is watching him, and reads out loud his complaint, which details how his love has been taken from him by Death, and how he is left alone with his sorrow. It is worth noting that the cause of his sorrow is unequivocally stated at this point: '… my lady bryght, / Which I have loved with al my myght, / Is fro me ded and ys agoon' (477–9). So ill does he look on completing this composition, that the Dreamer moves forward and stands 'ryght at his fete' (502) until his presence is acknowledged. The Dreamer describes the Knight's blood as rushing to his heart to succour him; the image chimes closely with ideas of the king as part of the body of state: a king who rules wisely and fairly is like a healthy body, but a king who is weakened by ignoble emotion or action weakens the whole state.

The relative status of the two characters is emphasised straight away. The Dreamer 'did of myn hoode' (516) and greeted him 'Debonayrly and nothing lowde' (518). The succeeding lines present us with a dialogue of mannered, courtly conversation that fits with an understanding of communication between two people of unequal social standing in the period; the Knight uses the second-person singular pronouns *thow* and *thee*, and the Dreamer not only takes off his hat but also uses the more formal second-person plural pronouns *ye* and *you*. The way he praises the Knight reveals a deference tinged with wonder and awe:

> Loo, how goodely spake thys knyghte,
> As hit had be another wyghte;
> He made hyt nouther towgh ne queynte.
> And I sawe that, and gan m'aqueynte
> With hym, and fonde hym so tretable,
> Ryght wonder skylful and resonable,
> As me thoght, for al hys bale,
> Anoonryght I gan fynde a tale

---

[37] For efforts to untangle the chess metaphor in this poem, see Margaret Connolly, 'Chaucer and Chess', *Chaucer Review* 29 (1994) 40–4, and Guillemette Bolens and Paul Beekman Taylor, 'The Game of Chess in Chaucer's *Book of the Duchess*', *Chaucer Review* 32 (1998) 325–34.

To hym, to loke wher I myght oughte
Have more knowynge of hys thoughte. (529–38)

The Knight's courtesy is a marker of his superior quality, and is signalled as such by the marvelling tone of line 530. The Black Knight is quite clearly not just 'another wyghte', but his manners are so well-bred that he is able to disconnect instantly from his grief and respond with the utmost civility to an intrusive companion. The gloss on this line in other editions of the poem interpret it as pointing to his change of stance, from emotionally charged to collectedly polite, as if he had become a different person,[38] but a representation of courtesy fits in better with the emphasis in the following lines in the Knight's lack of haughtiness.

Chaucer portrays the Knight as a man of noble birth and approachable mien; he later calls the Dreamer his 'goode frende' (line 560) and though this clearly does not imply an intimacy of equals, it does imply an acceptance of the Dreamer's sympathy, which in turn implies a positive relationship between them. The Dreamer never oversteps the bounds of courtesy when he is speaking to the Knight; he refers to him repeatedly as 'sir' (lines 714, 721, 746, 754, 1046, 1047, 1111, 1126, 1298, 1308) even when moved by the intensity of the Knight's narrative. The Knight, for his part, candidly reveals his love-story, and debates the Dreamer's points with unfeigned deliberation and no sign of hauteur. This 'franchise' and courtesy are characteristics of the ideal knight, described in medieval romances and mirrors of kingship. They were part of a group of traits that would identify the truly noble; they are two of the virtues symbolised by the pentangle on Gawain's shield in *Sir Gawain and the Green Knight*, and they are qualities urged as necessary to good kingship in the popular pseudo-Aristotelian *Secreta Secretorum*.

The Black Knight's story is full of woe: in the first section he lets the Dreamer how Fortune has cheated him by taking his queen at a game of chess. Fortune, personified as a fickle woman turning her 'false whel' (644), has the ability to overthrow anyone, of whatever status: 'Ther be but fewe kan hir begile' (674). The Knight's sorrow is without end because he cannot see a way out of his grief. The Dreamer urges him to have pity, and to remember Socrates, who did not consider Fortune to be worth worrying about. The Dreamer's chiding of the Knight for making such a fuss – 'ther is no man alyve her / Wolde for a fers make this woo' (740–1) – elevates him to the status of a counsellor, from which position he can better engage with the Knight's grief.

The Knight responds by explaining his relationship with the 'goode faire White' (948), revealing how he had seen her among a company of ladies and fallen in love. The description he gives, both of White's physical characteristics and her superlative inner graces, provides the eulogy for Blanche of Lancaster that the poem promises. Her perfections embrace an emotional and spiritual discipline that we have seen so celebrated by Gower, and she contrasts

---

[38] Benson's *Riverside Chaucer* does not gloss this line, but see Helen Phillips and Nick Havely, eds, *Chaucer's Dream Poetry* (London, 1997) 74.

starkly at this point with the Knight, who is unable to control his emotions. The Dreamer, however, now aware that White was the Knight's lady, reacts with more sympathy:

> 'By oure Lord', quod I, 'y trowe you wel!
> Hardely, your love was wel beset;
> I not how ye myghte have do bet.' (1042–4)

This encourages the Knight to provide a more detailed narrative of his courtship of White, a difficult challenge that tested his worth to the limits until she finally takes him 'in hir governaunce' (1286). Their love was a blissful union: 'Al was us oon, withoute were' (1295); the emphatic syllables *al* and *oon* underline the complete joy their love created.

This point of harmony, so carefully crafted by Chaucer's manipulation of the Knight's story, fairly blazes out of the misery the Knight has surrounded us with earlier. It is a union so perfect that the Dreamer's question, 'Where is she now?' (1298) seems abruptly intrusive, and the Knight reacts as if he has been jolted out of a trance. He reveals that White is dead, a horn sounds to signal the end of the hunt, and he rides away to his 'long castel with walles white, / Be seynt Johan, on a ryche hil' (1318–19). The Dreamer awakens and the poem ends.

The conclusion poses some textual dilemmas: the Dreamer describes the Knight as 'this kyng' (1314) and the long white-walled castle on a rich hill is a puzzle until it resolves itself into allusions to John of Gaunt's titles as duke of Lancaster and earl of Richmond.[39] In the Dreamer's landscape, these features may also indicate some heavenly destination towards which the Knight/King journeys: the reference to St John and the colour white hint at reference to the Book of Revelation. The poem finishes on an oblique note, which nevertheless contains clues to both the identity of the Knight and to a continuing spiritual relationship with loved ones after death.

Throughout this poem, as can be seen, there are constant allusions to the courtly life of a ruling lord in the transformed conventional motifs of the setting, the language in the dialogue between the Knight and the Dreamer, and the courtly depiction of the love affair with the lady White. The ambiguous references to kings show an awareness on the part of the poet that defining this royal status is not a concern here; indeed, definition, as I have tried to show, is antithetical to the spirit of this work. Chaucer uses conventions, dreams and chess images in order to create a work to console the duke of Lancaster, who was an important royal prince, in a way that does not transgress boundaries of courtesy and status, but still recognises his essentially human, and therefore identifiable, grief:

> On one level, the Duke is the great man whose private life continues: the hunting king. On the other, he becomes the grieving private man (not in this representation a prince, for grief is not the privilege of royalty), in the black of mourning – the lamenting lover whose grief is expressed through the double imagination of the poet Chaucer and his dreaming persona. The

[39] See Benson, *Riverside Chaucer*, 976.

poem acknowledges that continuing public life and private grief co-exist: the great man hunts, the bereaved husband mourns – and the man in black is left mourning.[40]

The subject of the poem is Blanche's death, and the subtlety with which Chaucer manages her eulogy shows how effective inexplicit imagery can be in offering tactful sympathy. Kingship is part of that structure of consolation, but does not, despite the royal nature of its central mourner, dominate it. Chaucer's other dream poems, written for less specific occasions, also show the poet's skill at showing kings through the refracted lens of characters who are aware of their royal status, but who are still unmistakably human beings who face experiences common to everyone.

The House of Fame, The Legend of Good Women *and* The Parliament of Fowls

In the *House of Fame*, Chaucer is carried in a dream by an eagle to a great rock of ice, upon which the palace of Fame stands. Though the eagle is used in medieval literature as a symbol of royalty,[41] it has other connotations as well, and in this instance probably indicates contemplative thought, one of the major themes of the poem. The eagle may be a magnificent bird, but in this poem he is a comic companion and mentor to the bewildered and terrified Chaucer: his tone is not that of a regal superior, but rather a scornful and impatient intellectual 'tourist guide and pedagogue'.[42]

Once at his destination, the poet is shown a gallery of different groups of people, all coming to petition Fame to grant them renown forever. She is a ruler who approves some and rejects others, but her status as ruler is difficult to define. She admits that she has 'no justice' (1820) in her, but nonetheless has power to dispense judgement according to her own wilful perspective. She is portrayed as a tyrant, a mythological creature covered in eyes and ears and tongues, product of Chaucer's dream world and his reading of classical legends. Her arbitrary actions are unsettling, as actions in a dream world very often are; the overall effect of the poem, described as a 'free-floating, gratuitous display of talent and of humour, thoroughly Chaucerian in its quality',[43] is to leave the reader reeling from the 'hilariously contradictory movement and noise, verging on hysteria'[44] contained in the final part.

Her realm is similarly chaotic, and Spearing points out that the references made to Boece's *De Consolatione*, where heaven is described as being the only true administrator of meaningful reward, show that Chaucer was pointing to a comparison between the two kingdoms: 'the order of the heavenly kingdom is thus described as being the very opposite of the disorder of earthly affairs,

---

[40] Cooper (2001) 63.
[41] See below in discussion on *The Parliament of Fowls* (**0**).
[42] Muscatine (1957) 111.
[43] Muscatine (1957) 113.
[44] Spearing (1976) 82.

ruled by the sisters Fortune and Fame'.[45] However, this is not an issue that is developed further, as the poem continues to put more quickly changing images before the dreaming Chaucer.

Although this poem is about the reputation of the good, the brave and the highly skilled, kings feature very little; the pillars of the palace are all held up by historians, and though musicians and writers are mentioned frequently, no emphasis is placed on any real kings or their achievements. The tantalising reference to 'a man of gret auctorite' (2158) at the end of the poem, unfinished as we have it, certainly could provoke discussions if we knew any more, but we do not. For now, this can only be expanded upon by reflecting that the poet chooses not to make this a poem about different estates: this mysterious character is a 'man', and not a king. Though there have been attempts to date this poem and tie it in to specific royal events – either the announcement of Richard II's marriage to Anne of Bohemia or the betrothal of John of Gaunt's daughter – neither argument has sufficient weight to be conclusive.[46]

Ultimately this is a literary work that shows Chaucer's engagement with ideas of relevance and appeal to a wide audience, which probably included members of the royal family, but which does not take them in any obvious way either as its subject or as its principal audience. Chaucer does look at the idea of authority in this poem, its origins in books and words and deeds, and in the consequent unreliable dispersement of that authority by Fame and Rumour, but by placing this within a dream world he is deliberately moving these ideas outside of a recognisable reality: they have been 'displaced into a fantasy world of amorous play'.[47]

The *Parliament of Fowls* is most commonly held to have some connection with the suit of Richard II for the hand of Anne of Bohemia in 1381, although, as with the later *Legend of Good Women*, this association is not backed by sufficient textual evidence to make it conclusive.[48] Although St Valentine's day is mentioned in the poem as the time when Nature held her parliamentary court, analogies with any real courtly celebrations are hard to find;[49] with May Day, also described as a festival for convening courts of love in poetry of this period, it seems rather that the reality 'was confined to casually assembled groups of courtiers engaged in either public flirtation (love-talking) or informal discussions on amorous topics'.[50] This may go a long way to explaining the playful tone of the *Parliament*, charming in its reconstruction of such *cours amoureuses*, sophisticated in its argument that 'love is not only a feeling, but also a real culture, with its conventions and laws'.[51] Chaucer's portrayal of kingship in this

---

[45] Spearing (1976) 82.
[46] Benson's note, *Riverside Chaucer,* 978.
[47] Patterson 25.
[48] See Benson, *Riverside Chaucer* 994, and L. D. Benson, 'The Occasions of *The Parliament of Fowls*', in *The Wisdom of Poetry*, ed. L. D. Benson and S. Wenzel (Kalamazoo, 1982) 123–44.
[49] See Green (1980) 120–4.
[50] Green (1980) 122.
[51] Piero Boitani, 'Old Books Brought to Life in Dreams: *The Book of the Duchess*, the *House of Fame*,

poem is not a major theme, but there are touches, in the figures of the tercel eagles, which show royalty as part of a very tightly defined hierarchy.

The Dreamer begins by detailing the worthiness of old books, just as the Dreamer does in the *Legend of Good Women* and Gower does in the *Confessio Amantis*. After reading about the dream of Scipio, the Dreamer falls asleep and dreams that Africanus, Scipio's grandfather, visits him and leads him to a walled park with a curious gate, half covered in black writing and half in gold. Africanus reassures the Dreamer that, since he has lost his taste for love, he need not be intimidated by what he sees; Africanus will allow the Dreamer to roam as an observer within the gates, so that he can gather new experiences to write about.

The garden is teeming with birds, animals and different kinds of trees, described in detailed lists that celebrate the beauty and variety of forms and colours. Beyond this, the Dreamer finds a temple made of brass, and enters, wonderingly registering the gods and goddesses resting and enjoying themselves all around him. Among them is a sensuous reclining Venus, half-naked and with golden hair unbound, surrounded by the broken bows of maidens who had dedicated their chastity to Diana. The natural profusion of the garden gives way to 'the human cosmos, an artificial world where myth and courtesy – civilisation as distinct from nature – are in full bloom'.[52] The paintings on the walls portray legends of tragic lovers, and the temple emphasises the double-edged power of love, which can both inspire great joy and great despair, be life and yet death, too.

The effect is of cloying claustrophobia; there is an inertia about the temple that seems unnatural. Like the Dreamer, the reader is relieved to escape into the open air, away from the realisation of the 'olde bokes' (24) praised so vehemently at the start of the poem. The garden brings him 'solace' (297), and he sees a hill of flowers, on top of which sits a queen: Nature herself. He becomes aware that it is St Valentine's day, and that all around the goddess are birds of every kind, making up her court.

The birds are arranged by species into a hierarchy,[53] so well organised that the contrast with the informal disarray of the temple is comical. The 'noble emperesse' (319) has an authority that her subjects respect without question: they perch ready 'to take hire dom and yeve hir audyence' (308), and accept her judgement in the matter of choosing a mate. This court, though outside the aesthetically sophisticated temple, has its own natural courtliness that reveals the ordered strength paradoxical in Nature's apparent freedom from such constraints.[54] Chaucer shows that Nature's fundamental governing policy, to

---

and the *Parliament of Fowls*', in *The Cambridge Companion to Chaucer*, ed. Piero Boitani and Jill Mann (Cambridge, 2003) 68.
[52] Boitani (2003) 69.
[53] Chaucer's source for this presentation is Alan of Lille's *Plaint of Nature*: see Benson, *Riverside Chaucer* 1000.
[54] However, as Spearing notes, 'the temple is set within Nature's garden: Nature is more inclusive than sexuality': Spearing (1976) 99.

create new life in all its forms, is allied to the mannered love paradigms of an aristocratic court:

> For her, the social order, and hence the courtly culture which it includes as an aspect of the ideal of the upper classes, is but a part of the natural order. The perfection of the universe requires plenitude and plurality – the increase and multiplication of living beings proclaimed by Genesis – as well as 'inequality'.[55]

This natural order is something Chaucer's work reflects constantly. Kings are at the top of this ranking, but they are bound by those below them to rule wisely and responsibly. Subjects, for their part, must support their monarch by leading good lives on Christian principles. It is a view shown more overtly in Gower, but still evident throughout Chaucer, as this section of the *Parliament* shows. Above all human states reigns God, to whom everyone owes allegiance; even Nature is described as 'vicaire of the almyghty Lord' (379). She is God's instrument, a deputy who carries out His work.

The parliament is a parody of the real and troubled parliaments of Richard's reign. Yet here every voice has an audience, and the common profit (or 'comune spede' (507) of the cuckoo) of all of Nature's subjects is taken into consideration, although, just as in reality, Nature has the final say. Nature has a formel eagle on her hand, who is looking for a mate. Three tercel eagles put themselves forward as her suitors, and Nature decrees that, with the input of the other birds, the formel eagle has the right to choose which she will take. Once the royal eagles have settled their partnership, the other birds will be free to make their choices. The order is clearly defined:

> 'The tersel egle, as that ye knowe wel,
> The foul royal, above yow in degre,
> The wyse and worthi, secre, trewe as stel,
> Which I have formed, as ye may wel se,
> In every part as it best liketh me –
> It nedeth not his shap yow to devyse –
> He shal first chese and speken in his gyse.' (393–9)

The list of virtues that belong to the tercel eagle echo those of conventional good kings, as well as integrating others such as discretion, which belong to the ideal lover. The first eagle is the most appropriate partner for the formel eagle in every way, and the other two contenders are but paler, less forcefully detailed shadows of the first's royal distinction. Chaucer's characterisation indicates that among kings there are differences, and if this poem was written to represent the wooing of Anne of Bohemia, then clearly to privilege the first eagle (as Richard II) would be a tactful and logical move. Nature herself advises the formel eagle to take the first suitor: 'If I were Resoun, thanne wolde I / Conseyle yow the royal tercel take' (632–3), but in a neat twist, the formel eagle requests she have

---

[55] Boitani (2003) 70.

another year in which to make up her mind, and rejects the governance of the language of courtship: 'I wol nat serve Venus ne Cupid / Forsothe as yit, by no manere weye' (652–3). In her allegiance to Nature, 'I am evere under youre yerde' (640), Chaucer beautifully undercuts with playful tone the posturing of the complex codes that had arisen around the games of love in courts of his time. Nature will have her way; it is as simple as that, and love needs no rules or courts to sort itself out.

However, as one critic has observed, the formel eagle's refusal to choose until she is ready suggests a further idea: it implies that human love

> involves not merely the gods of sex and their temple of illicit passions, but the possibility of resisting Nature, or at least of gaining a certain margin of freedom within which to choose the time and manner of one's submission.[56]

In this way not only is Chaucer humorously looking at the courtly language of love, but he is also suggesting that humans have some element of self-control, or self-governance. This, ultimately, will determine the outcome of any debate about love.

The poem ends with the formal ending to the parliament; the Dreamer awakes with the cacophony created by the departure of the birds ringing in his ears, and immediately begins to read more books in order 'to mete som thyng for to fare / The bet' (698–9). Reading has not moved him much further along in his quest for 'a certyn thing to lerne' (20), but it has given him the material to create a new piece of fiction, cut from old books such as the *Somnium Scipionis* and the *Plaint of Nature*, and the *Parliament* shows that this fiction looks for its authority in the abstracts of love and Nature, not in the depiction of real kings.

As in the *House of Fame* and, as will be seen below, in the *Legend of Good Women*, Chaucer uses the dream-vision and birds to distance the topic of kings. Indeed, the eagle in the *House of Fame* is not representative of royalty at all, and the birds of the *Legend* are miscreant lovers. Humour helps to buffer the poet from any accusations of imitating real life too closely, a strategy that achieves its apotheosis in the *Nun's Priest's Tale*, as will be shown later in this chapter.

The *Legend of Good Women* has similar concerns with the idea of fame, but concentrates on elaborating exemplary stories of virtuous ladies who have suffered in love at the hands of men. Like the *House of Fame*, it is unfinished, and at present there is no consensus on the date of its composition, although the reference to King Richard's palaces at Eltham and Sheen involves a date around 1394. This was the year that Queen Anne died, and the grief-stricken king had the palace at Sheen destroyed.

There are twelve known manuscripts of the poem in existence, and of these one has a revised prologue, which shows Chaucer reworked the poem at a later date.[57] This discussion will concentrate solely on the Prologue of the *Legend*, for

---

[56] Spearing (1976) 100.
[57] Cambridge University Library Gg.4.27. This will be indicated by 'G' and the earlier Prologue by 'F'. See Appendix.

it is here that the references to kingship cluster, and the variant version G gives much scope for analysis. The differences may lend credence to the theory that the work was written for a specific occasion, and that Chaucer was reworking it to present before a new audience; the references to the courtly May game of the flower and the leaf, and the concentration on women and on love, point to an audience of a courtly nature. The Springtime setting gives a general time of year, but there is little else to link the poem to a precise event, although the annual celebrations of May Day can be plausibly said to provide both occasion and a possible reason why the poem could be so readily adapted to subsequent festivities.

Despite attempts to show that the poem was written for Queen Anne, there is no convincing proof that this is so; indeed, critics seem united in agreeing that its true inspiration will always remain hidden. A. C. Spearing muses that 'one cannot help suspecting that crucial elements in its meaning may relate to some situation outside itself, to which we no longer have the key',[58] Richard Firth Green observes 'we can sense the presence of a tight-knit group of initiates playing with literary and social conventions at which we can now but guess',[59] while more recently Julia Boffey and A. S. G. Edwards note that the references to courtly games

> remind us that court life was a form of shared intimacy, one in which poet and audience coexisted in a proximity that can infuse courtly works with a tone that is at the same time palpable yet historically unrecoverable in its precise implications.[60]

Importantly, these responses show, as I hope to reveal, that the *Legend of Good Women* is directly related to the royal court, and that it therefore contains relevant reflections on the nature of authority and kingship; these are useful in that, used as part of the vehicle of a light-hearted game, they show another, very different approach to kingship from any yet seen in the poets under discussion. The *Book of the Duchess* may also be a courtly poem, but its subject matter is of a sombre note; here Chaucer is in apparent playful mood and the images are, if no less difficult to define absolutely (we are still within the protective world of the dream-vision), at least strikingly different in tone. There is no need to stress the real or imagined connection between Anne and the figure of Alceste in the poem in order for these images to augment the discussion; Blanche's presence in the *Book of the Duchess* made such bonds with real events of relevance, but here the queen is an indistinct participant. What is crucial is to see that

> the key to the relationship between Alceste in the poem and the historical Anne rests less in the denial of affirmation of particular congruences than in a recognition of the environment of interpretative structures within which

---

[58] Spearing (1976) 104.
[59] Richard Firth Green, 'The *Familia Regis* and the *Familia Cupidinis*', in *English Court Culture in the Later Middle Ages*, eds V. J. Scattergood and J. W. Sherborne (London, 1983) 106.
[60] Julia Boffey and A. S. G. Edwards, 'The *Legend of Good Women*', in *The Cambridge Companion to Chaucer*, eds Piero Boitani and Jill Mann (Cambridge, 2003) 116.

Alceste was invented and within which Anne seems at least partially to have invented herself.[61]

The Prologue begins with a passage praising the worth of old books, which tell of 'holynesse, of regnes, of victories, / Of love, of hate, of other sondry thynges' (F 22–3). This may remind us of Gower's Prologue in the *Confessio Amantis*, where he, too, defends the usefulness of books in helping to ensure exemplary stories of the past do not disappear. Chaucer says: 'Wel ought us thanne honouren and beleve / These bokes, there we han noon other preve' (F 27–8), and goes on to admit that there is little that will part him from the pleasure of reading except the coming of Spring and blossoming of the flowers. This passage owes much to Chaucer's French sources,[62] but there is an underlying humour here that is not in the originals, for Chaucer, by using other texts so extensively in his descriptions of May and the daisy, is showing how reading is in fact never absent from his activities. Books provide the conventions – and as importantly, the authority – needed to express experience, and in love, as in everywhere else, Chaucer proves that exempla and description from existing material are part of the 'game'.

The adoration of the daisy was part of the conventions of French courtly poetry, and the flower was also associated with the Virgin Mary. In French, the word 'margarite' can mean both 'daisy' and 'pearl', thus giving Chaucer a good deal of allusive space to work within. Pearls were particularly associated with Queen Anne,[63] a point that neatly suggests the alignment with the figure of Alceste, who is seen crowned with pearl and looking 'lyk a daysie' (224):

> And she was clad in real habit grene.
> A fret of gold she hadde next her heer,
> And upon that a whit corowne she beer
> With florouns smale, and I shal nat lye;
> For al the world, ryght as a dayesye
> Ycourouned ys with white leves lyte,
> So were the flowrouns of hire coroune white.
> For of o perle fyn, oriental,
> Hire white coroune was ymaked al;
> For which the white coroune above the grene
> Made hire lyk a daysie for to sene,
> Considered eke hir fret of gold above. (F 214–25)

---

[61] Strohm (1992) 116.
[62] See Froissart's *La Joli Buisson de Jonece*, ed. A. Fourrier (Geneva, 1975) 786–92, *Paradys d'amours*, in Windeatt (1982) and also Benson's notes in *The Riverside Chaucer* 1061.
[63] However, pearls are also used as a conventional adornment in the French love poetry of this period: see Froissart's *Paradys d'amours*, in Windeatt (1982) 50. For further discussion of the association with Queen Anne, see Bowers (2001) 158–9; Strohm (1992) 116; David Wallace, *Chaucerian Polity: Absolutist Lineages and Associational Forms in England and Italy* (Stanford, 1997) 372–3.

Alceste's white crown is mentioned several more times, at lines 242, 299, 304 and 527, making it a noticeable image throughout the Prologue; as a symbol of Alceste's status as both authoritative and meek queen it directly confronts the representation of kingship that Chaucer creates in the god of Love. The prefiguring designs of the daisy, which the Dreamer hails as 'my gide and lady sovereyne' (F 94), and summer, which the birds welcome as 'oure governour and lord' (F 170), establish the virtues inherent in both ideal male and female rulers. The female daisy is 'al vertu and honour' (F 54), and the 'clernesse and verray lyght' (F 84) that 'wynt and ledeth' (F 85) the Dreamer. The Marian analogies are clear, and the transcendent goodness elevates the humble flower to being the 'emperice and flour of floures alle' (F 185).

There are some complexities in lines 125–70, where Chaucer details the end of winter and the coming of spring. Here images of lordship are tangled among the seasons, love and the abstractions of Pity, Danger, Justice, Mercy and Courtesy. Winter is a cruel tyrant, whose 'swerd of cold' (F 127) makes the earth naked and poor, but the sun comes and alleviates its condition so that the birds worship and praise love and St Valentine, 'yeldyng honour and humble obeysaunces / To love' (F 149–50). They repent of past transgressions against love, and harmony is re-established by the coming of the new governor, Summer. So far, so conventional; this scenario can be found repeated in many of the French poems already mentioned and love's association with warmth, sun and summertime is a securely familiar one. What is striking are the next four lines:

> Al founde they Daunger for a tyme a lord,
> Yet Pitee, thurgh his stronge gentil myght,
> Forgaf, and made Mercy passen Ryght,
> Thurgh innocence and ruled Curtesye. (F 160–3)

These lines are absent in the revised Prologue, and present challenges of interpretation. 'Daunger' is a character found in *The Romance of the Rose*, but the parallels with Chaucer's Daunger are difficult to distinguish.[64] He prevents the lover from approaching his lady, and is violent and threatening in his rebuffs. The reader of the *Roman de la Rose* finds that Danger is a 'vilains; that he is swarthy, huge, and hirsute; that his eyes burn like fire and that he bawls at the top of his voice'.[65] In Gower's *Confessio Amantis*, Daunger is a counsellor, and Amans explains why he feels him such an enemy to his cause:

> For evere he hangeth on hire Seil,
> And is so privé of conseil,

---

[64] See Benson's *Riverside Chaucer*, note to F 160 and F 153–74, 1062. That the references are 'of more or less uncertain significance' seems an extremely vague and unsatisfactory reason for linking them at all; for more detailed discussion of 'daunger', see W. R. J. Barron, 'Luf-daungere', in *Medieval Miscellany Presented to Eugène Vinaver by Pupils, Colleagues and Friends*, eds F. Whitehead, A. H. Diverres and F. E. Sutcliffe (Manchester, 1965) 118, and Lewis (1936) 123–4. 'Dangier' also appears in Froissart's *Le Jugement dou Roy de Behaingne* (in Windeatt [1982] 9), and as a counsellor in Gower's *Confessio Amantis* (Book III, 1538–1612).
[65] Lewis (1936) 124.

> That evere whanne I have oght bede,
> I finde Danger in hire stede
> And myn ansuere of him I have; (III 1555-9)

Chaucer has transformed the figure of Daunger by elevating him to the status of a lord. In so doing he displays a stylistic sleight of hand that underlines his opening defence of old books. For reinvented as a lord, Daunger is returning to his ancestral etymological roots. C. S. Lewis notes that 'dangier' comes from the Latin 'dominus': 'lordship',[66] and W. R. J. Barron, expanding on Lewis's work, finds that 'by the twelfth century, [dangier] was already diversified in terms of various manifestations of power, including that dominion which love gives one individual over another'.[67]

Daunger's appearance in such close proximity to that of the lord of winter with the sword of cold who keeps away love and the lord of summer, associates the season of ice and barrenness with the state of rebuff that a lady may decide to inflict upon her lover. This can only be defeated by courtly virtues of pity, mercy, justice and courtesy, attributes not only detailed in courtly poems of love as belonging to the lady, who wields power over her suitor, but also, as we have seen from looking at the *Confessio Amantis*, aspects of the ideal king, too.[68]

However, Chaucer is describing the effect of the seasons on birds, not humans, in this passage. The birds who offend their lady-loves have shown 'unkyndenesse'; they have not only acted unfeelingly, they have acted against the natural order of things, against kind. They must be taught a lesson and Danger is the deliverer of this punishment, having lordship over them until the gentler virtues of the females release them from their feathered vassalage. 'Ruled Curtesye' (F 163), together with innocence, are the armaments Pity uses with 'stronge gentil myght' (F 161) to overcome the tyrant lord.

There are four lords in this passage: winter, summer, Danger and Pity. The natural world of seasons and birds is bound, 'ruled' by the stylised and conventional realm of 'curtesye' and love, in a way familiar from *The Parliament of Fowls*. In the earlier poem, Chaucer also shows Danger allied with wintry landscapes; behind one half of the gate to the walled garden lies a place where 'nevere tre shal fruyt ne leves bere' (F 137), while 'grene and lusty May' (F130) welcomes true lovers through the other side. Yet in the *Legend of Good Women* the appearance of Lord Danger seems to stretch the courtly ideals further than the *Parliament* does. Danger has been redefined as a powerful magnate, the rough-spoken churl no longer the warrior at the black gate, or the kind of bodyguard shown in the *Roman de la Rose*. As a lord he is an upstart, out of place, as 'unkynde' in his way as the fickle birds are, and his defeat is part of the pattern necessary to maintain the harmonious idyll that Chaucer has created. His elevation helps to create a sophisticated courtly harmony. Chaucer's dream world is an idyllic one; even the rough-spoken churl that is Daunger must rede-

---

[66] Lewis (1936) 124.
[67] Barron (1965) 2.
[68] Gower, *Confessio Amantis*, Book VII. See above (0).

fine himself to fit within that context. Daunger thus becomes a universal enemy, the poem a general celebration of love's dominion rather than a narrative representing one man's desire.

The beautiful picture of summer's arrival that Chaucer details remains in the Dreamer's mind as he falls asleep, and in his dream he sees the god of Love and his queen approach across a meadow filled with daisies. They are both royally attired in the colours of spring, green and white, and the god is described as having 'gilte heer' (F 230) in the F Prologue, a detail that is missing from that of G. That Richard II is well known for having been fair-haired may provide an explanation for this physical point, and would lend weight that the poem was created for him and Queen Anne.[69] The god is powerful, with wings like angels' and a stern gaze; together with the brightness of his whole appearance, which seems to radiate light and heat, he is a figure of such presence that he turns the Dreamer's heart cold (F 240). This is the remote and god-like king that historians suggest Richard tried to become: not only was he 'the first English King to cultivate magnificence in the style of his court, self-consciously and on principle, as a means of reinforcing his autocratic rule',[70] but the description recalls 'Richard's political use of the gaze: his increasing demand for subjects' bows and averting of eyes, and his practice of sitting on his throne and expecting anyone whom his gaze caught to kneel'.[71]

In contrast, Love's queen is 'so womanly, so benigne, and so meke' (F 243) that she inspires comparisons with Esther and Penelope. The royal pair are followed by nineteen ladies, all true in love. The court stops to worship the daisy, and then arranges itself, everyone sitting 'as they were of estaat, ful curteysly' (F 305). It is comparable to Nature's court in the *Parliament of Fowls*; there, as here, the court is outside, yet still ordered by courtly rules of estate. Spotting the Dreamer, the god of Love challenges him:

> '... What dostow her
> So nygh myn oune floure, so boldely?
> Yt were better worthy, trewely,
> A worm to neghen ner my flour than thow.' (F 315–17)

This is not a propitious welcome, and Love goes on to denounce the Dreamer's attempts to write love stories, judging that his work shows him to be a traitor to Love's cause. The Dreamer's future looks very bleak until the queen steps in and intercedes to calm her husband down. Her arguments begin with a detailed exposition of the behaviour of an ideal king, and she reminds Love that he must, out of courtesy, hear the Dreamer's own defence of his actions before he condemns him.

In a sense everything detailed to this point comes together in the versions of Alceste's speech that follows, as the wealth of intertextual allusions concentrate

---

[69] See Helen Phillips, 'Register, Politics and the *Legend of Good Women*', *Chaucer Review* 37 (2002) 119–20 for further suggestions about connections with Richard's physical appearance.
[70] Eberle (1985) 178.
[71] Phillips (2002) 120.

on the portrayal of perfect kingship that the queen talks about; the effect has been compared to the art of the Wilton Diptych.[72] What the reader has recognised, noted and responded to in this 'dynamic and discontinuous'[73] narrative will support the exposition of kingship without exposing it to necessary further reflection; it is, or can be, simply another field of register that combines with the others to continue this 'game' of courtly entertainment.

This passage has similarities to parts of Book VII in Gower's *Confessio*,[74] and reflects aspects of kingship common in Mirrors for Princes such as the *Secretum Secretorum*, Brunetto Latini's *Trésor* and Giles of Rome's *De Regimine Principum*. The material is not politically provocative in any way, and the readers of the time would have found no surprises, in the same way that the features of the seasons and love would have struck familiar chords. Yet there are also significant differences between the F and G versions, which indicate a subtle concentration on the representation of these kingly attributes and in places a shift of emphasis.[75] Its importance here is that in comparing the two, it can be seen that 'G adds an increased sense of negative and oppressive aspects of kingship and *auctoritee* (in both textual and political senses).'[76] A king's role is to avoid being a tyrant, 'that han no reward but at tyrannye' in the earlier Prologue (F 375), and 'that usen wilfulhed and tyrannye' in the later version (G 355). The more specifically accountable personal trait of wilfulness, altering the general comment that tyrants gain nothing except what they extort from their subjects, is remarkable, and might seem particularly applicable to Richard in the 1390s, yet this has been linked to other contemporary works, which suggests, again, that Chaucer was simply tapping into topical concerns, not offering a radical insight into Richard's rule.[77] The additional five lines added at line 359 in G emphasise the king's duty to show mercy to his liege-men, and to listen to them whenever they bring their grievances to him. A king must also have compassion on men of all estates, and like the lion who swats away a fly 'al esely' (F 394), must not be harsh with poor supplicants, but rather show his 'maistrye' (F 400) by being merciful: 'regard for the laws and justice was, as we have seen, a test of kingship as opposed to tyranny'.[78]

The reference to the tax-collectors may contain a glancing reference to Richard's unpopular tax policies of the 1380s, but again, the image is such a well-used convention that it is impossible to prove this convincingly. This diversion strengthens the opinion of writers such as Cicero, Boethius and Macrobius, as well as contemporaries such as Gower, in saying that

> Lordship, it was generally assumed, is primarily a duty; rulers were instituted for the sake of peoples, not peoples for rulers. Some writers even went so

---

[72] Phillips (2002) 121.
[73] Phillips (2002) 120.
[74] See Gower, *CA* VII 2695–3600.
[75] See Appendix for the two variants of this passage.
[76] Phillips (2002) 106.
[77] See Phillips (2002) note 10, 125.
[78] Schlauch 152.

far as to state explicitly: the right of lordship is based on the consent of the governed. It is subordinate to the laws, to which legitimate rulers are themselves 'subject'.[79]

In adding these lines Chaucer's emphasis can either be seen, in the light of their absence in F, as the poet's attempt to respond to a political climate he felt justified more forceful amplification of the king's role, or as a witty addition to the idea of the duality of the petitioning Dreamer / poet begging for favour at the court he relied upon for sustenance. In the scheme of the whole poem, this reading would not be out of place, but, just as Alceste does not have to be Queen Anne for the poem to work on different levels, so this passage operates on several possible and plausible, but not exclusive, understandings. When the 'deuwe tyme' comes when Chaucer / the Dreamer will offer his petition, then will be the opportunity for the king to show his greatness; though Chaucer's poem and Richard's kingship are already being tested in the real world they inhabit, within the safety of the protective allusive layers of the poem, both have their challenge still ahead. Neither has been judged yet; the passage is advice, not condemnatory comment, and the fact that Alceste is the speaker helps to broker that idea with status and more allusive distance. She has the right to counsel the king, and her role is admonitory harmonising: she can act as interceder for the Dreamer and talk to the king with a freedom not permitted for anyone else.

Paul Strohm has written persuasively about the links this has with the recorded actions of historical queens such as Queen Philippa, consort of Edward III, and Queen Anne, wife of Richard II. He suggests that the poem 'moves beyond intercessory images pleasing to autocracy in order to produce ideas of queenship that argue for the tempering of kingly power by good advice';[80] for the vital support position of counsellor Chaucer offers both queen and liege-men as potential candidates, and in so doing makes emphatic that kingship is dependent upon a system of co-operative government. This is the other side of the coin from the Dreamer's initial response to the god of Love as a terrifying and volatile figure, who appears capable of acting purely on his own caprice.

Love is so heedful of what his queen tells him that he turns the decision of what to do with the Dreamer completely over to her. This capitulation loses the king no authority because by graciously admitting the admirable qualities of charity in his consort, he is able to unite with her powers of discernment to create a harmonious portrayal of perfect partnership. In the revisions of G Alceste's prominence is increased, and this may be because, if the later dating for this version is correct, after Queen Anne's death Alceste could more productively unite references to different ideas. Indeed, the queen

> represents qualities of good kingship as well. G's single royal, quasi-spousal pair, like the Wilton Diptych, may represent the king in symbolic relationship to important powers; to heavenly protection, wisdom, good judgement,

---

[79] Schlauch 134.
[80] Strohm (1992) 119.

mercy, and fidelity, including fidelity to his own commitments, to his national destiny – Anglia itself? – and to a semi-divine conception of kingship. Perhaps Alceste represents, in a real sense, the king's 'better half', that is, his own sacred duty and dignity.[81]

This strengthens the courtly ideas of love, while moving those references beyond and into the arena of governance and good kingship.

In maintaining a fictional dream world of such complexity, Chaucer manages to entwine images of authority in books, Nature, love, and kings, and I would argue that one particular virtue connects these together through mutual sharing of allusive references: Pity. In the courtly world of love, Daunger is the cruel lord who can be won over only by Pity; in Nature this is represented by the tyranny of winter and the bountiful transformation of summer, and pity is the virtue needed to enable a king to carry out his just duty to his subjects. This imaginary court gives a judgement of pity to the Dreamer, whose crime is apparently to have retold stories so that women and love are falsely represented. Alceste, who connects all layers as a fictional character, a queen, an allegorical image of the daisy and a courtly lady, sets the example and personifies, as noted, the ideal of all realms of reference in the poem. 'Pite renneth soone in gentil herte' pronounces the god of Love (F503), and reminds the Dreamer of her superlative qualities, which carefully draw out and together these allusions:

> No wonder ys thogh Jove hire stellyfye,
> As telleth Agaton, for hire goodnesse!
> Hire white corowne berith of hyt witnesse;
> For also many vertues hadde shee
> As smale florouns in hire corowne bee.
> In remembraunce of hire and the flour
> Cibella maade the daysye and the flour
> Ycrowned al with whit, as men may see;
> And Mars gave to her corowne red, pardee,
> In stede of rubyes, wette among the white. (F 525–34)

As the Prologue ends, this court of Love seems strong and full of the attractions of Nature and courtesy, 'gentilesse', that complement Chaucer's French sources. It is a court directly related to the real English one, yet it is also as safely removed as those other courts of Chaucer's dream poems. There are reflections, echoes of relevance, but kingship is treated, even when as a direct subject, with as many conventional references as sustain the background to the love debates. As ever, it is only in what is not being said, and when it is not being said, as the two versions of the Prologue here give us an opportunity to study, that we can begin to ask questions. To find answers is another matter entirely; like Chaucer's Dreamer, we can only conclude 'For by assay ther may no man it preve' (F 9). However, it is possible to see that even when Chaucer is writing entertaining fiction set in a dream world, the opposed images of arbitrary royal tyranny

---

[81] Phillips (2002) 122.

110 *Chaucer*

and restrained government by counsel show themselves a part of his system of values, a system that can be accessed by close reading of all his works.

Troilus and Criseyde

The tale of the Trojan War has claim to be 'the most persistent non-religious subject in Western literature';[82] from the *Iliad* and the *Aeneid*, the accounts of Dictys and Dares, and then down through Joseph of Exeter in the twelfth and Albert von Stade in the thirteenth centuries, the story has held constant appeal for writers of history and legend. Its popularity during the medieval period reflects the attraction that it held as an anchor point of reference for the foundation of European nations, struggling in a time of political and economic instability to link themselves to a more golden age. Its profundity of effect, like 'an originary moment analogous to the biblical moment of Genesis',[83] resonates particularly in England during Henry II's reign, where Geoffrey of Monmonth's *Historia regum Britanniae* tried to establish Aeneas, fleeing from Troy, as the antecedent of the king.[84]

Henry and Eleanor's court, a centre of culture and literary patronage, was the place where Benôit's *Le Roman de Troie* was composed; this provided the source for Boccaccio's later *Il Filostrato*, itself the inspiration for Chaucer's *Troilus and Criseyde*. In 1287 a Sicilian judge, Guido delle Colonne, reworked Benôit's achievement (though he never named his main source), successfully emphasising the historical details so that for a long time his book was thought to be a real history of Troy. The proliferation of the Arthurian legends, originating from Geoffrey of Monmouth's *Historia*, provided an alternative, more local hero with inspiring attributes who combined the skilled battle tactician with the more cultured and sophisticated courtly knight. Where the threads of Romance quickly wove the legends of Arthur into patterns of ever more individual and fantastical invention, however, the legend of Troy maintained by and large an integrity that its appearance of historical accuracy, or what passed for historical accuracy, attempted to preserve.[85]

Chaucer, writing during the reigns of later kings, therefore had a rich tradition, ultimately foreign in origin, of Trojan legend, historicisation and romance to build upon. The most important aspect of his building is that his interpretation of the lovers, and his choice of detail and emphasis, can be said to explore the internal lives of great lords in ways his sources do not, while avoiding any extended discussion of the public actions of kings, which many of them do. In contrast to writers such as Guido, Chaucer's world is that of the royal court,

---

[82] C. David Benson, *The History of Troy in Middle English Literature* (Cambridge, 1980) 3.
[83] Patterson (1991) 91.
[84] Patterson asserts that 'the location of historical authority in a single source naturally appealed to a medieval monarchy interested in promoting its own role as an exclusive source of political power, and the linearity of *translatio imperii* was convenient support for hereditary dynasties and genealogical claims': (1991) 92.
[85] See C. David Benson (1980) 5 for a more expanded argument on this topic.

with all its manners and conventions. He works with these to reflect the influence of the ruling forces of that sphere of experience, and by so doing his work complements quite deliberately the human elements common to both royalty and those ruled by them. Descriptions of the battles and of the progress of the war are distinctly subsidiary in Chaucer's poem; they are merely the dramatic backdrop against which the tragedy of the lovers is played out.

The idea of kingship, however, is unexpectedly pertinent to the poem's main theme. The idea of servitude to Love can be explored as part of that continuously recurring idea. At the start of Chaucer's *Troilus* the narrator sets up a complicated network of pagan and Christian references; he describes himself as one 'that God of Loves servantz serve' (I 15), an allusion to one of the pope's titles.[86] His humility in demurring that he has any real claim to be worthy to be an effective servant of Love's cause has also been said to have many echoes of saintly attitudes, particularly those of Augustine.[87] Nevertheless, despite his reluctance to bother Love with a petition for help in speedily completing his work, the narrator acknowledges that if any lover should find comfort from his words, it is the God's doing, and the narrator's mere contributory effort: 'if this may don gladnesse / Unto any lovere, and his cause availle, / Have he my thonk, and myn be this travaille!' (I 19–21) In combining the two systems of belief, Chaucer 'applies the ecclesiastical doctrine of merit to love – the doctrine that the merit applying to any good work may be imputed to the doer or to some other to whom he chooses to transfer it'.[88]

The dichotomy becomes more complex when the narrator asks his audience to pray to God for various causes: Troilus, himself, other lovers in hopeless situations, and those who are currently happy. However, the personification and deification of Love does not undermine the integrity of the passage; rather it sets up the dual pulls of earthly and spiritual allegiance that figure so largely in the poem, and provide it with the philosophical exhortation to all lovers:

> Repeyreth hom fro worldy vanyte,
> And of youre herte up casteth the visage
> To thilke God that after his ymage
> Yow made, and thynketh al nys but a faire,
> This world that passeth soone as floures faire. (V 1837–41)

This emphatically Christian viewpoint, and the denunciation of all the 'payans corsed olde rites' (V 1849) cannot take away the demands of Love that are described in *Troilus*; the rhetorical form of the final lines, formalising their

---

[86] See Benson's note in *Riverside Chaucer*, 1025. The pope's official title used in the introductory greetings of all papal bulls was 'servus servorum Dei'. The gloss also suggests this may allude to Ovid's more flippant description of himself as Love's charioteer at the start of the *Ars Amores*, but this seems a difficult connection to make. Chaucer's narrator adopts a stance of awe and unworthiness before Love; Ovid is boastfully sure he can master the god and handle him as a charioteer handles the horses. See, though, Chaucer's later reference to Bayard the horse (I 218), where this parallel could be an ironic influence.
[87] See William George Dodd, *Courtly Love in Chaucer and Gower* (Cambridge, MA, 1959) 192–4.
[88] Dodd 194.

contents, has an ironic strain that subtly acknowledges the difficulty of complying with that directive. The strain is perfectly exemplified through Chaucer's use of Love as a king who demands fealty. This is an image used early in the first Book of *Troilus;* the young prince is walking through the temple and scoffing at the lovers he sees there, when Love, angered by this, strikes him with his conventional arrow, and Troilus becomes aware of the charms of Criseyde. The folly of Troilus in so proudly feeling himself to be free from the rules of Love's governance are stressed by Chaucer's choice of analogy: Troilus is no better than a horse, who feels himself free to move as he wishes until he feels the whip reminding him of his servitude. He is a king's son himself, but he is bound by a ruler whose laws transcend those of his father: 'he that now was moost in pride above / Wax sodeynly moost subgit unto love' (I 230–1). Chaucer's narrator breaks off his narrative to stress this in stanzas that convey the key observation of the poem:

> Forthy ensample taketh of this man,
> Ye wise, proude, and worthi folkes alle,
> To scornen Love, which that so soone kan
> The fredom of youre hertes to hym thralle;
> For evere it was, and evere it shal byfalle,
> That Love is he that alle thing may bynde,
> For may no man fordon the lawe of kynde.
>
> That this be soth, hath preved and doth yit.
> For this trowe I ye knowen alle or some,
> Men reden nat that folk han gretter wit
> Than they that han be most with love ynome;
> And strengest folk ben therwith overcome,
> The worthiest and grettest of degree:
> This was, and is, and yet men shall it see. (I 232–45)

Within these two stanzas the language of service is recurrent; the idea of being in 'thrall' to Love, of being bound to Love's governance is not a state that can be resisted by anyone, whatever estate they are born into. It is the 'lawe of kynde', an immutable truth of human nature. Significantly these passages are absent from Boccaccio, whose telling of the story at this point is concentrated on the actions of Troilus, with no reflections on this powerful call of Love on the individual. Chaucer goes still further: his narrator, having exhorted his audience to take heed of Troilus' swift bondage to Love, advises that it is better to bend and submit than resist, as Love's power is so great that 'as hymselven liste, he may yow bynde' (I 256). A twig that can flex is better than a twig that breaks, remarks the narrator (I 257–8). Where any kind of ruler is concerned, this seems prudent advice; Chaucer's own adaptability to the many political changes he worked under exemplifies the realism of this policy.

Troilus cannot resist Love's call either, but Chaucer's Troilus is thoroughly aware of his royal status in a way Boccaccio's prince is not; after he sees Criseyde in the temple, he goes back to his palace with his retainers, and tries to hide his feelings while he attends to the business he must do there. It is something he finds impossible to sustain, however, and having struggled to maintain the fiction that he was concentrating on matters of domestic importance he 'bad his folk to gon wher that hem liste' (I 357). In Boccaccio Troilus makes merry with his friends at his palace, and then pretends that other business means he must send them away. This subtle reversal in circumstance divides the two manifestations of the prince; Chaucer shows him endeavouring to continue his duties, while Boccaccio showed Troilus using those duties as an excuse to separate himself from his followers and dwell on his love for Criseida. However, where Boccaccio's love-struck hero worries about the other kings and lords, and what they will think of him if they find out he is in love, especially at a time when he should be focused on fighting and the war, Chaucer drops this fear from Troilus' mind and instead gives him the 'Canticus Troili' in which to express his emotions.

The appeal to Love, thus translated into a rhetorical composition, layers tones in a way that allows the reader to feel sympathy for Troilus while also appreciating the comedy present in the dramatic musings of the pensive lover. As the imagery tells us, he is completely at sea: 'Al sterelees withinne a boot am I' (I 416) and floored by the conflicts of opposing feelings that assault him. 'Allas, what is this wondre maladie?' (I 419) he asks. Chaucer's Troilus is not concerned with his reputation, but rather is so transformed by the experience of love that his thoughts are concentrated on how best to serve Criseyde, and how to understand what this new loyalty means. At the start of the song, Troilus appeals to 'God' (I 400) for enlightenment in terms that suggest the God of Love, and yet several lines later it is to the Christian God that he prays. There does not seem to be a clash with the presentation of deities, however, perhaps because the God of Love is seen so clearly as a sort of feudal lord, and therefore on a separate scale of kingship from the Christian God. In the song Troilus surrenders himself to the God of Love, telling him that 'now youres is / My spirit, which that oughte youres be' (I 422–3). He goes even further than this and adds that 'myn estat roial I here resigne' to Criseyde, 'and with ful humble chere / Bicome hir man, as to my lady dere' (I 432–4).[89]

In relinquishing his royalty, Troilus makes a sacrifice that he is unable to truly give, but in the private world of Love's rule, whose servant Troilus has become, he can give up his privileged state and serve the cause of Love as best as he is able. It is what he wants to do, and it is, as Chaucer has stressed, what 'kynde' impels him to do. He is Love's 'thral' (I 439) and is bound to behave that way. The rest of the story shows him, as the hero, doing just that until the real responsibilities of a larger world force themselves on his attention:

> For the English Troilus loving and serving, loving as serving, are inseparable, for service gives expression to devotion and hence to the suffering and self-sacrificing disposition of Chaucer's hero.[90]

---

[89] This finds a parallel in the *Franklin's Tale*, when Dorigen submits her high noble status to that of her knight, Arveragus. (See below, 129–31.)
[90] Barry Windeatt, *Oxford Guides to Chaucer: Troilus and Criseyde* (Oxford, 1992) 230.

He is ultimately unable to forget his royal status and obligations, and make any opposition to Criseyde's exchange for Antenor. Kings, rulers and lords are subject to higher laws than Love's, after all. They are vulnerable to the same desires but have duties that, Chaucer's poem argues, can cause great private tragedies.

Criseyde also reveals more ways that kingship is a particular issue to Chaucer in this love affair; she is described by Pandarus as having virtues that well suit her to holding a 'kynges herte' (I 889), and to begin with her own fears revolve around the realisation that Troilus' royal rank means that should she resist his advances, he could force her anyway (II 710–11). However, she persuades herself that his superlative qualities, and his high rank means that she would be within her rights to love him back. This reasoning, so different from Troilus' overwhelmingly emotional reaction to love's attack, is very telling, and Chaucer's sense of irony is well exhibited in the contrasts of the internal struggle she undergoes. There is a frank and calculating appraisal of Troilus as the best knight whom she could love; the best except for Ector, she says (II 739–40). Ector is the older brother and already her protector, but married and therefore unobtainable. She reminds herself of how beautiful she is, and how all men in Troy talk about her fairness (II 748), and with the same confidence that enabled her to look haughtily back at Troilus in the temple (I 292) she boasts:

> 'I am myn owene womman, wel at ese –
> I thank it God – as after myn estat,
> Right yong, and stonde unteyed in lusty leese,
> Withouten jalousie or swich debat:
> Shal noon housbonde seyn to me "Chek mat!"
> For either they ben ful of jalousie,
> Or maisterfull, or loven novelrie. (II 750–6)

She is wary of losing that independence, and the irony is heavy in these lines, which deal with her worries about the unfaithful natures of men, and the damage to her reputation that will follow from any affair that she embarks upon. There is further play on the idea of freedom, here very narrowly defined by Criseyde, who as we have seen already, is very far from being her 'owene womman' in Troy. She too has obligations, which are to shape her destiny in a way her own attempts to influence succeeding events make poignantly ineffectual. There is a gently humorous element to her vanity that parallels the proud boasts of Troilus against love earlier in the poem; Chaucer uses both characters to balance and test these ideas of freedom and service, ruler and ruled.

The dream that Criseyde has that same night, of the royal eagle who comes and tears out her heart leaving his own in its place, is another Chaucerian addition. The eagle does not cause her any pain in the dream, a detail that could be interpreted as a sign that Criseyde need fear nothing from the physical onslaught of love, a reassurance that the experience should be submitted to without fright. It is difficult to see her in any sense as a victim of the eagle's attack, however, because of the preceding insights Chaucer has given us about her character. She is both subject and monarch herself in this poem; subject to the laws of Troy and the society she lives in to conform to the demands made on her, and also lady and ruler of her lover, Troilus.

When the two are finally together, Criseyde is clearly more in control. Troilus is overcome, immediately promising service and passionate loyalty:

> 'And I to ben youre – verray, humble, trewe,
> Secret, and in my paynes pacient,
> And evere mo desiren fresshly newe
> To serve, and ben ylike diligent,
> And with good herte al holly youre talent
> Receyven wel, how sore that me smerte;
> Lo, this mene I, myn owen swete herte.' (III 141–7)

His desperate need to convince her of his seriousness is touching; the hardness of Crisyede's response is sharp in contrast. The presence of Pandarus, encouraging her to greater warmth, stresses this absence of corresponding passion. She responds 'ful esily and ful debonairly' (III 156), politely and with deliberation. This is a woman who has calculated, is calculating, the position that she finds herself in, and is determined to try and wield some power. Her speech is quite remarkably audacious:

> 'But natheless, this warne I yow', quod she,
> 'A kynges sone although ye be ywys,
> Ye shal namore han sovereignete
> Of me in love, than right in that cas is;
> N'y nyl forbere, if that ye don amys,
> To wratthe yow; and whil that ye me serve,
> Chericen yow right after ye disserve. (III 169–75)

She demands the surrender of Troilus' royalty, a status he had already given up freely in his supplications to Love. The demand emphasises the levelling effect of love again; there is no status, no difference of birth or background, that counts for more or less in love. Troilus shall only have sovereignty when 'right in that cas is', a sovereignty he ironically never chooses to invoke because of his own princely obligations.

This insight into the private life of a member of the royal family, already focused upon in the *Book of the Duchess*, is naturally concentrated on the character of Troilus, but there are details in the portrayal of his brother Ector that can also lucidly illustrate Chaucer's knowledge of and response to the dilemmas facing the responsible ruler. Both Boccaccio and Chaucer show the compassion of Prince Ector to Criseyde as one of the earliest interactions of their poems. Boccaccio has Criseida throwing herself at Hector's feet, and begging for mercy, after the departure of her father left her vulnerable and unprotected in the city; Hector is moved by her beauty, and promises she shall be safe. Chaucer follows this line very closely: Ector is an exemplary princely lord, who treats the piteously vulnerable Criseyde with courteous generosity, reassuring her that despite the treacherous actions of her father

116 *Chaucer*

> Al th'onour that men may don yow have,
> As ferforth as youre fader dwelled here,
> Ye shul have, and youre body shal men save,
> As fer as I may ought enquere or here. (I 120–3)

His offer importantly places Criseyde under royal protection, a position Chaucer later uses to stress the harshness of fate, which decrees that Criseyde must go over to the Greek side to be with her father again.

In the negotiations for hostages Benoît does not mention the part that Ector plays at all; rather it is King Priam who, angry and disgusted by Calchas' treason, sends Criseyde back with no shred of compunction. In Boccaccio's version, Ector is part of the discussions, but not noted for any particular part of their outcome; but in Chaucer the incident is drawn out into a drama of heightened tensions and emotional complexity. Here, the protection that Ector offered at the start of the poem creates a pivotal point in the decision-making process. Ector argues that because Criseyde is not a prisoner, but stays in Troy of her own free will, she cannot be made into a bargaining counter in hostage exchange. He has promised, in true knightly fashion, to protect her, and cannot in conscience allow her fate to be overruled by the Greeks' demands. His voice is heard 'sobrely' (IV 178) and contrasts effectively with the uproar his response provokes:

> The noyse of peple up stirte thanne at ones,
> As breme as blase of straw iset on-fire;
> For infortune it wolde, for the nones,
> They sholden hire confusioun desire.
> 'Ector', quod they, 'what goost may yow enspyre,
> This womman thus to shilde and don us leese
> Daun Antenor – a wrong wey now ye chese –
>
> 'That is so wys, and ek so bold baroun?
> And we han nede to folk, as men may se.
> He is eek oon the grettest of this town.
> O Ector, lat tho fantasies be!
> O kyng Priam', quod they, 'thus sygge we,
> That al oure vois is to forgon Criseyde.'
> And to deliveren Antenor they preyde. (IV 183–96)

Ector's knightly courtesy is initially drowned out by the people, who think only of the tactical advantages of having the skills of Antenor back within their walls. Their lack of chivalric honour is to cost them dear: Chaucer's narrator reminds them in his assertion that the people are demanding 'hire confusioun', that it is Antenor who is to prove to be Troy's ultimate traitor, while Criseyde 'which that nevere dide hem scathe, / Shal now no lenger in hire blisse bathe' (IV 207–8).

Boccaccio's barons have no voice of dissent to stand in the way of their decision; in Chaucer's more complex description, Ector's persistent interventions become an ironic reference to the effective power of the royal family. Once the parliament had deliberated the question, and the outcome 'pronuncede by the precident' (IV 214) this becomes the ruling. As Chaucer says, 'And fynaly, what wyght that it withseyde, / It was for nought: it moste ben, and sholde, / For substaunce of the parlement it wolde' (IV 215–17). Though Ector may be a superlative prince whom Pandarus praises, saying, 'in al this world ther nys a bettre knyght / Than he, that is of worthynesse welle; / And he wel moore vertu hath than myght' (II 177–9), he cannot resist this influential body.

King Priam, like the distantly felt Octavian in the *Book of the Duchess*, does not appear to engage actively with the course of events at all; his part in the story is minimal, and he is left as a remote figure. There are good reasons for this: what Chaucer gives us is a representation of a fourteenth-century model of government where the king's part is to endorse what the parliament decided, and not to undermine the working of that governing body by exerting his own will as he pleased. To have been more detailed in description would have made the analogy to Richard II too close for comfort, and so Priam's depiction is handled with great care: Chaucer gives no indication of Priam's reaction to the ruling, nor do we hear of Ector appealing to his father to exert any power over the decision. The king is, however, an importantly felt influence on the actions of Troilus, and in this his role is vitally tied in with, although not central to, the tragedy that ensues.

Chaucer had other literary precedents he was following, which he developed further by replacing Priam with Ector at the start of the negotiations. This distancing emphasises the poet's lack of narrative focus on real kings, and though he could have explored the political potency of a popular story that shows Priam 'as a medieval monarch, a tragic figure who gradually loses the power to fulfil his military and political responsibilities',[91] he deliberately does not.

Chaucer's primary focus is on garnering sympathy for Troilus, and it is this prince's inner conflicts that support the tragic love story with conflicting drives of duty and passion. At this key moment in the story, duty overrides what passion dictates. Troilus is silently present at the meeting of parliament, and leaves after everyone else. Devastated as he is by the decision to send Criseyde back to her father, he clings to his honour despite Pandarus' vigorous attempts to persuade him to take oppositional action. His friend urges Troilus to abduct Criseyde, saying that it is no more than his brother Paris did to secure Helen (IV 608), but Troilus has several objections to this plan. His first, significantly, is that the war was begun by Paris's decision to take Helen, and that to duplicate that would be to lose all respect and honour among the Trojan people: 'I sholde han also blame of every wyght, / My fadres graunt yf that I so withstode: / Syn she is chaunged for the townes goode' (IV 551–3). The wording stresses his recognition of his position as Priam's son, and the personal pronoun is used again a few lines later when the prince acknowledges the serious political nature of the exchange: 'For syn my fader in so heigh a place / As parlement hath here eschaunge enseled, / He nyl for me his lettre be repeled' (IV 558–60). Duty to his father, who also happens to be the king, is keenly felt by Troilus. He cannot

---

[91] Malcolm Hebron, *The Medieval Siege: Theme and Image in Middle English Romance* (Oxford, 1997) 106.

see a way of betraying that principle, no matter how cruelly he might feel fate has dealt events. The need to maintain royal integrity effectively negates any special favours his position might be thought to incur.

Though this episode is fairly close to the corresponding passage in the *Filostrato*, there are small changes that carefully slant Chaucer's retelling. In Boccaccio, this understanding of honour as upholding his father's word is slightly undercut by Troilus' following comment that he knows any attempt to challenge the ruling would not further his cause, as his father wants him to marry a lady of royal birth. The lack of any mention of the parliament's part in the decision also makes the issue a more local, personal and selfish one; Chaucer enlarges it to encompass a noble view of how Troilus, as a royal prince, is aware that his actions have great implications for the king and the land that he rules. His refusal to act dishonourably, for his father's sake, shows a prince who is bound so completely by his sense of duty that he cannot escape from the duties and demands of his rank. This, Chaucer explores, is the difference for kings; they may, indeed, be subject to the same emotions as everyone else, but they have higher responsibilities that must temper those feelings always with the examination of how they will affect those beneath them in status. Even if a man 'a worthi Kynges sone were' (I 226) love is a state 'that alle thing may bynde – / For may no man fordo the lawe of Kynde' (I 237–8). However, a king may not allow that love to cause distress to his people. The whole story of Troy is an exemplum of the truth of this. Paris did not resist his desire for Helen, but put his own passions before those of his country, and thereby caused cataclysmic results; Troilus cannot follow the example of this brother, and must instead be seen to be more akin to Ector, whose knightly virtues we have already discussed.

Love as a universally levelling experience is arguably the *sentence* of Chaucer's work in *Troilus and Criseyde*; as C. S. Lewis pointed out in an influential essay, the areas in which Chaucer augmented or changed Boccaccio's version of the story reveal him to be interested in this exploration of theme as a reflective exercise, and the defencelessness of Troilus to the arrival of love provides a splendid vehicle for examining the potency of the effects it can have.[92] Chaucer's conclusion, that heavenly love should energetically be the subject of devotion, not earthly desires, is tugged from beneath by this assertion that no-one is immune to the sudden capitulation that love compels. That Troilus, so convinced that he is safe from falling where his companions have fallen before him, should fall so far and so fast, is a great testimony to the power of love.

The focus on the love story of Troilus rather than on the details of the Trojan War itself really began with Benoît's development of the character of Briseis, who was to become the Criseida of Boccaccio, and then the Criseyde of Chaucer. In narratives before Benoît, Troilus himself was an important but minor character in the Trojan War; his death at the hands of Achilles his plot function, and little else: 'he is his death and the fall of Troy in that war which, being the

---

[92] C. S. Lewis, 'What Chaucer Really Did to *Il Filostrato*', *Essays and Studies* 17 (1932) 56–75.

first and most famous of all, constitutes the archetypal World War'.[93] However, the twelfth century saw a shift of interest towards more courtly romance tales, crafted to entertain the demanding court of Henry and Eleanor, whose sophisticated tastes helped to turn the emphasis increasingly to the thoughts and feelings of the protagonists, rather than their actions; Wace's *Brut*, for instance, begins to investigate the motivating emotions of the Arthurian heroes. These early manifestations of the story of Troilus and Criseyde show their love foregrounded against the Trojan War, a tendency that became ultimately translated in the 1380s into Chaucer's 'litel bok' (V 1786). Just as the love of Arthur and Mordred for Guenevere in Wace ultimately causes the downfall of the kingdom, so Troilus and Criseyde's affair prefigures the destruction of Troy.

Chaucer seems to recognise all these inherited impulses, and rework them for his own times. A court poet himself, he reveals a strong impetus to entertain and enhance the educated audience's perception of themselves as capable of appreciating detailed layers of allusion and invention. His Troilus, royal lord and skilful warrior, is fated to love a woman whose fickleness will cost him his life, a woman whose birth, lower than his own, plays no small part in this predestined outcome. Though she seems, when Troilus first sees her in the temple, to exemplify all the traits of 'Honour, estat, and wommanly noblesse' (I 287) her family background is suspect. Her father, after all, though a 'lord of gret auctorité' and 'a gret devyn' (I 65–6) – though it appears not skilled enough in prophecy to see the fate of his own daughter – was a traitor. Her own betrayal of Troilus is a constant presence from the beginning of Chaucer's tale. His 'matere', he reveals, is to tell of 'the double sorwes here / Of Troylus, in lovyng of Criseyde, / And how that she forsok hym er she deyde' (I 53–6).

Chaucer's controlled sense of his sources cuts out any dedicatory persona and concentrates overtly on an implied listening audience, leaving him free to explore the nature of the betrayals in the relationship without fear of offence. He can also draw upon his self-deprecating narrator to acknowledge the potential for disturbance that his themes might provoke:

> N'y sey nat this al oonly for thise men,
> But moost for wommen that bitraised be
> Thorugh false folk; – God yeve hem sorwe, amen! –
> That with hire grete wit, and subtilte
> Bytraise yow. And this commeveth me
> To speke, and in effect yow alle I preye,
> Beth war of men, and herkneth what I seye! (V 1779–85)

Chaucer's audience has become the subject of much scholarly debate, and in *Troilus* it seems particularly eclectic. The many tone shifts, combined with the direct and indirect addresses to different groups of people, and even to specific individuals (Strode and Gower in V 1856–7) make very pertinent Kittredge's assertions that Chaucer's 'specialty was mankind' and that 'society, in all its

---

[93] Piero Boitani, 'Antiquity and Beyond: The Death of Troilus', in *The European Tragedy of Troilus*, ed. Piero Boitani (Oxford, 1989) 5.

aspects, is the continual theme of Chaucer's verse'.[94] Paul Strohm's work on Chaucer has highlighted in more detail the types of audience that are implicated in *Troilus,* and it is an impressively diverse list:

> Fictional audiences of lovers, scoffers, historians, those unsophisticated in history, ladies and gentlewomen, and young people on the brink of love jostle with actual (though exemplary) addressees in Gower and Strode, and also with implied audiences of courtiers, mature people able to keep love in perspective, rakes, embarrassed or vexed women, flirts, devout moralists whose devotion is nevertheless constrained within human limits ...[95]

That the list is so wide is worth emphasising; though the continued popularity of Chaucer's work is often cited as evidence of his universal appeal, and though this is a truism so well worn that to revisit it may seem to be unnecessary, in *Troilus* it especially rewards the reader who looks for topics contained within the poems that have a universal relevance. Here, Kingship, or the inner lives of rulers and the experiences that they may share with those they rule, of whatever estate, is one of these themes that I would argue shows itself most thoroughly in Chaucer's treatment of Troilus.

The poem is not just a political treatise, or a religious sermon, or a romance, or even simply the tragedy that Chaucer describes it as being. Its appeal lies in its breadth of associations of style and its crafting of influences so masterfully that no one asserts itself above the rest. It is an amalgam, reflecting the society it was written within, and with such tactful appreciation of the human condition that Kittredge's declaration of it as 'the first novel, in the modern sense, that ever was written in the world, and one of the best',[96] still seems a justified claim.

Chaucer's engagement with kings in this poem, therefore, illustrates their vulnerability to the human experience of love, and shows how this is complicated into matters that can become tragic in outcome by their royal duties and obligations. Paris's lack of restraint precipitates the Trojan War, and although there is nothing in the poem to encourage us to think that Troilus' actions with Criseyde could in themselves have affected the eventual outcome of the political conflict, this other son of Priam nevertheless feels himself obliged by his position to resist any further disgrace of honour and let Criseyde go to the Greeks, as his father and the Parliament have decreed she should. Criseyde's fickle nature causes Troilus' private tragedy, but it is still, importantly, just that: a private affair that affected only those immediately involved. He contains his love within a private sphere, which becomes open to the audience in a privileged way through the tactfully interrogative structure of Chaucer's narration.

Troilus is, according to Chaucer's retelling, granted a place in heaven after his heroic death fighting the Greeks, a detail in neither Benoît nor Boccaccio. 'Swich fyn hath al his grete worthynesse; / Swich fyn hath his estat real above'

---

[94] George Lyman Kittredge, *Chaucer and His Poetry* (1915; Cambridge, MA, 1967) 10.
[95] Strohm (1989) 62.
[96] George Lyman Kittredge, 'Troilus', in *Chaucer's Troilus: Essays in Criticism,* ed. Stephen A. Barney (London, 1980) 2.

(V 1828–9); it is a lament for a prince whose life was curtailed by the events catalysed by love. In the pre-Christian world of Troy Love could not be enlightened by the spiritual love of God. Love that could not flourish, the narrator seems to mourn, as a result:

> The poem states, what much of Chaucer's poetry states, the necessity under which men lie of living in, making the best of, enjoying, and loving a world from which they must remain detached and which they must ultimately hate: a little spot of earth that with the sea embraced is, as in Book Three Criseide was embraced by Troilus.[97]

Troilus is still a tragic hero, and though the narrator struggles to reconcile, as Donaldson says, the sympathies his story has evoked for Troilus with the fact that it appears to end so hopelessly, there is in this conclusion a very important truth: that

> the simultaneous awareness of the real validity of human values – and hence our need to commit ourselves to them – and of their inevitable transitoriness – and hence our need to remain uncommitted – represents a complex, mature, truly tragic vision of mankind.[98]

Men from all walks of life, including princes, kings and rulers, are subject to the same paradoxical challenge of fulfilling as best they are able the responsibilities of the lives they have been dealt, while also acknowledging the powerfully irresistible emotions that make those lives meaningful on other levels. Or to put it another way, 'all human experience – for Troilus' love comes to represent any worldly commitment – is conditioned and modified by the process of time and change'.[99]

This opinion firmly transcends the historical value of the Trojan story placed on it by earlier writers, and also goes beyond the courtly tale of Boccaccio's love complaint. Though studies have been made of the poem's political significance, linking its supposed dates of composition in with the Peasants' Revolt, and the so-called Merciless Parliament of 1388, attempting to see it as a Utopian work that 'offers a vision of a prelapsarian old Troy that coincides with a moment of prelapsarian but foredoomed new Troy, before the fall of Richard II and its inevitable entry into the chronicles',[100] these theories seem distractions from the innately tactful, consummately universal achievement of Chaucer's work. His position as an employee of the king, and the nature of his own relatively high-profile public responsibilities, make it extremely unlikely that he would risk subversive works foretelling the fall of that king and his reign. If the tortuous theoretical notion that 'like the mechanics of negation as outlined in Freudian

---

[97] E. Talbot Donaldson, 'The Ending of *Troilus*', in *Chaucer's Troilus: Essays in Criticism*, ed. Stephen A. Barney (London, 1980) 129.
[98] E. Talbot Donaldson, ed., *Chaucer's Poetry: An Anthology for the Modern Reader* (New York, 1975) 980.
[99] Windeatt (1992) 299. See also 310–13 for a summary of the major critical opinions on the ending and its meaning.
[100] Sylvia Federico, *New Troy: Fantasies of Empire in the Later Middle Ages* (Minneapolis, 2003) 71.

psychoanalysis, utopian figures stand in for what has been repressed and replace the objectionable truth with something that is at once less distasteful but also thoroughly transparent in its motivation',[101] is reflected upon, it should immediately be obvious that such transparency would cost its author dear; there are many examples among Chaucer's contemporaries to illustrate this, the fate of Thomas Usk and the former mayor of London Nicholas Bembre perhaps most pertinent. These two were executed in 1388, along with several of the king's friends, for being too obviously partisan to Richard's supporters. It was not a safe time to show public political commitment. Nicholas Bembre, often mentioned in studies of Chaucer's *Troilus* because of his wish to rename London 'Little Troy', was in a more influential position than Chaucer, but it did not save him. It would therefore be highly unlikely that Chaucer would parallel the Trojan/London analogy in public, particularly at this time.

Troilus and Criseyde reveals a great deal of what poetry of the time said about kings and kingship precisely because of what it does not say. It is a story that could have lent itself to extended reflections on the powers of the monarch, but it concentrates instead on human morality and human emotion. It leaves behind its sources to make a poem that is a 'new thing', an achievement that was remarkable because 'nothing like it was ever in the world before'.[102]

The Canterbury Tales

The analysis of Chaucer's works has so far shown that the poet chose to write about kingship, as he chose to write about other themes, through a glass darkly. The impossible juxtapositions available to the dream-visions and the distancing provided by history and myth in *Troilus* make any references refracted. Even in *The Book of the Duchess*, which is inspired by a real event, historical veracity is deliberately avoided. It is not until we turn to the *Canterbury Tales* that this approach is modified to give what has been called 'the shrewdest and most capacious analysis of late medieval society that we possess'.[103]

The *General Prologue* describes a heterogeneous group of characters who come together voluntarily to share a pilgrimage to Canterbury. They 'form themselves into a corporate unity and regulate their affairs without reference to external authority',[104] and despite the fact that Chaucer does not speak explicitly about political matters in the *Tales*, he seems to 'speak to us through his characters – including the fictional persona of Chaucer the pilgrim'[105] so that the portraits of the pilgrims as well as their tales reveal attitudes and values their author wanted to put forward. However, it is important to note that there are no representatives of the highest levels of nobility, and only one (the Ploughman)

---

[101] Federico 74.
[102] Kittredge (1980) 2.
[103] Patterson (1991) 26.
[104] Wallace (1997) 65.
[105] S. H. Rigby, 'Society and Politics', in *An Oxford Guide: Chaucer*, ed. Steve Ellis (Oxford, 2005) 35.

who might be said to be part of the very lowest stratum. The *General Prologue* gives little in the way of any sense of national identity (the enthusiasm for the Knight and the Squire's experience of war, and the comment on maritime policy in the portrait of the Merchant are chivalric and commercial respectively rather than patriotic), but it does give us a presentation of a world view from the perspectives of a range of different characters, who come not just as types, but as people with places at different levels in a hierarchically structured society. Because of this, the presentation is made

> in terms of worldly values ... their views on the world are not individual ones, but are attached to their callings – in medieval terms, their estates.[106]

In this way Chaucer can illustrate a wide range of viewpoints, and projected through the particular narrator's voice he chooses for each tale, his own thoughts become incidental to those outlooks.

Harry Baillie, tavern keeper, becomes the leader of the group at the start of their journey, and is elected by everyone 'with ful glad herte' (*GP* 811). They swear to abide by his judgement: 'and we wol reuled been at his devys / In heigh and lough' (*GP* 816–17). This decision is to provide plenty of scope for reflection upon ideas of rulership as the pilgrimage progresses, for despite the oath, Harry's decisions are often challenged, ignored and overturned. His status is not sufficient to make any real impact on his companions, despite their initial willingness to follow his wishes. It is a humorous depiction of the perils of group leadership that acknowledges on a very human level the difficulties of pleasing every member of the party; as such the fluctuating balance of power as the journey progresses can reveal a very shrewd sense of the difficulties facing those who attempt to govern real people in the real world, difficulties of which the structured ideals portrayed in the Mirrors for Princes give only a faint intimation. It is fitting – and perhaps no accident – that the first tale should be told by the Knight, as the most noble member of the pilgrims. The courtly world in which his tale is set contrasts sharply with the rambunctious riot of colour and noise that has been shown in the *General Prologue*; here we are back in the distant world of cultured elegance and royal circles, familiar from Chaucer's earlier works.

This courtly world is reflected in several of the *Canterbury Tales*, and these provide a first group for discussion. The *Knight's Tale* presents us with an ideal monarch in Theseus, duke of Athens. Though he is not a king in name, he rules as independently as any king, and his position in the story has been the source of a great deal of critical debate. Some see him as a tyrant,[107] and others as powerless in the face of Fortune;[108] but he is usually agreed to be a dominating

---

[106] Jill Mann, *Chaucer and Medieval Estates Satire: The Literature of Social Classes and the General Prologue to* The Canterbury Tales (Cambridge, 1973) 201.
[107] Terry Jones, *Chaucer's Knight: The Portrait of a Medieval Mercenary* (London, 1994).
[108] Jill Mann, 'Chance and Destiny in *Troilus and Criseyde* and the *Knight's Tale*', in *Cambridge Companion to Chaucer*, eds Piero Boitani and Jill Mann (Cambridge, 2003) 107.

figure in the English poem.[109] Chaucer's retelling of an Italian story, told originally by Boccaccio and then by Petrarch, removes a great deal of detail from the beginning, where Theseus is fighting against the Amazons and the Thebans. In Chaucer's *Knight's Tale*, all that is in the past: the story starts when Theseus is on his way home from the war. A deputation of queens and noblewomen meets him on the road, and begs him to revenge the deaths of their husbands at the hands of the tyrant king of Thebes, Creon. Theseus, moved by their piteous state, swears to help them, and rides straight away to Thebes. The war itself is not detailed, except for the horrors of the battlefield after the fighting has finished, when the scavengers work over the bodies to salvage what they can. Among these bodies are found the half-dead royal cousins Arcite and Palamon, who are brought before the duke. He decrees that because of their noble blood they should be healed and then kept as prisoners in Athens for the rest of their lives. These insights into Theseus help to form an opinion of him 'as variously the ruler, the conqueror, the judge, and, not least, the man of pity'.[110]

In this opening section the duke's merciful side has been emphasised, his knightly warrior prowess pushed to the background. Chaucer's tale is concerned with pity and mercy in ways recognisable from his other works, such as the *Legend of Good Women*, and Theseus sets a good example in exercising these virtues, in contrast to the fated lover-knights and the capricious planetary gods. Although the tale is set in antiquity, 'and while its pagan protagonists worship the planets as gods, Chaucer takes pains to remind us that they are in fact planets'.[111] They function according to their astrological natures, and therefore, unlike the human characters we admire in Chaucer, have no sense of pity. They do, however, have enormous power, which means that Theseus' decisions are only as effective as the gods allow them to be: 'Al is this reuled by the sighte above' (*KT* 1672). Wise and measured as his governance ultimately is, he can only hope that the heavenly powers will not destroy what he is trying to achieve.

His concluding speech, in which he commands Palamon to marry Emily, reveals that his own response, drawn from observations of the unpredictable natures of the gods, is that man should 'maken virtue of necessitee' (*KT* 3042). In this he shows that he 'speaks not as a philosopher but as a governor'.[112] It is a view that, read cynically, comes dangerously close to that of Langland's tale of the belling of the cat: hardly one that inspires confidence in the efficiency of any king, no matter how exemplary his behaviour. However, the tone at this point in the tale is far from negative. There is behind all other forces, 'The Firste Moevere' (*KT* 2987), who has set down the life span of everything that lives. All must die at some point: 'He moot be deed, the kyng as shal a page' (*KT* 3030), but this should provoke not despair, but a humble acceptance of one's place in the universe. This 'Firste Moevere' is vaguely conceived by Theseus, as is

---

109 See, for example, J. A. Burrow, 'The *Canterbury Tales* I: Romance', in *Cambridge Companion to Chaucer*, eds Piero Boitani and Jill Mann (Cambridge, 2003) 156: Helen Cooper, *Oxford Guides to Chaucer: The Canterbury Tales* (Oxford, 1989) 81.
110 Muscatine (1957) 183.
111 J. A. Tasioulas, 'Science', in *Chaucer: An Oxford Guide*, ed. Steve Ellis (Oxford, 2005) 181.
112 Burrow (2003) 158.

fitting in his pre-Christian world, but Chaucer's audience would have identified it with the God they know, whose influence is supreme. Jupiter, representing the secondary influence of the planets, may be the 'prince and cause of alle thyng' (*KT* 3036), but he too is accountable to this higher power, just as humanity is subject to his. To try and rebel against his order is to deploy that enemy of good governance and harmony, 'wilfulnesse' (*KT* 3057). The two heavenly rulers are distinct, yet part of the same overall system of governance.

However, far from being as set and ordered as Theseus tentatively tries to describe, the gods are fractious and wilful, as the battle between Venus and Mars shows, even while their impulses are paradoxically entirely restrained by their astrological positions. It is this 'subsurface insistence on disorder [which] is the poem's crowning complexity, its most compelling claim to maturity'.[113] Ultimately it is Saturn who sorts out the dispute, and not Jupiter, whom Theseus hails as the 'stable' and 'eterne' king (*KT* 3004), a point that confuses any attempt to see a coherent portrayal of planetary supremacy in the duke's scheme. Saturn is 'the colde' and it is 'agayn his kynde' to try and sort out disputes; he is of all the gods the most disturbing and dark. His powers are destructive and negative:

> Myn is the drenchyng in te see so wan;
> Myn is the prison in the derke cote;
> Myn is the stranglyng and hangyng by the throte,
> The murmure and the cherles rebellyng,
> The groynynge, and the pryvee empoysonyng;
> I do vengeance and pleyn correccioun ...
> And myne be the maladyes colde,
> The derke tresons, and the castes olde;
> My lookyng is the fader of pestilence. (*KT* 2456–69)

His influence is exerted in a sort of parody of Theseus' earlier defence of the queens injured by Creon, in that his astrological context presumably makes his intervention not only possible, but inevitable. As such it opens a gap between Theseus' sense of the world he inhabits and that world as portrayed by the narrator/Knight. Despite his enormous power, Saturn cannot control his own movements, and neither can the other planets; Theseus, though he cannot control their influences, is free to choose how to respond to them. Throughout the *Knight's Tale* Theseus acts with consistent good sense, courtesy and careful justice; he reflects openly on the duties of lordship, emphasising his active pursuit of good governance:

> And softe unto himself he seyde, 'Fy
> Upon a lord that wol have no mercy,
> But been a leon, bothe in word and dede,
> To hem that been in repentaunce and drede,
> As wel as to a proud despitous man

---

[113] Muscatine (1957) 189.

> That wol mayntene that he first bigan.
> That lord hath litel of discrecioun,
> That in swich cas kan no divisioun
> But weyeth pride and humblesse after oon.' (*KT* 1773–81)

Despite his wisdom and his goodness, however, he is not able to prevent Arcite and Palamon's feud from ending in Arcite's death, even after decreeing that the beaten knights should be taken off the field, not killed: 'it were destruccioun / To gentil blood to fighten in the gyse / Of mortal bataille now in this emprise' (*KT* 2537–40). Arcite wins the battle, but fate in the shape of Saturn takes a hand, and he is fatally injured by a fall from his horse. Theseus' faith and acceptance of this, adapting to what he must, ultimately point to a profounder truth and a complex presentation of governance, whether personal or political. The harmony that is presented is hardly without difficulties; technically Palamon did not win Emily, Arcite did, and as Emily's plastic will favours Arcite over Palamon at the point he seemed to be victorious – 'she agayn hym caste a freendlich ye' (*KT* 2680) – Palamon's victory in love is no real victory at all, at least at this point in the story. However, the symmetry and order of the structure of the tale offer another view, that in fact each knight does get exactly what he asked for: Arcite prayed to win the battle, and Palamon to win Emily. This is precisely what happens.[114] On a practical level, the whole situation is a mess of courtly conundrums, which makes it a difficult situation for Theseus to sort out. The best solution is that Palamon and Emily marry: this will cement relations between two countries and reflect the harmony that Theseus wishes to provide for his people. Whether the gods or fate interfere with that harmony is unpredictable; Theseus does not, however, simply abdicate responsibility and let events take their natural course. As Jill Mann has pointed out, he does not imply that accepting the gods' will means mere passivity, but recognises the need to transform necessity *into* 'vertu'.[115] He acts as a king should, trying to order his realm despite the forces of the heavens that can disrupt these efforts; though he begins the tale under the banner of Mars, god of war, he ends it 'as the follower of Providence in the guise of Jupiter, bringing joy rather than death and accord in place of conflict'.[116]

Chaucer's Knight shows a universe of inscrutability, of mysteries unfathomable, in which one of the most important of the ways that humanity can try to cope with the uncertain future is by good kingship. Theseus' wisdom can shape some positives out of the death of Arcite, seeing those chances for good as continual opportunities to transform chaos into order, or as one critic has put it: 'When the earthly designs suddenly crumble, true nobility is faith in the ultimate order of all things.'[117] By implication, these opportunities will be available

---

[114] For an elaboration of these two critical standpoints, see Derek Pearsall, *The Canterbury Tales* (London, 1985) 124–5, who argues that Chaucer shows 'hesitancies and inconsistencies' in his style, and Muscatine (1957) 178–90, who argues that the tale is characterised by a sophisticated unity and symmetry.
[115] Mann (2003) 109.
[116] Cooper (1989) 81.
[117] Muscatine (1957) 190.

to everyone who has power and rule in society, according to his or her situation. We may not know what darkness lies beyond our realms of knowledge and understanding, although the 'faire cheyne of love' (*KT* 2991) ultimately holds all together, but we should strive to make sense of what we have, and a good lord will constantly try to harness events for the good of his people.

The *Squire's Tale*, as is fitting, is also set in the world of courtly manners, and follows the conventions of the romance genre. However, it appears to be unfinished, and so the complete structure of its themes is difficult to realise: whether this was a deliberate move on Chaucer's part or not, we have no way of telling. Despite this, what does exist still furnishes a little evidence of attitudes to kings for, like the *Wife of Bath's Tale*, this tale begins in a king's court. King Cambyuskan of Turkey is an ideal ruler, beloved of his people for his wise and just governance:

> ... ther was nowher in no regioun
> So excellent a lord in alle thyng:
> Hym lakked noght that longeth to a kyng.
> As of the secte of which that he was born
> He kepte his lay, to which that he was sworn;
> And therto he was hardy, wys, and riche,
> And pitous and just, alwey yliche;
> Sooth of his word, benigne, and honurable;
> Of his corage as any centre stable;
> Yong, fressh, and strong, in armes desirous
> As any bachelor of al his hous.
> A fair persone he was and fortunat,
> And kept alwey so wel roial estat
> That ther was nowher swich another man. (*SqT* 14–27)

The repetition of the adjective 'noble' and the repeated superlative references to the fact that 'ther was nowher' another king like him idealises him, in the same way that the beauty of his daughter Canacee renders the Squire conventionally speechless. The king's reign is unblemished and secure; he has every blessing that he could want, and so he holds a feast to celebrate. At this feast, arriving in a manner reminiscent of the Green Knight in *Sir Gawain and the Green Knight*, a strange knight rides into the hall and, after showing his own nobility by courteously greeting everyone there 'by ordre, as they seten in the halle' (*SqT* 92), he gives the king a message from the king of Arabia and India. This message congratulates the king on his long reign, and offers gifts for the occasion. These gifts are magical and marvellous objects: a mechanical brass horse, a truth-telling mirror, a ring that will enable Princess Canacee to understand the speech of birds, and a naked sword that will cut through anything with its sharp edge, and heal any wound it has made with its flat side. The ring enables Canacee to listen to a wounded falcon, who has been betrayed in love, and she attempts to heal it. Although the Squire begins to explain that he has much more to say, he is then interrupted by the Franklin, and it is at this point that his tale peters out.

King Arthur's court in the *Wife of Bath's Tale* has a function like King Cambyuskan's in that it provides the setting for the initial action, but really has no more influence on the tale other than to provide a background. It is another well-known folk tale, and Gower, as we have seen, was among other medieval writers who retold it. King Arthur does not even receive the laudatory description that King Cambyuskan does, although the Wife of Bath says that the British speak of him with 'greet honour' (*WBT* 858), nor does he figure as a major character in the tale. The focus is on the nameless knight and his quest for what women most want, and it is Arthur's queen who dispenses justice and asks for the power to administer the knight's punishment. The female authority figures in this tale reflect the Wife of Bath's character and interests, so it would be incongruous for there to be more on men or kings or political rule in general. The Wife of Bath is concerned with the sort of governance a woman can have over her lover, and explores in the tale how a harmonious relationship can be achieved if there is a balance of authority, or 'sovereynetee' in it. She also examines the idea of nobility, and whether this comes from being born into a higher estate or from leading a virtuous life. This debate puts Christ at the centre of all claims to gentility (*WBT* 1117), and states, as the Parson does at greater length later on in the *Tales*, that all are equal by His grace. The old woman in the tale declares that nobles who do immoral acts only debase themselves:

> He nys nat gentil, be he duc or erl,
> For vileyns synful dedes make a cherl. (*WBT* 1157–8)

and says that those who are poor and do good deeds like Tullius Hostilis, should, as he did, rise into the *gentil* class: 'He is gentil that dooth gentil dedis' (*WBT* 1170). This seemingly egalitarian argument then goes on to urge the ruling classes to behave with 'gentillesse' and the poorer levels of society to be contented with their lot: 'the recipe for social wellbeing is not social or economic change, but individual moral reform'.[118] Greater social and personal accord will come from successful 'sovereynetee' over oneself and one's actions.

This sovereignty is of the same general kind as that which the Parson speaks of in his tale; rules, boundaries and hierarchies are social constructs everyone has to negotiate, and the exercise of justice, mercy and pity is a skill that all estates should try and learn. The Wife of Bath, a contrast to the courtly ladies of her tale, exemplifies this universal applicability. Both the *Squire's Tale* and the *Wife of Bath's Tale* use the courtly setting of romance to initiate a kind of textual authority, that of a conventional setting and basic plot elements that will help to foreground their particular manipulation of the details. The Squire's king is functional, just as King Arthur is in the *Wife of Bath's Tale*, and it is his rather bungled handling of the direction of his tale that, like the gender bias of the Wife of Bath, reveals more about the character telling the tale than the tale itself reveals about themes and ideas. The Squire is young, as yet untried

---

[118] Helen Phillips, *An Introduction to* The Canterbury Tales*: Reading, Fiction, Context* (Basingstoke, 2000) 102.

in battle and with little courtly experience; if the tale is deliberately unfinished, this could indicate that his attempts to tell a long and sophisticated interlaced romance are too ambitious. Though he starts enthusiastically and shows some promise in his style, he does not manage to complete his task.

The Wife of Bath also uses style to impress. Although her tale does explore the nature of the relationships between men and women, it remains dominated by the long Prologue that precedes it. Though the romance genre might seem a rather unexpected choice for a voluble gap-toothed cloth-seller, it provides the opportunity for a 'replacement of beautiful antique myth with exploitative modern reality';[119] the Wife can invert convention to reiterate her personal belief in the need for a woman to have an active role in marriage, and by working within such an old and respected tradition of stories still imply that the structures that they contain are necessary and stable. As such, there is little that is really outrageous in her tale, despite the impression the colour and noise of her description in the Prologue might seem to promise. Neither of these tales shows any desire to destroy convention, but rather shows how the romance genre can argue for a conservative continuation and preservation of the ideals they promote. Kings are distant and exemplary images, but they are part of a picture that contains important instruments of discourse in the romance genre, and that does not concern itself with political undertones of any sort.

The *Franklin's Tale* is based on a type of folk tale called the 'Damsel's Rash Promise', a story that has many variations in medieval romance. Chaucer's Franklin claims his version is based on a Breton lai, a form of short narrative popular at the French court of Marie de France; this raises expectations about its contents, and alerts the listeners to the courtly context the Franklin apologetically tries to recreate. His deprecatory comment at the start, that he is but a 'burel' man (*FranT* 716) puts immediate distance between the audience and any elements it might find offensive: the rhetorical device of *diminutio* Chaucer often uses to indicate that topics of a provocative nature will be included. Here the Franklin, as one of the higher-status characters of the group of pilgrims, is perhaps apologising to the Knight for attempting a story set in a world similar to that of Theseus and Emily, but the apology also works if it is taken as Chaucer's offering to his own courtly audience. Perhaps this is because, like the *Wife of Bath's* and *Clerk's Tales*, this story is concerned with the definition of nobility, and sovereignty in love and marriage.

In many ways, this tale is very close to that of the Wife of Bath; it begins with a description of Arveragus and his courtship and marriage to Dorigen that stresses their agreement to serve and obey each other. This is detailed in terms that follow the pattern of the Wife of Bath's knight and his lady; once the knight has given governance to the lady, she gives it back again to him, and the result is harmony. Arveragus makes one proviso, however: that he should retain in

---

[119] Phillips (2000) 100.

public 'the name of soveraynetee' (*FranT* 756), to stop knowledge of this oath bringing shame upon him. Like the knight in the *Wife of Bath's Tale*, who is horrified to find he has pledged himself to marry the ugly old woman, Arveragus is concerned with appearance, yet here it is of a kind that is very proper in the chivalric world. By defending his reputation he can protect Dorigen's, too; as Prudence notes in the *Tale of Melibee*, 'certes he sholde nat be called a gentil man that after God and good conscience, alle thynges left, ne dooth his diligence and bisynesse to kepen his goode name' (*Mel* 1640). This reflects the character of the Franklin, whose social position as part of the landed owners of the minor gentry, and his description in the *General Prologue* as a 'worthy vavasour' (*GP* 360) made him appreciate the attributes of 'gentil' behaviour. In this way it does not undermine Arveragus's worthiness, for at the end of the tale he and Dorigen 'in sovereyn blisse leden forth hir lyf' (*FranT* 1552) and he 'cherisseth hire as though she were a queene' (*FranT* 1554). This final note emphasises his submission to his wife, whose value in terms of love has now increased her status from a lady to a queen; Arveragus appears to appreciate her worth even more now that he knows the extent of her faithfulness, for in 'cherishing' her he reveals an awareness of her extraordinary qualities that make active the more abstract promises to 'take no maistrie / Agayn hir wyl, ne kithe hire jalousie' (*FranT* 748–9) which he gives at the start of the tale. Those were the extravagant but untried promises of courtship; the 'cherishing' he now provides reveals a more deeper, fully understood commitment to marriage.

This is a story not about kings, but about class and love. Dorigen is of higher status than her husband and of Aurelius, but she willingly accepts her new status as a married woman in an unconventional marriage where each partner promises the other obedience:

> She thanked hym, and with ful greet humblesse
> She seyde, 'Sire, sith of youre gentillesse
> Ye profre me to have so large a reyne,
> Ne wolde nevere God bitwixe us tweyne,
> As in my gilt, were outher werre or stryf.
> Sire, I wol be youre humble trewe wyf –
> Have heer my trouthe – til that myn herte breste.' (*FranT* 753–9)

Arveragus swears to maintain his lover's position of servitude to Dorigen's will after marriage, at least in private, and by doing so, gains a new status of lordship:

> Thus hath she take hir servant and hir lord –
> Servant in love, and lord in mariage.
> Thanne was he bothe in lordshipe and servage.
> Servage? Nay, but in lordshipe above,
> Sith hi hath bothe his lady and his love;
> His lady, certes, and his wyf also,
> The which that lawe of love acordeth to. (*FranT* 792–8)

Though the language in this passage has been criticised for using 'incompatible terms' that 'chop and change in a dizzying manner',[120] there is no real incompatibility in the ideas described. The oppositions only emphasise the strength contained in their appropriation of both areas of reference, and therefore also in their relationship.

Aurelius, as a squire, has the lowest social status of all three. Yet in the final instance, in releasing Dorigen from her promise to him, he proves

> Thus kan a squier doon a gentil dede
> As wel as kan a knyght, withouten drede. (*FranT* 1543–4)

Even the magician acts with gentilesse when he refuses to take Aurelius's money. Chaucer has

> extended and deepened the courtly concepts involved in the definition of a 'gentil' man until their class-basis, their narrowly conceived aristocratic tenor, becomes irrelevant. Chaucer's courtliness, more evidently than that of other romancers, is Christian at root.[121]

The *Franklin's Tale* argues, as the *Wife of Bath's Tale* does, that individual actions define the nobility of a person, and not their birth into a particular class. The social hierarchy, however, remains inviolable, and a large part of attaining sovereignty comes from pursuing that gentilesse within the confines of social class. Each division has its own responsibilities to the estates around it, and Chaucer's tales of romance make use of the genre to show this. The more times this model is proposed in Chaucer, the more the proposal increases the sense that this is very far from a paradoxical view. Indeed, in claiming distinct modes of operation for earthly and spiritual living there is an effort to recognise the duties owed as subjects of secular and heavenly worlds that are, to any Christian believer, inseparable.

That it is the socially ambitious Franklin who tells this tale becomes extremely pertinent, for his self-defined state as a 'burel' man given at the start of his narrative is clearly linked to his final question to his audience: 'Which was the mooste fre, as thynketh yow?' (*FranT* 1622). He invites the listeners to judge who was the most generous in spirit, and therefore to recognise the worthiness of the squire and the philosopher, whose actions show them to be as 'gentil' in this respect as the noble-born knight and his lady. And yet the question itself admits that socially there is a different kind of gentilesse, which is rarely transcendable; the *Franklin's Tale* and the Franklin himself conserve the boundaries they seek to transform, both of the romance genre and of social estate.

Chaucer's courtly stories illustrate a concern with how to act within this framework of tensions; he chooses to focus on themes of gentilesse and nobility and not on the role of kings, as Gower often does, so that his work is more applicable to all listeners, whether of the mixed but lower estates represented

---

[120] Helen Phillips, 'Love', in *A Companion to Chaucer*, ed. Peter Brown (Oxford, 2002) 288.
[121] John Stevens, *Medieval Romance* (London, 1973) 58.

within the text of the *Canterbury Tales* itself, or the aristocratic lords and ladies of the royal court viewing that text from outside.

A second group of tales uses the role of a king more directly in extending these ideas, showing how a bad ruler, or tyrant, can upset the balance of harmony. All of them contain portraits of or comments on tyrannical rulers: the *Man of Law's*, the *Clerk's* and the *Physician's* tales present these lords in different ways, and the response of the subjects to their actions is as revealing as the actions are themselves. The *Man of Law's Tale* shows what happens when kings do not put the good of their people first. Chaucer's sources for this Tale have been traced to Nicholas Trevet's Anglo-Norman *Chronicle*, written for Marie, the daughter of Edward I, in 1334; his reworking of elements of the popular plot of a princess being exiled for refusing to marry her father, and a queen exiled for giving birth to a monster are transformed into a more complex story by the Man of Law's emphasis on the persecution of Constance and her steadfast Christian faith.[122] Throughout, Constance is the epitome of strength, faith and nobility, while the male characters fall foul of their desires. In this tale, the Man of Law describes the characters of three male rulers: the Roman emperor, the sultan of Syria, and the king of Northumberland. All three are flawed in some way, and these weaknesses have serious repercussions for the lands they govern. At the start of the tale Constance's qualities are revealed as being so exemplary that the common voice of the Roman people wishes that she should be 'of al Europe the queene' (*MLT* 161). Her fame spreads to Syria, where the sultan, hearing of her virtues, decides he must marry her. So convinced is he of his desire that he converts to Christianity in order to secure her hand. This reckless and dramatic conversion appals his mother, who is horrified by her son's impetuous betrayal of his faith. She concocts a brutal plan to murder him and his retainers at a feast, leaving only Constance alive. The sultan is portrayed as a king ruled by his passions (*MLT* 204–10): he acts less like a powerful potentate than like a courtly lover. His pagan 'Otherness' is tempered, sublimated by his love for Constance, but he is vulnerable to rebellion, which comes swiftly by courtesy of his own mother.

In contrast to her son, the sultan's mother is a ruthless tyrant who butchers everyone at the feast, including her own offspring, rather than see Christianity replace the Moslem faith of Syria. She is described initially as 'welle of vices' (*MLT* 323) and then later, directly addressed as 'roote of iniquitee! / Virago, thow Semyrame the secounde! / O serpent under femynynytee, / Lik to the serpent depe in helle ybounde!' (*MLT* 358–60) The classical and Biblical references underline the Man of Law's sympathies, setting her heathen evil against the Christian goodness of Constance, who has been saved from the sultan's mother by God's good mercy. Constance is put in a boat and set adrift, but she is kept alive by God, who 'sente his foyson at hir grete neede' (*MLT* 504). She arrives in Northumberland, and is rescued by the constable and his wife, whom she converts to Christianity. However, a wicked knight decides to seduce her, and

---

[122] Benson, *The Riverside Chaucer* 857.

when she rejects him, cuts the constable's wife's throat and blames Constance, who is then brought before King Alla for justice to be done. The king sorts out the truth, falls in love with Constance's goodness himself, and asks her to marry him. Here is another pagan ruler, but this one, unlike the sultan, has compassion and pity; Alla also becomes a Christian, but once again, the mother disapproves of the match and schemes to make Constance disappear. Eventually, despite her plotting, husband and wife are reunited in Rome, and can present themselves to the emperor, who is full of wonder at seeing his daughter again.

As a result of decisions taken by kings, Constance is accused of murder by one spurned admirer, and has to fight off a rapist later in the story; her only true supporter is the constable's wife, Hermengyld. As a victim of these decisions, Constance exemplifies the tragic consequences of orders that are made without proper wisdom. The fact that the kings in this Tale are portrayed as mostly vulnerable through their own emotional instability strengthens the portrayal of Constance's Christian fortitude and providential salvation. If you are suffering under the rule of a tyrant king, or a foolish one, you should throw yourself on God's mercy and ask Him to 'governe us in his grace' (*MLT* 1161). This tale's theme is of God's ultimate kingship; He is the only king that can be relied upon, because, as the various rulers of this story show, earthly kings are vulnerable to evil influences that all too often prevent them from ruling wisely.

This tale has a disturbing sense of the humanly flawed potential of kings; even the emperor misjudges the wisdom of sending his daughter to marry a Syrian sultan who rules over a heathen land. However, his powerful paternal joy harmonises the ending, and the succession is set upon Constance's son, so that the future looks hopeful. This makes it hard to find a coherent pattern in the ending of the story.[123] The final blessing recombines the Christian theme with that of kings: 'now Jhesu Crist, that of his myght may sende / Joye after wo, governe us in his grace' (*MLT* 1160–1), yet

> it is hard to credit so serious a thinker as Chaucer ... with believing that the naïve folk piety of the tale, with its miracles provided to order, answered any serious questions; nor would such an attitude explain the blanket appeal to determinism in the first part, or the reversion to patterns of unstable fortune at the end.[124]

One answer would be to credit the Man of Law with what is being said, and not Chaucer. The narrator's voice is hard to grasp in this tale, and his views, struggling to make a neat conclusion, perhaps reflect this. He has been seen as a 'sentimental (albeit sympathetic) narrator' who is used to make a powerful comment on the popular piety of Chaucer's time: 'with its misdirected veneration of the saints, threatened to obscure the true, exemplary power of their holy lives through "golden legends" and sensational display'.[125] Alternatively, it has

---

[123] Cooper (1989) 131.
[124] Cooper (1989) 131.
[125] Ann W. Astell, 'Apostrophe, Prayer, and the Structure of the *Man of Law's Tale*', *Studies in the Age of Chaucer* 13 (1991) 96.

been said that the tale 'has no deeply necessary congruity with what we know of the character of the speaker'.[126]

Whatever the reason for its narrative ambiguities, it nevertheless maintains the strength of God's rule above all others in the world. Constance will finish her days doing good deeds and living with her family. Through this, God brings joy that can ultimately ameliorate all the tragedies that came before. In this way

> the vision of the world, the vision of tragedy, is set in sharp juxtaposition with the conventions of hagiography, with their insistence on miracle and unmediated divine intervention, and on a simple triumph of God over Satan.[127]

In this sense, it is naïve in its approach, but this is because compared with the *Knight's Tale*, the Man of Law's dominant philosophical influence is 'not *De consolatione philosophiae* but *De contemptu mundi*'.[128] In this context, the unreliability of earthly rulers becomes an integral part of the Man of Law's perspective, and justifies the emphasis on God's power as the only real stable source of governance.

In the *Clerk's Tale*, another virtuous woman is tested to her limits by a tyrannical lord. The ruler, a marquis called Walter, decides to marry Griselda, a woman of low birth from the nearby village. Once married she exemplifies some of the best qualities of queenship:

> Nat oonly this Grisildis thurgh hir wit
> Koude al the feet of wyfly hoomlinesse,
> But eek, whan that the cas required it,
> The commun profit koude she redresse.
> Ther nas discord, rancour, ne hevynesse
> In al that land that she ne koude apese,
> And wisely brynge hem alle in reste and ese. (*ClT* 427–33)

Though she was born of lowly stock, her natural virtues transform her into a queen of grace and peace. Like Alceste in the *Legend of Good Women*, her role as intercessor and consort is carried out with success, and like Constance in the *Man of Law's Tale*, she is uncomplaining and obedient to the dictates of her husband: harsh as his treatment is to her, she bears it with a fortitude that is remarkable. Griselda takes Constance's Christian attributes to another literary level when the Clerk suggests that she is a symbol of how all Christians must behave under God's design:

> For sith a womman was so pacient
> Unto a mortal man, wel moore us oghte
> Receyven al in gree that God us sent;
> For greet skile is he preeve that he wroghte. (*ClT* 1149–52)

---

[126] Muscatine (1999) 160.
[127] Cooper (1989) 132.
[128] Alfred David, 'The Man of Law vs. Chaucer: A Case in Poetics', *PMLA* 82 (1967) 223.

This tale is an allegory, and the king-like rulers in it exemplars of how God's actions can often seem arbitrary and unfair; it does not matter that Walter is a bad ruler, because he is not the focus of this story. The focus is on how his subjects react to his decisions. Not only does Griselda illustrate the perfect pattern for such subjection, but she reveals the reward to be gained from it. Using the language of ideal kingship, Chaucer shows how the consequence of Griselda's patience resulted in a world of joy for all: 'Ful many a yeer in heigh prosperitee / Lyven thise two in concord and in reste' (*ClT* 1129–30). Walter's realm is a peaceful one, and there is a strong emphasis on this in the repetition of certain phrases: Griselda's father is looked after 'in pees and reste' (*ClT* 1132) and her son rules 'in reste and pees' (*ClT* 1136). This is not the picture of a country that has been blighted by this marquis's allegorically charged actions, but rather one that has been made harmonious by Griselda's responses to them.

This is pulled more sharply into focus with the inclusion of the reactions of the marquis's other subjects. Here the Christian allegory retreats to let a more politically potent aspect intervene, for the story is 'on one level, a political myth about a theory Chaucer often offers as the optimal solution to social conflict'.[129] When it is announced that their leader will be marrying again, and they see the fair young maid brought to be the new bride, the people stop their unhappy murmurings about Walter's treatment of Griselda and instead start 'commendynge now the markys governaunce' (*ClT* 994). The narrator interjects at this point to denounce their fickleness:

> 'O stormy peple! Unsad and evere untrewe!
> Ay undiscreet and chaungynge as a fane!
> Delitynge evere in rumbul that is newe,
> For lyk the moone ay wexe ye and wane!
> Ay ful of clappyng, deere ynogh a jane!
> Youre doom is fals, your constance yvele preeveth;
> A ful greet fool is he that on yow leveth.' (*ClT* 995–1001)

Unlike Griselda, they are inconstant in their loyalty, and lack the integrity to maintain their love of their lovely and talented lady; she is a commoner, just as they are, and her elevated status may explain why she is vulnerable to their changing respect. As has been seen, Chaucer's *Canterbury Tales* shows a world ordered by the three estates, a system that the poet seems consistently to assert is vital for the structure of a co-operative and successful society. Here Griselda exemplifies this, for as a villager she is unquestioningly obedient to her lord's demands. If social peace is to occur 'all classes should accept their situation, the rulers should act for the common good and the subjects should give their submission voluntarily'.[130] It is a world ordered also by love and by gentilesse; Griselda is obedient as wife and consort, too. She is bound by all three of these different states to her lord, and the tale therefore explores, in a harsher way than the *Franklin's Tale* does, the effects of entrusting these obediences to an unreli-

---

[129] Phillips (2000) 121.
[130] Phillips (2000) 121.

able recipient. The marquis 'acts high-handedly, and as a feudal master'; it is ultimately Griselda's fortitude and constancy that make her 'the rock on which Walter breaks'.[131] Griselda's story shows how individual integrity is the only weapon successful against the actions of a tyrannical overlord, and that passive obedience can be a powerful agency for change.

The *Physician's Tale* displays the people in a more flattering light; here they effect the punishment of the corrupt judge, exacting justice for the death of Virginia, the 'constant in herte' (*PT* 56), just as they do in Gower's version of this story. As Strohm has noted, 'Apius is actually an agent of social dislocation, setting a "cherl" against a worthy "knyght"'.[132] Just as in the *Clerk's Tale*, the upset of hierarchical norms cause serious consequences. In this story, however, the balance is remade by the people themselves, outraged by what has happened. They are suspicious 'By manere of the cherles chalangyng' (*PT* 264) and break into the courtroom to save the knight, condemned to death for decapitating his daughter to prevent Apius from obtaining her. The subjects in this story interfere to protect justice and order; governed by a ruler (or judge, in this instance) who has betrayed their trust and corrupted the natural order of society, they act to restore the status quo. Read as a group, these three tales embody a broadly consistent view about the role of tyrants, and the necessity for virtue, patience and maintenance of social order to counteract their destabilising effects.

The final six tales share an interest in the topic of advice, and have been grouped together for this reason. The first three, the *Merchant's*, *Manciple's* and *Parson's* tales, treat this theme in a rather more abstract way, whereas the last three, *Melibee*, the *Monk's* and the *Nun's Priest's* tales, have a more specific engagement with it.

The *Merchant's Tale* contains a representation of lords and their advisers through the story of January and his decision to marry a young wife. Placebo and Justinus show contrasting sides of counsel, and the dangers of vanity that lead to attending to the wrong sort. Placebo demonstrates the opposite approach to this role from the crow in the *Manciple's Tale*: he is keen to tell January only what he thinks he wants to hear, trying at all times to keep his lord happy. This course of action he proudly defends, saying that though Solomon himself advised everyone to act only upon good counsel, he believes that January's wisdom is 'the beste' (*MerT* 1490):

> For, brother myn, of me taak this motyf:
> I have now been a court-man al my lyf,
> And God it woot, though I unworthy be,
> I have stonden in ful greet degree
> Abouten lordes of ful heigh estaat;
> Yet hadde I nevere with noon of hem debaat.
> I nevere hem contraried, trewely;

---

[131] Cooper (1989) 195.
[132] Strohm (1989) 159.

> I woot wel that my lord kan moore than I.
> What that he seith, I holde it ferme and stable;
> I seye the same, or elles thyng semblable.
> A ful greet fool is any conseillour
> That serveth any lord of heigh honour,
> That dar presume, or elles thenken it,
> That his conseil sholde passe his lordes wit.
> Nay, lordes been no fooles, by my fay! (*MerT* 1491–1505)

He boasts of his familiarity with the court and with great men, and his obsequious flattery of the wisdom and reliability of a lord's judgement is a parody of the sort of court hanger-on that Chaucer and his noble audience would have been all too familiar with.

Though the Merchant is one of the strongest and most revealing narrative voices Chaucer creates, the poet can manipulate this to create humour more applicable to his audience. It is witty for Chaucer to suggest that lords can be very great fools, by showing January's deception and literal blindness to the truth of his marriage. That the Merchant is the narrator ostensibly protects Chaucer from accusations of presumption; the foolishness of January's character is contained mostly within the context of a fabliau, a genre usually containing cruder humour that distanced the proceedings from reality. Of course, there is the more sophisticated effect that in fact compliments the intelligence of the courtly audience by implying that they would get the joke about foolishness and be able to laugh at it. They can see beyond Placebo and the Merchant, from their privileged position as listeners, so that they can appreciate the entertainment from an indulgent distance.

Chaucer is also himself a 'court-man', so he inserts a joke at his own expense alongside this one about lordship. He is no more suggesting that he is like Placebo than that his listeners are like January – or is he? The darkness of the tale that has made some critics uncomfortable with its 'tone of voice that persistently expresses bitterness, cynicism and sardonic humour'[133] may provoke consideration into whether beneath the comedy lies something more critically biting. The Merchant's character and experiences make much of this tone appreciable, but in the larger context of Chaucer's social position there are details that call for investigation as well.

Justinus is not only learned, but practical, and his good sense prompts him to advise January that marriage is not a good idea. January rejects his help – 'Straw for thy Senek, and for thy proverbes!' (*MerT* 1567) – and decides, supported by Placebo, to follow his own inclinations and marry anyway. What proceeds is a treacherous subterfuge that is directly caused by his self-deception and which will indicate the corruption at the heart of the marriage. Despite the intervention of the god Pluto, the self-deception that caused January's initial error of judgement is too deep-rooted for him to escape from its effects. Pluto protests against May's scheme, and declares he will make January see again so that he

---

[133] Derek Pearsall, *The Canterbury Tales* (London, 1993) 194.

realises what is going on. His word is seemingly final: 'My word shal stonde, I warne yow certeyn. / I am a king; it sit me noght to lye' (*MerT* 2314–15). Yet even the authority of the king of the underworld is subverted by the defiance of the queen, who replies that nevertheless she will have her way. The discord among the royal pair is a further indication that all things are out of joint in this tale; not even strong, good lordship from a determined supernatural power acting out of mercy and pity can stand against the combination of male vanity and female cunning. Though January appears to be a 'worthy knyght' (*MerT* 1246), living so that 'His housynge, his array, as honestly / To his degree was maked as a kynges' (*MerT* 2026–7), his vanity prevents him from controlling his desires and listening to reason. As a result, even though his physical blindness has been miraculously cured, he condemns himself to living with an unfaithful and deceitful wife, still spiritually blind to the truth.

It is a bleak tale: May jeeringly makes a parody of the line 'pitee renneth soone in gentil herte' (*MerT* 1986). Chaucer used it in the *Legend of Good Women* and the *Squire's Tale* to demand the reader's whole-hearted approval for this unselfish sympathy, but May uses it as an excuse to justify taking a worthless lover. Like Phoebus Apollo in the *Manciple's Tale*, January is self-deceived. Both lords had voices of reason to advise them, and both chose to ignore the truth because it was not what they wanted to hear. In this Chaucer forcefully drives home the view that good counsel, though it may not be palatable, is essential for effective rule of self and of others. Nevertheless the portrayal of January, like the portrayal of Phoebus, is very far removed from that of any actual king, and the moral impetus of the tale is once again kept general rather than specific.

The *Manciple's Tale* and the *Parson's Tale* appear at the end of the sequence of the *Canterbury Tales*, and they also have elements that relate to kingship, although it is not their main focus. The *Manciple's Tale* has been seen to contain ideas on different matters, kingship among them; although it is short, an allegorical interpretation of the god Phoebus can view him as a kind of ruler whose wisdom is so limited he cannot discriminate between a trustworthy subject (the crow) and a disloyal traitor (his wife). He is introduced in terms that show him as a courtly lord:

> He was therwith fulfild of gentillesse,
> Of honour, and of parfit worthynesse.
> This Phebus, that was flour of bachilrie,
> As wel in fredom as in chivalrie (*MancT* 123–6)

but his role is 'utterly undignified, as a jealous husband who is cuckolded and then foolishly punishes the truth-teller'.[134] The Manciple himself is an unsavoury character, bullish and inflammatory; he undercuts the Host's decision to ask the Cook to tell a story next, and scoffs at any idea that the Cook might

---

[134] A. C. Spearing, 'The *Canterbury Tales* IV: Exemplum and Fable', in *Cambridge Companion to Chaucer*, eds Piero Boitani and Jill Mann (Cambridge, 2003) 209.

take revenge for all the sarcastic comments he throws at him. His story has a boldness about it that echoes the teller; it is the shortest of the completed tales, but has been called the most baffling, with a clear exemplum whose function is nevertheless 'strangely distorted'.[135] The language itself seems to defy fluency; first using courtly descriptions as shown in the lines depicting Phoebus, above, and then colloquial interjections that emphasise the Manciple's coarseness and vulgarity: 'I am a boystous man, right thus seye I' (*MancT* 211). Though this does not in itself make a disconnected sense of narrative, the direction of the plot itself does:

> Various speeches pull in opposing directions; the tale seems to offer not a stable, even if inverted, hierarchy of story and meaning, but a cluster of divergent discourses in unstable equilibrium.[136]

One of those discourses is relevant to kings, not only in that Phoebus and his crow are a parodic image of the prince and his adviser portrayed in Mirrors for Princes, including that of Prudence and Melibee earlier in Chaucer's own work, but in the positively scornful judgement the Manciple gives on the morally lax aristocracy and tyrant kings. A faithless wife is the same, he declares, whether she is born into a high estate or a low one, except that the language used is different: a gentlewoman will be called a 'lady' and a peasant-woman a 'wench' or a 'leman'. In a similar way, a tyrant king and a common thief are no different from each other, except in their titles. This, he adds, was pointed out to Alexander (something Gower also included in his *Confessio*[137]) as part of his education on how to become a great ruler. The appeal of this line of argument to the voluble Manciple is obvious; what Chaucer does is to utilise the language of different contexts (the court, exemplum, Mirrors for Princes and ordinary speech) and put them in opposition to each other to illustrate the conflict of meaning between them. The Manciple's argument is daringly seditious in arguing that all estates are the same under the trappings of status, and Chaucer acknowledges this by making the Manciple suddenly back-pedal, excusing himself by a plea of lack of education that is confusingly, perhaps ironically, at odds with the sophisticated handling of meaning and style Chaucer has shown his character demonstrating elsewhere:

> But for I am a man noght textueel,
> I wol noght telle of textes never a deel;
> I wol go to my tale, as I bigan. (*MancT* 235–7)

There is a sense of embarrassed awareness that he might have gone too far, and a witty play on words in his protest that he is 'a man noght textueel' that deflects attention away from any shock such radical views might evoke from Chaucer's noble listeners.[138]

---

[135] Spearing (2003) 208.
[136] Spearing (2003) 210.
[137] *Confessio Amantis*, Book VII.
[138] See Phillips (2000) 215.

Because of the difficulty of interpreting the tale, it is difficult to conclude how pertinent to kingship are the references to tyrants and lords who do not listen to wise counsel; what is evident once again is Chaucer's care, when his characters suggest a controversial subject, to redress the balance towards less incendiary topics. The Manciple's Phoebus is a strange hybrid of characteristics, and his outburst against his crow is full of bluster and comic dismay at having slain his wife and broken his bow. The tirade he launches against his faithful bird, denouncing him as a traitor, and sending him to the devil, is less engaging. This portrait of incensed power, out of control and irrationally blaming bad fortune on a bird, is a sobering image of the fate that can befall a subject who upsets his king, or a servant his master: 'The message seems to be that society is so ordered that underlings waste their time if they try to speak truth or give advice.'[139]

The final lines conclude that this example proves that the best course of action to take is that of silence, for anything other than this invites personal disaster:

> My sone, if thou no wikked word has seyd,
> Thee thar nat drede for to be biwreyed;
> But he that hath mysseyd, I dar wel sayn,
> He may by no wey clepe his word agayn.
> Thyng that is seyd is seyd, and forth it gooth,
> Though hym repente, or be hym nevere so looth.
> He is his thral to whom that he hath sayd
> A tale of which he is now yvele apayd. (*MancT* 351–8)

This theme is reiterated over fifty-three lines. This may be mild comedy at the Manciple's expense; it may even be a serious warning, coming at such an emphatic length after Apollo's tyrannical outburst, of the dire consequences of speaking up in front of social superiors. It may even have prompted contemporary readers to put themselves in the position of the crow and see Richard II as Phoebus, but if that happened, Chaucer, whose own brevity of comment within the tale is exemplary, could plead that he had no part in making it happen. In this the *Merchant's Tale* and the *Manciple's Tale* share an agility that makes them able to look at the role of the court adviser, but disguise with comedy any precise application to Chaucer's world and his audience. The unsettling comedy in both tales alerts us to possibilities of reference, but cannot, or will not, concretely establish them.

In contrast to the hectic composition of the *Manciple's Tale*, the *Parson's Tale*, which follows immediately afterwards, comes as an antidote. Where the former is short and energetic, the latter is long and confidently collected. There could not be a better way to draw any sting from the Manciple's cynical view of the world than to listen to the Parson's Christian principles for good living and self-governance. The *Parson's Tale* shows points of contact with all the

---

[139] Phillips (2000) 217.

other Ricardian poets that we have looked at: the *Gawain*-poet in *Cleanness* shows similar concerns with spiritual truth, Langland emphasises good deeds and moral living, and Gower's *Confessio* has enough parallels with this tale to prove that a relationship existed between these texts, even if we cannot be sure of their relative order of composition. The *Parson's Tale* also manages to compress the 'sentence' of all the other *Canterbury Tales* together in a finale that shows the essentially Christian scope of Chaucer's opus. As Helen Cooper has said,

> As a *summa* in miniature, the Parson's Tale in one sense encapsulates the various *moralitees* of the whole work into a single treatise just as the tale of the other priest on the pilgrimage, the Nun's Priest, encapsulates the aesthetics of all the tales, their styles and genres.[140]

Academics have argued about the tale's place in the *Canterbury Tales*, its cohesiveness, its dullness or otherwise, and even whether Chaucer wrote it at all. Keeping in mind the sensible observation that 'we cannot banish works from the canon just because we don't like them',[141] however, we can turn to the tale itself.

The structure of this tale is bound by three parts of the sacrament of Penitence: being sorry, making a formal confession to a priest, and then doing penance, or Contrition, Confession and Satisfaction, as they appear in the text.[142] Within this structure is a digression on the Seven Deadly Sins, a theme comprehensively worked out in Gower's *Confessio*.[143] Chaucer uses the same theme, but works much more closely with the vehicle of the penitential manual,[144] a genre that 'envisions Christian faith as an endless internalisation accomplished against continual resistance'.[145] Gower's narrative has a different inspiration: his whole work is centred on the seven sins, and he makes use of the continuing confession of the Lover to explore them with exemplary stories that constantly reiterate the need for more rational self-control. There is a sacramental confession that confirms the authority of Amans's spiritual journey, but the sacramental element is not an integral part of the poem in its entirety. In Chaucer, the sacrament, introduced at the start of the tale, never really leaves the centre of the narrative; it is always before the reader, emphasising that the end of the pilgrimage for the characters in the *Tales*, as well as for himself, lies just ahead. Canterbury, the spiritual capital of England, is figuratively reminding us of the need for reflection and repentance, as well as the spiritual life that continues after earthly life

---

[140] Cooper (1989) 405.
[141] Muscatine (1999) 34.
[142] The fourth part, absolution, which comes between confession and satisfaction, is necessarily excluded by the format of the tale. See George D. Smith, *The Teaching of the Catholic Church* (London, 1952) 955–89.
[143] Morton W. Bloomfield, *The Seven Deadly Sins* (East Lansing, MI, 1952) 157–201 discusses this theme in fourteenth-century literature.
[144] The tradition of the penitential manual began after the Fourth Lateran Council of 1215 prescribed yearly confession for all Catholics. The earliest English penitential manuals were not available until about 1340: Scanlon 12.
[145] Scanlon 13.

is done. The entertainment on the road is now in the past; it is the time to focus on the goal of the pilgrimage itself, a goal that the Parson does not allow any irony to undermine. Christian authority and spiritual power become the ultimate theme, and Chaucer's distinctive transformation of sources is respectfully held in check for most of the tale. This may be because

> it expresses a deep and orthodox piety, in the practice of which, as a man, Chaucer would not have wished to be separated from his fellow men. He does little to make it his own, as a writer, nor to carry alive its truth into the heart by passion or the power of his imagination. No attempt on Chaucer's part should be detected in this to 'distance' himself from these orthodox pieties: only a recognition, perhaps temperamental in origin, that they are not the appropriate material for his art.[146]

The argument for Chaucer's maintenance of respectful treatment of Penance seems plausible, but that does not mean Chaucer chooses to step away from the text completely. Truth need not, indeed should not, rely on passion and imagination to be felt and believed; Chaucer works instead with small details to show his artistic presence in the tale, aware all the time of his audiences inside and outside the text.

In the character of the Parson Chaucer gives us an exemplary portrait of a man whose life is dedicated to serving his parish. Like a good king, he exhibits all the best tenets of humanity: he is humble, does not stand on ceremony and puts his parishioners before himself at all times. However, his voice

> although it is obviously meant to embody clerical authority ... cannot be specified even so generally as the voice of the Church. He is not a monk or a friar. Still less is he a bishop or a pope. He is a parson, occupying the lowest position within the hierarchy of the secular clergy.[147]

This is true, yet even so he has in his possession a very powerful authority indeed, to minister the holy sacraments to those in his parish and teach them how to improve their spiritual lives. His vocation puts those spiritual lives under his direction, and it is a responsibility that he takes as seriously as any ideal king would take governing his country. The *General Prologue* emphasises his fairness as well as his complete devotion to God. He sees his duty to follow the pattern of moral living as essential; without his example, as he says, the people have no real spiritual model:

> For if a preest be foul, on whom we truste,
> No wonder is a lewed man to ruste;
> And shame it is, if a prest take keep,
> A shiten shepherde and a clene sheep.
> Wel oghte a preest ensample for to yive,
> By his clennesse, how that his sheep sholde lyve. (*GP* 501–7)

---

[146] Pearsall (1993) 289–90.
[147] Scanlon 7.

The Parson may be humble and poor, with little ostentation to show for his role, but it is an influential one; in appearing the antithesis to a great lord, his spiritual richness can radiate out unobscured by the trappings of power. He is not in any sense a mere 'ventriloquist's dummy', as one critic has claimed;[148] Chaucer makes him very aware of the gravity of his words. His guidelines for avoiding sin have an authority of their own that his character need not strongly interact with, although this does happen at times, for instance in the discussion on Pride, in which ornate clothes and riding paraphernalia are severely criticised (*PT* 415–35), which may be criticism of the notorious pursuit of extravagant new fashions by Richard and his courtiers. In one of those imaginative touches that alert us to Chaucer's control of the narrative, the Parson also denounces as Pride the fashion for wearing too few clothes: the people 'showen the boce of hir shap, and the horrible swollen membres, that semeth lik the maladie of hirnia, in the wrappynge of hir hoses' (*PT* 422), a comic detail that gives individuality to this Parson. He may have exemplary virtues, but Chaucer does not deny him a voice of his own. His fascinated horror at such fashions reveals an unworldliness that would protect this presentation from insulting the contemporary courtly listeners. It provides a moment of carefully placed humour that shows Chaucer's awareness of their presence, and subtly indicates that awareness is of listeners whose engagement with his work was on different levels. The humour helps draws attention from the easily bored, for whom a sermonic tale on the deadly sins might not inspire engagement; its satire would evoke sympathy from those listeners whose views might very well coincide with that of the Parson, and who might be drawn from that group of well-educated, intellectually curious men Derek Pearsall calls the 'Chaucer Circle',[149] and its striking imagery might stir ideas in those whose own beliefs were undefined and unsure, and inspire greater thought on issues of faith than had existed in them before.

The examination of Pride becomes more uncomfortably pertinent to rulers and lords when at line 450 the distinction between the goods of the body, soul, fortune and grace is made. The Parson says that it is good to remember that too much pride in any of these areas will cause inevitable distress, and that it is necessary to treat such bounties with humble gratitude:

> ... remembre hym of bountee that he of oother folk hath receyved. / Another is to be benigne to his goode subgetis; wherfore seith Senek, 'Ther is no thing moore covenable to a man of heigh estaat than debonairetee and pitee, / And therfore thise flyes that men clepen bees, whan they maken hir kyng, they chesen oon that hath no prikke wherwith he may stynge'. ... Certes also, whoso prideth hym in the goodes of fortune, his is a ful greet fool; for somtyme is a man a greet lord by the morwe, that is a caytyf and a wrecche er it be nyght; / and somtyme the richesse of a man is cause of his deth;
>
> (*PT* 465–71)

---

[148] Robert Swanson, 'Social Structures', in *A Companion to Chaucer*, ed. Peter Brown (Oxford, 2002) 407.
[149] Pearsall (1992) 181–3.

A great lord (whether a king or not) must have kindness and pity on his followers, because they are more likely to be loyal if treated with those qualities. This example is characteristic of the tale as a whole: though, as Gower as shown, each of the deadly sins provides ample opportunity for an application to kings, Chaucer does not link them in this way. The discussion of the sin of anger, which can lead to murder, brings no condemnation of tyrant kings, and the examination of greed does not focus on covetous monarchs. The reason for this is explained by the Parson himself:

> But certes, sith the dom and grace cam, God ordeyned that som folk sholde be moore heigh in estaat and in degree, and som folk moore lough, and that everich sholde be served in his estaat and in his degree. / And therfore in somme contrees, ther they byen thralles, whan they han turned hem to the feith, they maken hire thralles free out of thraldom. And therfore, certes, the lord oweth to his man that the man oweth to his lord. / The Pope calleth hymself servant of the servantz of God; but for as muche as the estaat of hooly chirche ne myghte nat han be, ne the commune profit myghte nat han be kepte, ne pees, and rest in erthe, but if God hadde ordeyned that som men hadde hyer degree and som men lower, / therfore was sovereyntee ordeyned, to kepe and mayntene and deffenden hire underlynges or hire subjetz in resoun, as ferforth as it lith in hire power, and nat to destroyen hem ne confounde. / Wherfore I seye that thilke lordes that been lyk wolves, that devouren the possessiouns or the catel of povre folk wrongfully, withouten mercy or mesure, / They shul receyven by the same mesure that they han mesured to povre folk the mercy of Jhesu Crist, but if it be amended. (*PT* 770–5)

The Parson, unlike Chaucer, does not have access to royal circles. His perspective is from the other end of the social spectrum, and his words try to emphasise the integral part all people have in the structure of society; their spiritual state makes the issue of which estate they belong to irrelevant in the after life, but an essential part of it while they are on earth. These lines make very explicit that class hierarchy is in accordance with God's will, and that even the church needs this structure if it is to function. It also argues that all estates are equal, but only in their spiritual state. It rejects the idea of a democracy, but the obligations due to each estate as a result of this order mean a strengthening of society, rather than a weakening of it: 'community not only depends on hierarchy, it is hierarchy'.[150] The mention of 'sovereyntee' in line 773 is deliberately unspecific. It could mean lordship in general, or kingship specifically; the weak passive construction also lessens the ordinance from God that is given to the church. Scanlon points out that Chaucer could, in this respect, be referring to the gradual consolidation of power structures under Richard II happening in England in the late 1300s. Parliament, the judicial system and the royal bureaucracy all became

> newly emergent national forms of sovereignty [and though they] could not be presented as divinely ordained in the same way as the general principle

---

[150] Scanlon 19.

of social inequality, they could nevertheless be seen as following in the same spirit.[151]

Sovereignty is therefore important to the Parson in that as a principle it upholds the Church and keeps safe the common good of all the members of the lower estates that his role makes him particularly responsible for. His scope of reference is so different from that of Chaucer, or Chaucer's courtly audience, that the distance is insurmountable. In itself the layering of narrators and listeners perfectly exemplifies here the hierarchical boundaries Chaucer, through the Parson, is describing. The Parson would not imagine coming within the orbit of a king, and so his images of lordship are more localised, more applicable to those he is used to addressing.

This creates a complex representation of individuality, for earlier in the tale the Parson defines man's three estates as being innocence, sin and grace, which come after penitence (*PT* 680). In this expression

> The Parson's Tale turns away from both individuality and social and professional distinctions; for him all men are descendents of Adam, and difference of estate lies in the eyes of God.[152]

However, the later passage re-establishes those earthly estates as a different system of social order that must separate individuals. Chaucer does not turn away from them because the two are not incompatible, but rather complementary. Both assert God's creation of all things in their rightful order. The distinctive voice of the Parson, marking him as an individual with firm beliefs and a strong faith, gives a provocative image of a kind of ruler that is far removed from any seen so far, but which can be seen to have an authority beyond but still dependent upon earthly systems of rule. It is a compelling portrait, whose strengths make Chaucer's Retraction, which follows it, more effectively powerful. Here Chaucer asks for forgiveness if he has offended any of his listeners, and asks them to pray for his soul. He ends by beseeching 'hym that is kyng of kynges and preest over alle preestes' (*PT* 1090) to send him grace to live the rest of his life in a way that will enable his soul to be saved at the Day of Judgement.

In this prayer Chaucer's ultimate image of kingship is revealed; God is the only king he is willing to celebrate unequivocally. His is the rule under which the poet works to celebrate life in all its forms and with all its foibles. Kings are as much a part of that life as any other individual, and they have neither more nor less spiritual accountability than other men.

The final three tales to be considered represent the most complex reflections of Chaucer's approach to the idea of kingship, and as in the three tales above, these reflections appear in the manipulation of different modes of advice that seem more directly adapted from sources specifically intended for a royal audience. The *Tale of Melibee*, the *Monk's Tale* and the *Nun's Priest's Tale* all focus

---

151 Scanlon 20.
152 Cooper (1989) 407.

on kings, but in different ways. That focus 'depends on the moral authority of the narrative discourse that produces it, and each of these tales will make their affirmation of kingship inseparable for their affirmation of narrative'.[153] The narrative forms are very different: *Melibee* is written in prose, the *Monk's Tale* is a *compilatio* of exempla, and the *Nun's Priest's Tale* is a melting pot of genres and stylistic parodies. The shifting nature of these narratives protects the views of the poet from direct analysis; as we have already seen, we cannot expect securely proven links to specific events. What can be gleaned, however, is the range of ideas presented about kingship; these are sometimes closely related to what can be learnt about Richard II's reign, but are more often approaches applicable to any king, or ruling lord.

The *Tale of Melibee* is a reasonably close translation of the *Livre de Melibée*, which is a version of Albertanus of Brescia's *Book of Consolation and Counsel*. Like the *Manciple's Tale*, it has as one of its major themes the importance of distinguishing between good and bad counsel, especially for lords. Richard II saw himself as a peacemaker, but was vengeful towards those who displeased him, and so suggestions that this tale could be offered to him as an instrument of counsel cannot be dismissed out of hand. In adopting the female persona of Prudence as a vehicle for these conciliatory ideas, Chaucer could address 'in safely indirect, fictional fashion, some issues relevant to Richard II's style of government'.[154] Prudence is an authority figure, but she is also less of an abstraction than, for instance, Lady Philosophy is in Boethius' *Consolation*. She is a medieval housewife, who always speaks in respectful and humble terms, with an authority that derives from the wisdom and reliability of her words:

> 'My lord', quod she, 'I beseke yow in al humblenesse that ye wol nar wilfully replie agayn my resouns, ne distempre your herte, thogh I speke thyng that yow displese. / For God woot that, as in myn entente, I speke it for youre beste, for youre honour, and for youre profite eke. / And soothly, I hope that youre benyngnytee wol taken it in pacience.' (*Mel* 1235–8)

Melibee is a lord whose passions rule his reason, and even after all that Prudence has taught him about the need to choose supportive and truthful counsellors, when finally confronted with transgressors his initial response is to disinherit them and exile them forever. He is wilful, and Prudence carefully asks that he put this trait aside, so that he can really listen to what she is saying. Wilfulness will prevent her words having any real effect; it is the enemy of reason, and so ultimately the enemy to good governance, of self and subject. Then she reminds him that mercy and pity are the best ways to win a good name, which is what every good ruler should strive to obtain:

> And therefore, if ye wole that men do yow obeisance, ye moste deemen moore curteisly; / this is to seyn, ye moste yeven moore esy sentences and juggementz./ For it is written that 'he that moost curteisly comandeth, to hym men

---

[153] Scanlon 206.
[154] Phillips (2000) 178.

moost obeyen.'/ And Tullius seith, 'Ther is no thyng so comendable in a greet lord / as whan he is debonaire and meeke, and appeseth him lightly.'

(*Mel* 1854–62)

The importance of pity as a quality all good kings should have has been noted several times, and the stress on the vitality of a good name recalls advice in Book VII of Gower's *Confessio*. Melibee's lordship is transformed by Prudence's teaching, and he is persuaded to work for reconciliation with his former enemies.[155] Chaucer concentrates on temperance, good governance and the necessity of honest counsel, and it could be seen that

> the tale thus concerns itself literally with issues that were important throughout Richard II's reign; the king's need for counsel, the principles guiding the proper or improper influence over the king, his receptivity to their advice, and the questions of taking revenge against, or seeking reconciliation with, one's enemies.[156]

These are indeed important issues, but not ones uniquely relevant to Richard. English history is littered with kings who suffered because of rash actions and bad counsellors. One of the passages that Chaucer deleted from his sources is a Biblical reference to the miseries a land can suffer if ruled by a child, a nicety, it may be remembered, that Gower did not follow in his *Confessio*. As Judith Ferster observes,

> This shows that Chaucer knew that the tale could be taken as a reference to Richard II's accession to the throne when he was still a young boy.[157]

It also

> may suggest that Chaucer wrote *Melibee* with a consciousness of its applicability in the contemporary context to a monarch who was unwarlike abroad but could be capricious and vindictive where his own domestic power and royal dignity were threatened or criticised.[158]

Both these views are plausible, but do not allow for the possibility that in deleting that reference, Chaucer was deliberately avoiding any specific connection, so revealing that his focus was not on Richard, but on a more encompassing examination of lordship; Melibee is, after all, a great lord, but not a king. The tale contains an exhaustive quantity of references, and these strengthen it, for constantly re-enacting ideas of medieval authority, as Scanlon has said, was the

---

[155] See Scanlon 214: Scanlon argues that Melibee achieves a kind of sovereignty by renouncing his desire for vengeance, but admits that this is 'implicit and figural, nor can it ever move beyond that indefinite state'. It is a 'kind of' sovereignty, but it is also very clearly not named as sovereignty by Chaucer, which is surely more to the point.

[156] Ann W. Astell, *Political Allegory in Late Medieval England* (Ithaca, 1999) 101.

[157] Judith Ferster, *Fictions of Advice: The Literature and Politics of Counsel in Late Medieval England* (Philadelphia, 1996) 92.

[158] Phillips (2000) 178.

148 *Chaucer*

medieval writer's way of consolidating and transforming previous works into new and more provocative ones:

> Translation was one form of such re-enactment, which most medieval writers viewed not solely as submission to previous authority, but precisely as a means of appropriating it. The production and acceptance of *counseil* was another. The *Tale of Melibee* defines and explores both of these forms of reiteration in narrative terms, translation in its characterisation of Chaucer's own voice, *counseil* both in its production by Prudence and its acceptance by Melibee, and in the exemplary transformation that acceptance will effect in his social position.[159]

By proposing himself as the teller of the tale, Chaucer is also claiming a measure of authority as a court writer; the successor to generations of minstrels who is made fun of in *Sir Thopas* is in *Melibee* reinterpreted as the adviser to princes who can manipulate exempla with deep appreciation of their worth. The juxtaposition of the two tales also suggests the ironies inherent in either role; these ironies resurface in the themes of lordship in the perceived gap between the real Chaucer and the narrator-Chaucer and the imagined lord Melibee and the shadowy real King Richard. In its evocation of the *Fürstenspiegel*, the *Tale of Melibee* can reasonably be supposed to have been written for an audience that had the king in mind; Chaucer's appropriation of it certainly reveals that 'the writer in the *familia regis* might hope to demonstrate his particular worth and claim for himself a more substantial role that that of mere amateur entertainer'.[160] What it carefully refuses to do is become a personalised mirror written specifically for Richard. This distinction denies the tale many of the arguments for relevance to contemporary political events, such as war with France and opposition to Richard in the late 1380s that have characterised so much of its criticism,[161] but it does allow for a more fruitful comparison with other Mirrors for Princes and a wider appreciation of Chaucer's interpretation of that genre, that, by stepping inside of the frame of the story himself, he seems to be requesting.

Melibee is concerned with the relationship between an adviser and his lord / king, which could and could not be about Chaucer's relationship as a writer with King Richard. He has therefore translated the mirror form through the vehicle of the *Canterbury Tales* so that it functions on an entirely new level; part of a game, an entertainment on a pilgrimage, where its royal associations are out of place in the company of the pilgrim listeners. The Host's reaction is to focus on Prudence, saying that he had rather she were his wife than the scold he has at home. There is no comment on the exempla, or the morals implicit in them. Here, Chaucer's use of irony works to contrast the estates concerned; without a royal or wholly noble audience, the mirror becomes simply a collection of moral injunctions told by a wife whose wise forbearance is the only

---

[159] Scanlon 207.
[160] Green 143.
[161] For a summary of these views, see Helen Phillips, "The French Background", in *Chaucer: An Oxford Guide* 308.

remarkable element about it. It becomes a comic aberration, not a serious intellectual construct. Yet, as already noted, that royal audience does exist for the real Chaucer; each narrator is therefore telling the story with a distinct and very different awareness of the social location of his text. This complex narratology further complicates a cohesive reading of the tale, like the collection of genres used in the *Nun's Priest's Tale*; by playing with identity like this Chaucer can once again deny the reader a comprehensive and secure appreciation of the subtleties of his narrative.

The *Monk's Tale* consists of a collection of stories that all focus on the foolishness of trusting in material success. The exempla begin by retelling how all things were made, and how both the Fall of Lucifer and the Fall of Man came to pass. Adam is described as a powerful ruler: 'Hadde nevere worldly man so heigh degree / As Adam' (*MT* 2011–12). He had everything, but lost it all through 'mysgovernaunce' (*MT* 2012), and as such his is the supreme example of loss. The string of summaries of the reigns of Biblical and classical kings, emperors, and queens that follows all reiterate this theme of Fortune's indiscriminate power: both exemplary rulers such as Zenobia and Alexander, and tyrants such as Nero come to the same end. There is no commentary between the exempla, and it is hard to see the structuring force behind their order, but that very randomness underlines the unpredictable nature of Fortune. All are subject to the same force: 'Fortune alway wole assaille / With unwar strook the regnes that been proude' (*MT* 2763–4).

There is, however, another, more political way of understanding this lack of order. At the beginning of the tale, the Monk says that he will tell the story of the life of St Edward, a promise that he does not fulfil. St Edward was a saint whom Richard II closely identified with; he appears by Richard's side in the Wilton Diptych, and there is other evidence to prove how devoted Richard was to his predecessor's memory.[162] So committed was he to emulating Edward that he was crowned in the saint's robes, and 'saw the Confessor as his partner: his mentor in spirituality and guide in matters of government'.[163] Ann Astell has argued that Chaucer's Monk gives us Edward's history, albeit allegorically. She suggests that St Edward can also remind readers of King Edward II, Richard's ill-fated great-grandfather. Through the addition of the more nearly contemporary histories of Peter of Spain, Peter of Cyprus, Ugolino of Pisa and Barnabò Visconti, lord of Milan, who were all murdered by envious enemies, it is possible that 'the "lyf of Seint Edward" to which the Monk refers is, simply put, a recognisable code for the life of Richard'.[164] These perhaps make the analogy more specific than the bloody deaths by assassins of rulers such as Nero and Julius Caesar. Astell's argument relies on an assumption that the placing of these four more modern deaths at the end of the tale, just before the Knight's interruption, was Chaucer's preferred order, rather than the alternatives presented in other manu-

---

[162] See Saul (1997) 311.
[163] Saul (1997) 311.
[164] Astell (1999) 103.

scripts. She says that this would then force the reader to 'think of Edward II and to wonder about the fate of Richard II'.[165]

There are many different manuscript versions of the stories, and it is hard to prove which order was intended by Chaucer.[166] The Monk himself admits that he will not be telling the exempla in any particular order, 'but tellen hem som bifore and som bihynde' (*MT* 1988), and this statement of random composition warns us against critical attempts to synthesize it. This may be another effort of Chaucer's to deflect attention from any more subversive analysis, but it may also just reflect the theme of Fortune in its lack of formal cohesiveness.

The inclusion of the more contemporary examples has been said to show that

> Chaucer had – boldly for his place and time (the period of the *Canterbury Tales*, c1385–1400) – used contemporary figures as *exempla* for the insecurity of rulers' hold on power.[167]

It is not only the legendary leaders of the past that have suffered, but men whom readers would still remember. As a warning to any current ruler, this format clearly points to the necessity for prudence, an attribute urged in the previous tale of *Melibee* and consolidated here with more forceful and graphic illustrations of what could happen without it. The *Monk's Tale* concentrates on emphasising the fall of great men and women rulers most of whose falls come in gruesomely detailed ways; there are stabbings and starvings, decapitations and poisonings. These famous figures do not experience temporary setbacks but feel the full weight of Fortune's power; this is necessary in the scheme of the tale, for 'the complete loss of personal autonomy drives home the essential uncontrollability of political power'.[168] There is less distance between the reader and Ugolino of Pisa than there is between the reader and Alexander the Great, who was so powerful that 'Comparisoun myghte nevere yet been maked / Betwixe hym and another conquerour' (*MT* 2639–40). This catalogue of disasters concerning exclusively royal or noble examples is interrupted by the Knight, himself the highest-status pilgrim of the group, who says that he has had enough of hearing about such woeful deeds. He would rather hear about the opposite side of Fortune, 'As whan a man hath been in povre estaat, / And clymeth up and wexeth fortunat, / And there abideth in prosperitee' (*Pro NPT* 2775–7). It is difficult not to sympathise with the Knight's impulse to stop the relentless cataloguing of gloomy endings: the tale

> refuses to admit the possibility of any other vision of the world, apart from its own narrow and belittling definition of tragedy: it is the other tales that provide such extras as human relationships, happy endings, searching philosophy, salvation.[169]

---

[165] Astell (1999) 108.
[166] For a discussion of the variants, see Benson's *Riverside Chaucer*, 930.
[167] Phillips (2000) 184.
[168] Scanlon 225.
[169] Cooper (1989) 334.

The *Knight's Tale* in particular handles tragedy in a particularly sophisticated way, so it is surprising that the Knight desires to hear of more auspicious stories, when his own tale was set in a courtly world where Fortune was a far more mysterious figure; there are more complex ironies in the implications that rulers can only suffer from Fortune, whereas subjects have more to gain by it, and in the alignment of woe with high status and joy with lower status.

The *Nun's Priest's Tale* fulfils the Knight's requirements by using one specific exemplum rather than a whole host of them. This single base-line, however, contains within it a seemingly infinite amount of readings, so that it becomes a brilliantly inverted paradigm of the inexorable sequence of tales offered by the Monk. By using comedy to subvert the learned authority of the writers who have written about Fortune, as well as creating a farmyard kingdom where status becomes a provocatively unstable commodity, Chaucer's Nun's Priest triumphantly transforms his earnest endeavours into a rhapsodic portrayal of Fate's often unpredictable management of worldly affairs.

I would like to complete this appraisal of Chaucer's work, therefore, by looking at the *Nun's Priest's Tale*, which 'in style as in theme and structure ... is the *Canterbury Tales* in miniature'.[170] Its unrivalled combination of the ludicrous with the serious and the courtly with the natural means that it can sum up everything that has been looked at so far.

In following the *Monk's Tale*, Chaucer performs a juxtaposition of narratives that complement and conflict with each other; in this, as has been noted, the effectiveness is 'not in any dramatically conceived confrontation between the Monk and the Nun's Priest as pilgrim-characters', but in the stories themselves.[171] The Nun's Priest has an edict from the other pilgrims to tell them something merry; the Host condemns the Monk for annoying them all with a tragic view of life that is always 'covered with a clowde' (*Pro NPT* 2782). The Monk's glass is always half-empty; the Nun's Priest will show the glass half-full. His tale concludes with the wheel of Fortune on the upward turn, and though there are ambiguities present in this, the overall effect is much lighter than that of the Monk's concentration on dire portents for the future.

The sources for this tale lie in the anti-clerical and anti-monarchical twelfth- and thirteenth-century French beast-fables, the most well-known being the *Roman de Renart*. In this source the farmyard is described, but it is under the ownership of a wealthy landowner, and not a poor widow, as in Chaucer. The protagonist is Reynard, while Chaucer makes Chauntecleer the main character, and he also adds the large discussion on dreams, which is not in the French tale. The Renardian stories were produced for lesser provincial French nobility, a sort of sub-class who had an uneasy relationship with both the church and the crown. The tale's popularity grew from the opportunities for satire of those secular and religious overlords that these listeners would have most appreciated. However, the tale's sources go back to much older roots, like Aesop's fables, and the story also circulated in England in the earlier medieval period. It found a place

---

[170] Cooper (1989) 352.
[171] Pearsall (1985) 230.

in moral writing as an exemplum against vanity, and was included in Chaucer's lifetime in John Bromyard's preacher's anthology, the *Summa praedicantium*. It has, therefore, a mix of associations that make it an appropriate choice both for a Nun's Priest to tell, and as a means for subtle commentary on politically pertinent as well as moral matters.

This eclectic narrative approach draws on all of Chaucer's skills to work these implications through in a way that will appeal to his varied audience. Like the Canterbury pilgrims themselves, Chaucer's courtly circle consisted of many different types of courtly people; the cacophony of ideas and lively action in the *Nun's Priest's Tale* would entertain these listeners, but also prevent close scrutiny of each reference: like Chauntecleer, our attention is distracted by the variety of images so that we move from one topic to another without resting on any for long:

> The *Nun's Priest's Tale* ... preserves the variety of the complete work, its interplay of voices and styles, its refusal to stand still.[172]

In this, and in the sense that the more times this particular tale is read the more stylistic masterstrokes become recognisable, Chaucer's final laugh is on us. Like Chauntecleer, the reader has plenty of warnings to pay attention to what is happening, to pick the fruit from the chaff, but there is so much to delight in and respond to, imaginatively and intellectually, that it is intentionally made an impossible task to do this with any degree of confidence. It is better to see its effect that of a wonderful tree covered in many different kinds of fruit, any one of which will taste delicious, but none that will define the type of tree itself. The humour flatters, in its reliance upon a wide knowledge-base to appreciate its nuances; the description dazzles, in its magnificence of reworked conventional imagery. No other tale in the collection works so hard to appeal to all listeners, and that could in itself be a signal of danger. It is not difficult to be seduced, like Chauntecleer, by the glamour of the language and the signs of conventional familiarity into feeling prematurely secure with our response. There is a sense of repletion created by the many courses the narrative serves up: almost too much of a good thing. 'Rhetorical pyrotechnics'; 'a humane masterpiece'; 'brilliant, varied, a virtuoso performance':[173] these are all responses that demonstrate the universal enthusiasm the tale provokes. Yet, as critics also have all agreed, 'one is apt to come away from this feast feeling that one has been abundantly fed, but one is not sure on what kind of food'.[174]

Analysis of the tale has been attempted from every sort of interpretive angle and, like academic chickens pursuing grains of textual meaning around a literary farmyard, critics have expended an enormous amount of very eminent time and energy trying to define it. Kingship provides scope for some of that research, in both general and contemporarily relevant terms. The tale is set in the familiar

---

[172] Cooper (1989) 405.
[173] Cooper (1989) 350; Speirs 185; Muscatine (1957) 237.
[174] E. Talbot Donaldson, *Speaking of Chauce* (London, 1970) 146.

surroundings of a humble farmyard, complete with pigs, cows and a sheep called Malle. The poor widow's 'ful symple lyf' (*NPT* 2826) is carefully recorded: what she ate, what her house was like, what she did. The muted colours and the lack of luxury show the very antithesis of royalty, and so does the vocabulary, which is plain in comparison with the courtly French adoptions of the description of Chauntecleer. In contrast, he is a king in his realm, enjoying the sun and his wives and crowing with his voice 'murier than the murie orgon' (*NPT* 2851). His exquisite colouring, and the courtly elaborations of its effects, may suggest that what we see is not a cockerel but an *icon* of a cockerel,[175] but eagerness to associate the formal and heraldic qualities with Richard II's depiction in the Wilton Diptych are to stretch the significance of this too far.[176] Chauntecleer's life is one of leisured privilege; the widow's, one of quiet struggle for survival. The farmyard therefore presents us with a microcosm, with extremes of both high and low estate being described.

This picture of a miniature society has attracted critical attention to the hierarchies it creates: a recent study has argued that the whole of the narrative is 'about the authority of utterance' and that it has 'a single shape. It is patriarchal and monarchical: its position is occupied by Chauntecleer.'[177] This approach connects the authority of the tale's exemplum with the images of royalty portrayed; the language shows both that 'Chauntecleer is threatened throughout by the discourse of his subordinates'[178] and that the concept of flattery it reveals stakes out 'a zone of completely degraded, completely false discourse against which more authoritative political discourse could be defined'.[179] However, the subordinates, in the shape of Pertelotte and the fox, the only other two speaking characters in the piece, are not greatly distant in status from Chauntecleer's princely one in the hierarchy of the farmyard. Pertelotte's attempt to advise with learning and wisdom shows a queen-consort unique in Chaucer's works; she is no Griselda or Alceste, and chides her husband for his lack of courage and manliness: 'Have ye no mannes herte, and han a berd?' (*NPT* 2920). Nevertheless, she is still 'Madam Pertelote' (*NPT* 3200) and 'trewely' holds the love of Chauntecleer (*NPT* 2874), above the other six hen-wives he possesses. The fox suavely ingratiates himself with Chauntecleer by praising his father's singing ability and by claiming a polite social acquaintanceship with both parents – 'My lord youre fader – God his soule blesse! – / And eek youre moder, of hire gentilesse, / Han in myn hous ybeen to my greet ese' (*NPT* 3295–7). This shows a mastery of courtly speech so complete that it implies a status of at least equal to Chauntecleer's. The reader of course responds to the sustained chilling irony of the fox's words, an irony that goes straight over Chauntecleer's head. In this respect at least it is Chauntecleer who is, in both senses of the word, outclassed.

---

[175] Staley (2005) 142.
[176] Staley (2005) 142.
[177] Scanlon 234.
[178] Scanlon 234.
[179] Scanlon 241.

In its final stages, the language returns to the theme of lordship. The frightened Chauntecleer, clutched in the fox's jaws, remarks: 'Sire, if that I were as ye, / Yet sholde I seyn, as wys God helpe me, / "Turneth agayn, ye proude cherles alle!"' (*NPT* 3407–9). For the vain fox, this enticement to show his power over those beneath him far outweighs, for one diastrous moment, the desire for a chicken dinner; he opens his mouth to speak, and the cock escapes. Apparently unruffled, the fox asks Chauntecleer to come down from the tree and listen to his innocent explanation: 'I dide it in no wikke entente' (*NPT* 3423). Chauntecleer is not as witless as that, and the fox reflects, with his final words of the story: 'God yeve hym meschaunce, / That is so undiscreet of governaunce / That jangleth whan he sholde holde his pees' (*NPT* 3433–5). Here is Chaucer at his most sublimely provocative; the fox's French counterpart in the *Roman de Renart* displays violent emotions at finding himself outsmarted before running off into the woods, but Chaucer's fox appears to be meekly accepting the lesson he has been taught: lords or men who have so little self-control that they cannot discipline their speech deserve to be punished. It is hard to believe that the fox is transformed so easily. He is far too eloquent, far too acquiescent, and so his quickly reasserted 'governaunce' evokes a sense of latent danger. Words are slippery things, which can mean the opposite of what they seem to be saying: just like people, especially in the houses of the great.

It can be no coincidence that these lines appear so soon after the reference to Jack Straw (*NPT* 3394). The association of the Peasants' Revolt with the noisy hens creates a connection between the transference of the image of king to the fox and the other animals as the 'cherles'; Richard, like the fox, tricked Wat Tyler and his followers with placating words, and then took merciless vengeance on them. The parallel seems clear, and yet is safely subsumed by the comic reversal in this tale where the cock manages to outsmart his natural intellectual superior.

However, on closer scrutiny there are difficulties with this analysis. It could be argued that the animals may be called 'proude cherles' (*NPT* 3409) by Chauntecleer, but this is a deliberate over-exaggeration of their lowly state in order to flatter the fox's vain sense of superiority, and not a description meant to represent what they are actually like. Though the noise they create is compared to that of 'Jakke Straw and his meynee' (*NPT* 3394), this is surely meant no more seriously than the preceding image of their cries being as anguished as 'feendes doon in helle' (*NPT* 3389), or the comparison of the upset hens being like the ladies of Ilium, or Pertelotte like Hasdrubale's wife. Indeed, the reference 'seems naked of political or social significance, as if Chaucer were almost unaware of such'.[180] Drawing back from the individual images and seeing them together, there is a consistency in the mixture of genres that fits with the style in the rest of the tale: the topical reference is as comic a comparison as the others,

---

[180] Muscatine (1972) 28. However, this is not to deny the slipperiness of this seeming political innocence: Steven Justice, for example, has argued for links with the Jacquerie, France's own peasants' revolt. See his *Writing and Rebellion: England in 1381* (Berkeley, 1994) 222–3.

for rebels the pursuers of the fox are clearly not. It is not as an 'anarchic mob'[181] that the humans and animals run after the fox, but some as concerned defenders of Chauntecleer's safety and some because they are frightened by the hullabaloo. Though this chase 'draws every member of his community, including the bees who swarm from their hive, away from their accustomed places',[182] the dislocation is provoked by a single cause, and that cause is the noise created by Chauntecleer's capture.[183] In this it is a portrayal of a naturally ordered world, with a hierarchy that supports and defends its ruling monarch from intrusive aliens. Indeed, it could be said to show, if any political analogy were to be made at all, a secure antithesis to the discontented mob of 1381.

The reference to Jack Straw therefore cannot justify the view that 'Chauntecleer's fascination with his own magnificent image almost brings his realm into utter ruin, into the type of chaos reminiscent if the Rising of 1381.'[184] Terms like 'ruin', 'chaos' and 'anarchy' over-exaggerate the implications of this passage. There is no evidence that any of these states threaten to become real as a result of Chauntecleer's capture, or that this is one of the issues the narrator, whether he is the Nun's Priest or Chaucer, invites speculation about. The event creates a great deal of noise, but the suggestion that its imagery evokes ideas of social revolution is as unlikely as the one that suggests it evokes a vision of hell, and the context of the passage means that to infer one must bring with it inference of the other. Chauntecleer is a king-like figure in the farmyard, but he is also a chicken in a beast fable; his authority as a king is comic because it is unrealistic, exaggerated and inconsistent. Any comparisons we are tempted to make to real kings, or a philosophy of kingship, must therefore be tempered with this understanding, for no secure proposition can be made without it foundering on the same rocks of vanity that Chauntecleer himself encounters.

The reference to St Kenelm at line 3110 has also been used to try to yoke the tale to Richard II and make it into a political allegory. Kenelm was a boy king murdered by his trusted tutor; Richard was crowned on the eve of St Kenelm's day. 'By God! I hadde levere than my sherte / That ye hadde rad his legende, as have I' (*NPT* 3120–1) Chaunticleer exclaims to the unsupportive Pertelotte. The inclusion makes emphatic that there is some relevance in this saint's life and this might lie in the connections with Richard. Chaucer, it is argued, would have known his audience would realise the link: he 'calls on them to observe parallels between Kenelm's legend and the tale of Chauntecleer, on the one hand, and between the adventures of Chauntecleer and Richard, on the other'.[185] However, this puts an undue stress on the quickness of the listeners' powers of recall, and there does not seem enough evidence to suggest this would have been a natural

---

[181] Scanlon 242.
[182] Scanlon 241.
[183] It is the cacophony that prompts the analogy with the mob, and the other parallels fall into place around that; the allusion is neatly executed, but it is the pleasure of seeing the device unfold rather than the pinpointing of taut historical significances that makes the evocation most successful here. I am grateful to Ad Putter for illuminating this point for me.
[184] Staley (2005) 143.
[185] Astell (1999) 110.

link for them to have made. There are differences, which Astell claims create the ironic comedy of the comparison: while both Kenelm and Chauntecleer are captured while singing, Kenelm is singing to God, and Chauntecleer is singing out of pride. It is true that

> crowned in 1377 on the eve of Saint Kenelm's feast, King Richard strikingly resembled Kenelm in his youth, his kingship, his vulnerability, and his need for wise counsel[186]

but unless Chaucer had the gift of prophecy, he cannot have been suggesting that Richard would meet the same end as Kenelm. After all, Chauntecleer escapes from death at the end of the tale.

There is another, more reasonable explanation, however: Kenelm's age, seven, was the same as that of the martyr the Prioress describes in her story, so this provides another connection to set with Astell's theory.[187] The two associations are certainly not incompatible, and it would be no surprise to find Chaucer exploiting layered meanings in this way, but the strength of the political associations seems on balance to be unjustifiable. They are just part of that multi-referential bank of ideas we have to draw upon, all pulling in different ways. The Jews of the *Prioress's Tale* listen to 'oure firste foo, the serpent Sathanas' (*PrT* 558) and are as a consequence incited to murder the little boy; both of these examples suggest the inclusion of Kenelm, whatever other analogies it might create, was principally a warning against listening to flatterers, a major theme of the tale. If those tragic deaths linger in the memory, as it especially does if the *Monk's Tale* is read immediately before, then any warning of the vulnerability of kings to an assassin's hand can be no more than a discreetly muffled one.

Chauntecleer may be the monarch of his yard, as vain and proud as the fox, but is a less darkly devious creature, and the comedy of his creation makes sympathy with his weakness hard to resist. His realm has boundaries, and he is secure as long as he does not stop maintaining them; by lazily allowing his attention to wander his governance lapses, and the predator tyrant fox can strike. The fox's sphere is far wider, and as such is more unsettling. He roams at will, and is ruled by will, a quality that was consistently criticised in advice to princes: this is emphasised when Chauntecleer tells the fox that 'he that wynketh, whan he sholde see, / Al wilfully, God lat him nevere thee!' (*NPT* 3431–32).

Chauntecleer does learn his lesson, and so does the fox, but the tale surely implies that both will transgress again, because it is in their natures to do so. Chauntecleer will go back to his hens, and the fox will retreat to attack again another day. This is a maintenance of order that either realistically or rather darkly illustrates the fundamental and perpetual tendency of man to sin again. It can in this way be seen to support the Parson's detailed explanation of the need for penance in his tale. Seen in terms of a battle for authority, the fox is forced by Chauntecleer's flattery to

---

[186] Astell (1999) 112.
[187] Cooper (1989) 344.

face the impossibility of any form of authority other than the one he would destroy, and ultimately returns Chauntecleer's world to the position of stability from which the narrative began.[188]

Chaucer manages to celebrate this return to order and offer a critical perspective at the same time. Humans, like farm animals, are dealt a destiny that they must handle as best they can; the Nun's Priest widens the Monk's moral exempla so that all estates are seen as vulnerable to temptation and Fortune's hand, but still includes, in the form of a beast-fable parody, an interrogation of those ideas of the fates of kings contained in the previous tale.

It is difficult to defend reading this poem as an allegorical offering to Richard, as is also the case with other poems of Chaucer's that have been alleged to have political implications. It has been suggested that they are politically oblique because the 1352 Statutes of Treason made it treason to imagine the death of the king, his queen or the heir to the throne.[189] Even if we know, however (as we do not), that Chaucer wanted to tell stories about the deaths of kings but was too frightened to do so, there is a logical absurdity in claiming that he was 'really' writing about a subject he did not dare to mention, even before we consider how unlikely it is that his customary tact and respect for the status of the king and the nobility would really be a cover for sedition. Chaucer is concerned with society at all its levels, and his commentary is that of a sympathetic close observer of people and the human experiences, common to all, that they face.

In this we see the embodiment of Chaucer's social view, where maintaining the structure of high and low status is vital to good governance, but where rulership is a fluid position that is not just the preserve of the king. Husbands and wives, parents and children – even animals, in this tale – live and work within the confines of a small kingdom, which has to support rules and courtesies like any larger realm. The ideas of authority that Chaucer continuously examines through *The Canterbury Tales* therefore does not concentrate on the role of the king alone, but focuses on how these many conflicting structures work within the larger moral and Christian context that contains them all. Everyone, whoever or whatever they are, must try and work against ingrown tendencies to indulge selfish vanities: this is a tale about individual, personal kingdoms, and how the governance of self can affect those around you.

At the end of the tale, the Nun's Priest finishes with a blessing:

> 'Now, goode God, if that it be thy wille,
> As seith my lord, so make us alle goode men,
> And brynge us to his heighe blisse! Amen.' (*NPT* 3444–6)

The referent 'my lord' has caused a large amount of critical attention, because it raises the question of who the lord could be. Early scribes glossed it as referring to the archbishop of Canterbury, and later critics suggested variously the bishop

---

[188] Scanlon 243.
[189] See Ferster 33–8.

of London, St Paul, the devil, the Pater Noster and God. The most convincing argument, however, proposes that 'my lord' is Christ,

> for although the 'heighe blisse' cannot belong to God as the Father or as the Trinity, it can and indeed must belong to Christ. The grammar implies theological distinctions very like those made in Chaucer's Retractions; in this case, the bliss of heaven can be attributed to Christ with greater theological propriety than it can to any or all of the other persons of the Trinity, since Christ earned that bliss for the redeemed by his death on the cross.[190]

If the lord is Christ, then this would put a Christian focus, as would befit a narrator who is a priest, securely at the centre of the tale. The conclusion, read with this interpretation in mind, seems to bear this out, for there is a repeated use of appeals to God in the exchange of words between the cock and the fox – 'God helpe me' (*NPT* 3408), 'God help me so' (*NPT* 3425), 'God lat him nevere thee' (*NPT* 3430) and 'God yeve hym meschaunce' (*NPT* 3433) – and the repeated phrase 'goode men' (*NPT* 3402 and 3445), first as an exhortation to the listeners, and then in the prayer to God, makes another potential gap of meaning open before us. It is only 'goode God' (*NPT* 3444) who can truly make us 'goode men'. Chauntecleer's fate was because 'what that God forwoot moot nedes bee' (*NPT* 3234). The 'heighe blisse', like the 'heighe' tree Chauntecleer escapes to, is where our eventual salvation will be found, figuratively above us, in heaven. The Nun's Priest concludes with St Paul's teaching that everything that has been written is for our education, if we can learn to take the fruit and leave the chaff. His tale points to the difficulties of gaining that skill of discernment. If we cannot even be sure of understanding completely all the resonances of this puzzle of a tale, how much less can we comprehend the mystery of God? Ultimately,

> Like the figure who appears at Chaucer's shoulder to interrogate him in the *House of Fame*, or the 'man of great auctorite' who never gets around to speaking at the end of that poem, 'my lord' remains a shadowy figure who casts things into doubt; but we are never sure what things, or how much doubt.[191]

If 'my lord' is to be read as Christ, that enriches this view of this phrase, for Christ should be that presence felt behind everything, unfathomable and yet part of a hierarchy that holds the world together. There is a movement away from any debate about Chauntecleer's status, or that of the listeners, actual or imagined, in the Nun's Priest's audience at this final point; the brilliance of the cockerel, who becomes just a farmyard bird in the wider context of God's universe, is representative of the individual man, whose own tiny realm, whatever that may consist of in life, needs to be constantly defended and alert to attacks of temptation. This universal appeal, contained with clarity in the entreaty to 'goode

---

[190] Field (2002) 303.
[191] Cooper (1989) 350.

men', rather than lords (as the Nun's Priest used in his earlier, specific warning against false flatterers) shows this tale to be a 'meta-fable',[192] transcending any questions of earthly estate by combining so many different ideas that

> the freedom which the reader is apparently offered at the end to decide what part of the story is wheat and what chaff has the effect of creating greater uncertainty in our minds about the relationship between the pleasure of fiction, the nature of reality and the good of morality.[193]

The opportunities for political comment that the fable offers seem to be subsumed by these larger debates, all contained within a narrative that offers, as so many of the other *Tales* do, a reflective exercise on the individual's place in a world ordered by God, and maintained by those individuals' efforts to respect and improve the stability of the social estate they belong to. Above all, flattery and vanity must be avoided. These are aspects of pride, which the Parson speaks so vehemently against in his tale. Most of all, as literary critics, it would be well to appreciate the warning that

> the manner in which the *Nun's Priest's Tale* recoils upon all systematic attempts at interpretation is not a sign that more efforts should be made to find one that works. Its machinery is designed to defy such attempts: that is the point of the tale.[194]

---

[192] Tony Davenport, *Medieval Narrative* (Oxford, 2004) 83.
[193] Davenport 267.
[194] Pearsall (1985) 238.

Conclusion

> 'All places that the eye of heaven visits
> Are to a wise man ports and happy havens
> Teach thy necessity to reason thus;
> There is no virtue like necessity.'
>
> Shakespeare, *Richard II* I iii 275–8

Richard II's reign was marked by a particular concern to establish the king as a divinely confirmed ruler. This concern manifested itself in the construction of an image of powerful and authoritative majesty that was to prove ironically vulnerable and insubstantial under pressure. However, the poets who wrote during Richard's reign did not concentrate on portraying kings as possessors of a quasi-divine status, or directly reflect on or engage with Richard's governance; they did, as we have seen, unite instead in their focus on the individual subject's place in a kingdom beset with corrupt practices and unstable leadership. This kingdom is seldom recognisable as Richard's, and yet each poet clearly writes in response to what is happening within their immediate experience. Charles Muscatine, writing at roughly the same time that John Burrow was composing *Ricardian Poetry*, defined the period as one of 'culture in crisis',[1] and his work shows convincingly how Chaucer, the *Gawain*-poet and Langland illustrate that tension in their poems. Burrow also finds common elements between the poets, concluding that

> None of these poets ... shows much interest in public affairs; great matters of state or city, the matters of epic, lie outside their compass. But a *crowd*, a company of 'sondry folk' massed together and displaying – often to distinctly comic effect – rich varieties of behaviour, opinion or attitude, interests them very much, not as a political force but as a conglomerate of private persons.[2]

The crisis forced efforts to engage old conventions with new and original treatments; the structure of society, straining to encompass the new gentry and business classes, produced a great variety of people who now lived and worked together, and who had, as Burrow notes, distinct perceptions of their own. The poets were no longer writing for a consistently aristocratic audience, although there is plenty of evidence to suggest a courtly setting for much of their works' presentation. However, the way that these courtly ideals were reworked during

---

[1] Muscatine (1972) 145. Though Muscatine's book was published in 1972, the material comes from lectures he gave in 1969, before Burrow's work would have been available.
[2] Burrow (1971) 122.

this period shows the efforts that were being made to react poetically to the changes that were happening in society at large.

Gower is the poet most openly concerned with the theme of kingship, and his *Confessio* relentlessly examines the different types of king and the effect of their rule on their subjects. Yet even he contains this exploration within a very specific framework of an individual's journey towards greater self-governance, and one, moreover, who is not a king. Amans's behaviour is paralleled with the kings who Gower discusses, but he is never described as anything other than a rather lowly cleric; though Gower includes a Mirror for Princes in Book VII of his work, it is to Amans that Genius directs it, and Amans turns out to be none other than Gower himself. What Gower indicates is that such advice is universally applicable, and that kingship is not only the responsibility of the king himself. All subjects must try to be like an ideal king, like Apollonius, whom Gower holds up as the epitome of wise and effective governance. The moral governance is the vital aspect of Gower's treatment of kingship, and it is this that transcends any other relevance to real kings that he makes in his poem.

Langland and the *Gawain*-poet mention kings, but obliquely. *Piers Plowman* denounces corruption at all levels, including kingship, but is more consistently focused on the clergy and the misapprehension of their spiritual responsibilities. Langland puts Christ at the centre of his work; for him Christ is the ultimate king, and the majesty he describes makes clear that he feels no other ruler deserves the awe and wonder that his heavenly king does. The *Gawain*-poet, too, has this reverence as its prevailing tone. The earthly life is a preparation for what lies beyond that; his poems show a transcendence of earthly concerns that try to reconcile the responsibilities owed to both realms.

Chaucer's work contains elements from every conceivable reference point. His attention to detail, to characterisation and narrative structure, like that of his contemporaries, shows him to be responding vigorously to the demands of his time. The sheer volume and variety of his poetry makes a comprehensive assessment of one theme an audacious task; here I have simply tried to look at the major works and draw out as much of relevance as was possible. It is quite obvious that the wealth of material that is contained in Chaucer would furnish a separate study and not exhaust what can be found with close reading; his work is ambiguous, shifting and complex. However, read with the informing context of the other three Ricardians, similarities are definite, and reveal, despite the differences of style and structure, a closeness of response to kingship.

The conclusion is that the poets reacted to their world by turning away from the monarch and restating the importance of the individual, both as an English citizen and as subject to the most important ruler of all: God. Spiritual integrity lies at the heart of all four of our poets; self-governance is the main and often urgently stressed requirement that the poetry offers as a way to move forward successfully:

> Whatever achievement there may be seems a matter, not of changing the world by founding kingdoms or conquering enemies. . . but of coming to terms with everyday realities and better understanding one's own nature and that of the

world around one. The achievement, such as it is, is private and quotidian, rather than public and for all time.[3]

It seems fitting to finish with these words of Burrow, for this 'private and quotidian' view, characteristic of all four major Ricardian poets, is ultimately one that most successfully summarises their approach to kingship. Each poet offers a perspective very different to the next, and yet in this central belief in the harmonising influence of God shows how this provides all the stability that the world needs. Earthly kings may come and go, may be good, bad or indifferent, but it is the kingship of the inner self that truly matters. In this sense, though it may not be public, this poetry is, at least, absolutely and irrefutably 'for all time'.

[3] Burrow (1971) 101.

Appendix

Prologues to *The Legend of Good Women*

F
373–90

This shoolde a ryghtwis lord have in his thoght,
And nat be lyk tirauntz of Lumbardye,
That han no reward but at tyrannye.
For he that kynge or lord ys naturel,
Hym oghte nat be tiraunt ne crewel
As is a fermour, to doon the harm he kan.
He moste thinke yt is his lige man,

And is his tresour and his gold in cofre.
This is the sentence of the Philosophre,
A kyng to kepe his liges in justice;
Withouten doute, that is his office.

Al wol he kepe his lordes in hire degree,
As it ys ryght and skilful that they bee
Enhaunced and honoured, and most dere –
For they ben half-goddes in this world here –
Yit mot he doon bothe ryght, to poore and ryche,
Al be that hire estaat be nat yliche,
And han of poore folk compassyoun.

G
353–76

This shulde a ryghtwys lord han in his thought,
And not ben lyk tyraunts of Lumbardye,
That usen wilfulhed and tyrannye.
For he that kyng or lord is naturel,
Hym oughte nat be tyraunt and crewel
As is a fermour, to don the harm he can.
He moste thynke it is his lige man,
And that hym oweth, of verray duetee,
Shewen his peple pleyn benygnete,
And wel to heren here excusacyouns,
And here compleyntes and petyciouns,
In duewe tyme, whan they shal it profre.
This is the sentence of the Philosophre,
A kyng to kepe his lyges in justice,
Withouten doute, that is his office.
And therto is a kyng ful depe ysworn
Ful many an hundred wynter herebeforn;
And for to kepe his lordes hir degre,
As it is ryght and skyful that they be
Enhaunsed and honoured, and most dere –
For they ben half-goddes in this world here –
This shal he don bothe to pore and ryche,
Al be that her estat be nat alyche,
And han of pore folk compassioun.

Select Bibliography

Primary sources

Alan of Lille. *The Plaint of Nature*. Trans. James J. Sheridan. Toronto, 1980
Amis and Amiloun. In *Of Love and Chivalry: An Anthology of Middle English Romance*. Ed. Jennifer Fellows. London, 1993. 73–146
Beowulf. Ed. Fr Klaeber. Lexington, KY, 1950
Boccaccio, Giovanni, and others. *The Story of Troilus*. Trans. R. K. Gordon. Toronto, 1978
Chaucer, Geoffrey. *The Riverside Chaucer*. Ed. Larry D. Benson. Boston, MA, 1987
Chaucer's Dream Poetry: Sources and Analogues. Ed. and trans. Barry Windeatt. Cambridge, 1982
De Voragine, Jacobus. *The Golden Legend*. Trans. William Granger Ryan. 2 vols. Princeton, 1993
Froissart, Jean. *Oeuvres*. Ed. Kervyn de Lettenhove. 28 vols. Brussels, 1868–77
——. *La Joli Buisson de Jonece*. Ed. A. Fourrier. Geneva, 1975
——. *Froissart's Chronicles*. Trans. John Jolliffe. London, 2001
The Golden Legend. See De Voragine, Jacobus
Gower, John. *Confessio Amantis*. In *The English Works of John Gower*. Ed. G. C. Macaulay. 2 vols. EETS, Extra Series 81–2. London, 1900–1
——. *The Major Latin Works*. Trans. Eric W. Stockton. Seattle, 1962
——. *Confessio Amantis*. Ed. Russell A. Peck. Toronto, 1980
——. *Confessio Amantis*. Ed. Russell A. Peck. 3 vols. Kalamazoo, 2000–4
Hoccleve, Thomas. *The Regiment of Princes*. Ed. Charles R. Blyth. Kalamazoo, 1999 <http://www.lib.rochester.edu/camelot/teams/hoccfrm.htm>
Langland, William. *The Vision of Piers Plowman*. Ed. A. V. C. Schmidt. 2nd edn. London, 1978
La queste del Saint Graal: roman du XIIIe siècle. Ed. Albert Pauphilet. Paris, 1999
Legenda Aurea. See De Voragine, Jacobus
Malory, Sir Thomas. *The Works of Sir Thomas Malory*. Ed. Eugène Vinaver. 3rd edn, rev. P. J. C. Field. 3 vols. Oxford, 1990
Morte Arthure: A Critical Edition. Ed. Mary Hamel. New York, 1984
Ovid. *Metamorphoses*. Trans. A. D. Melville. Oxford, 1987
Pearl. Ed. E. V. Gordon. Oxford, 1953
Sir Gawain and the Green Knight. Eds J. R. R. Tolkien and E. V. Gordon. 2nd edn, rev. Norman Davis. Oxford, 1967
Sir Gawain and the Green Knight, Pearl, Cleanness, Patience. Ed. J. J. Anderson. London, 1996
Sources and Analogues of the Canterbury Tales. Eds Robert Correale and Mary Hamel. 2 vols. Cambridge, 2002–5
Walsingham, Thomas. *Historia Anglicana, Vol. I: 1272–1381*. Ed. Henry Thomas Riley. London, 1863

Secondary sources

Alford, John A., ed. *A Companion to Piers Plowman*. Berkeley, 1988
Antonelli, Roberto. 'The Birth of Criseyde'. *The European Tragedy of Troilus*. Ed. Piero Boitani. Oxford, 1989. 21–49
Archibald, Elizabeth. 'Incest in Medieval Literature and Society'. *Forum for Modern Language Studies* 25 (1989) 1–15
——. *Apollonius of Tyre: Medieval and Renaissance Themes and Variations*. Cambridge, 1991
——. *Incest and the Medieval Imagination*. Oxford, 2001
Armitage-Smith, Sydney. *John of Gaunt: King of Castile and Leon, Duke of Aquitaine and Lancaster, Earl of Derby, Lincoln and Leicester, Seneschal of England*. London, 1964
Astell, Ann W. 'Apostrophe, Prayer, and the Structure of the *Man of Law's Tale*'. *Studies in the Age of Chaucer* 13 (1991) 81–97
——. *Political Allegory in Late Medieval England*. Ithaca, 1999
Baldwin, Anna P. *The Theme of Government in* Piers Plowman. Cambridge, 1981
——. 'The Historical Context'. *A Companion to* Piers Plowman. Ed. John A. Alford. Berkeley, 1988. 67–87
Barber, Richard. *The Knight and Chivalry*. London, 1970
Barney, Stephen A., ed. *Chaucer's Troilus: Essays in Criticism*. London, 1980
Barr, Helen. *Signs and Sothe: Language in the Piers Plowman Tradition*. Cambridge, 1994
Barron, W. R. J. 'Luf-daungere'. *Medieval Miscellany Presented to Eugène Vinaver by Pupils, Colleagues and Friends*. Eds F. Whitehead, A. H. Diverres and F. E. Sutcliffe. Manchester, 1965. 1–18
——. *Trawthe and Treason: The Sin of Gawain Reconsidered*. Manchester, 1980
Benson, C. David. *The History of Troy in Middle English Literature*. Cambridge, 1980
——. 'Incest and Moral Poetry in Gower's *Confessio Amantis*'. *Chaucer Review* 19 (1984) 100–9
——. *Public Piers Plowman: Modern Scholarship and Late Medieval English Culture*. University Park, PA, 2004
Benson, L. D. *Art and Tradition in Sir Gawain and the Green Knight*. New Brunswick, 1965
——, and S. Wenzel, eds. *The Wisdom of Poetry*. Kalamazoo, 1982
Blanch, Robert J., ed. *Sir Gawain and Pearl: Critical Essays*. Bloomington, 1966
Bloomfield, Morton W. *The Seven Deadly Sins*. East Lansing, MI, 1952
——. *Piers Plowman as a Fourteenth Century Apocalypse*. New Brunswick, 1961
Boffey, Julia, and A. S. G. Edwards. 'The *Legend of Good Women*'. *The Cambridge Companion to Chaucer*. Eds Piero Boitoni and Jill Mann. Cambridge, 2003. 112–27
Boitani, Piero, ed. *The European Tragedy of Troilus*. Oxford, 1989
——, and Jill Mann, eds. *The Cambridge Companion to Chaucer*. Cambridge, 2003
Bolens, Guillemette, and Paul Beekman Taylor. 'The Game of Chess in Chaucer's *Book of the Duchess*'. *Chaucer Review* 32 (1998) 325–34
Bolton, W. F., ed. *The Middle Ages*. London, 1980
Bowers, John M. '*Pearl* in its Royal Setting: Ricardian Poetry Revisited'. *Studies in the Age of Chaucer* 17 (1995) 111–55

——. *The Politics of Pearl: Court Poetry in the Age of Richard II*. Cambridge, 2001
Brewer, Derek. 'Courtesy and the *Gawain*-poet'. *Patterns of Love and Courtesy: Essays in Memory of C. S. Lewis*. Ed. J. Lawlor. Evanston, 1966. 54–86
——, Derek, and Jonathan Gibson, eds. *A Companion to the Gawain-Poet*. Cambridge, 1997
Brown, Peter, ed. *A Companion to Chaucer*. Oxford, 2002
Bryan, W. F., and Germaine Dempster, eds. *Sources and Analogues of Chaucer's Canterbury Tales*. Chicago, 1941
Burgess, Glyn S., and Robert A. Taylor, eds. *The Spirit of the Court*. Cambridge, 1985
Burnley, David. 'Langland's "Clergial" Lunatic'. *Langland, the Mystics and the Medieval English Religious Tradition: Essays in Honour of S. S. Hussey*. Ed. Helen Phillips. Cambridge, 1990. 31–8
——. *Courtliness and Literature in Medieval England*. London, 1998
Burrow, J. A. *A Reading of Sir Gawain and the Green Knight*. London, 1965
——. *Ricardian Poetry: Chaucer, Gower, Langland and the Gawain-Poet*. London, 1971
——. 'The *Canterbury Tales* I: Romance'. *Cambridge Companion to Chaucer*. Eds Piero Boitoni and Jill Mann. Cambridge, 2003. 143–60
——. 'Lady Meed and the Power of Money'. *Medium Aevum* 74 (2005) 113–18
——. 'Politeness and Privacy: Chaucer's *Book of the Duchess*'. *Studies in Late Medieval and Early Renaissance: Texts in Honour of John Scattergood*. Eds Anne Marie D'Arcy and Alan J. Fletcher. Dublin, 2005. 65–76
Carruthers, Mary J., and Elizabeth D. Kirk, eds. *Acts of Interpretation: The Text in its Contexts 700–1600*. Norman, OK, 1982
Condren, Edward I. 'The Historical Context of the *Book of the Duchess*: A New Hypothesis'. *Chaucer Review* 5.3 (1971) 195–212
——. 'Of Deaths and Duchesses and Scholars Coughing in Ink'. *Chaucer Review* 10.1 (1975) 87–95
Connolly, Margaret. 'Chaucer and Chess'. *Chaucer Review* 29 (1994) 40–4
Cooper, Helen. *Oxford Guides to Chaucer: The Canterbury Tales*. Oxford, 1989
——. 'Chaucer's Self-Fashioning'. *Poetica* 55 (2001) 55–74
Crick, Julia. *The* Historia regum Britanniae *of Geoffrey of Monmouth: Dissemination and Reception in the Later Middle Ages*. Cambridge, 1991
Crow, Martin M., and Clair C. Olson, eds. *Chaucer Life Records*. Oxford, 1966
Davenport, Tony. *Medieval Narrative*. Oxford, 2004
Davenport, W. A. *The Art of the Gawain-Poet*. London, 1978
David, Alfred. 'The Man of Law vs. Chaucer: A Case in Poetics'. *PMLA* 82 (1967) 217–25
Dodd, William George. *Courtly Love in Chaucer and Gower*. Cambridge, MA, 1959
Donaldson, E. Talbot. *Speaking of Chaucer*. London, 1970
——. ed. *Chaucer's Poetry: An Anthology for the Modern Reader*. New York, 1975
——. 'The Ending of *Troilus*'. *Chaucer's Troilus: Essays in Criticism*. Ed. Stephen A. Barney. London, 1980. 115–31
Donavin, Georgiana. *Incest Narratives and the Structure of Gower's* Confessio Amantis. Victoria, B. C., 1993
Eberle, Patricia. 'The Politics of Courtly Style at the Court of Richard II'. *The Spirit of the Court*. Eds Glyn S. Burgess and Robert A. Taylor. Cambridge, 1985. 168–78
——. 'Miniatures as Evidence of Reading in a Manuscript of the *Confessio Amantis* (Pierpoint Morgan MS. M. 126)'. *John Gower: Recent Readings*. Ed. R. F. Yeager. Kalamazoo, 1989

Echard, Siân, ed. *A Companion to Gower*. Cambridge, 2004
Edwards, Robert R. *The Dream of Chaucer: Representation and Reflection in the Early Narratives*. Durham, NC, 1989
Ellis, Steve. 'The Death of the *Book of the Duchess*'. *Chaucer Review* 29.3 (1995) 249–57
——, ed. *Chaucer: An Oxford Guide*. Oxford, 2005
Epstein, Robert. 'London, Southwark, Westminster: Gower's Urban Contexts'. *A Companion to Gower*. Ed. Siân Echard. Cambridge, 2004. 43–61
Evans, W. O. '"Cortaysye" in Middle English'. *Medieval Studies* 29 (1967) 143–57
Federico, Sylvia. *New Troy: Fantasies of Empire in the Later Middle Ages*. Minneapolis, 2003
Ferguson, George. *Signs and Symbols in Christian Art*. New York, 1966
Ferris, Sumner. 'John Stow and the Tomb of Blanche the Duchess'. *Chaucer Review* 18.1 (1983) 92–3
Ferster, Judith. *Fictions of Advice: The Literature and Politics of Counsel in Late Medieval England*. Philadelphia, 1996
Field, P. J. C. 'A Rereading of *Sir Gawain and the Green Knight*'. *Studies in Philology* 68 (1971) 255–69
——. 'The Ending of Chaucer's *Nun's Priest's Tale*'. *Medium Aevum* 71 (2002) 302–5
Fisher, John. *John Gower: Moral Philosopher and Friend of Chaucer*. London, 1965
Fletcher, Alan J. '*Pearl* and the Limits of History'. *Studies in Late Medieval and Early Renaissance Texts In Honour of John Scattergood*. Eds Anne Marie D'Arcy and Alan J. Fletcher. Dublin, 2005. 148–71
Gallacher, Patrick. *Love, the Word, and Mercury: A Reading of John* Gower's Confessio Amantis. Albuquerque, 1975
Goodman, Anthony. *John of Gaunt: The Exercise of Princely Power in Fourteenth-Century Europe*. Harlow, 1992
——, and James L. Gillespie, eds. *Richard II: The Art of Kingship*. Oxford, 1999
Gransden, A. *Historical Writing in England*. Vol. 2 London, 1982
Green, Richard Firth. *Poets and Princepleasers: Literature and the English Court in the Late Middle Ages*. Toronto, 1980
——. 'The *Familia Regis* and the *Familia Cupidinis*'. *English Court Culture in the Later Middle Ages*. Eds V. J. Scattergood and J. W. Sherborne. London, 1983. 87–109
Hardman, Phillipa. 'The *Book of the Duchess* as Memorial Monument'. *Chaucer Review* 19.4 (1985) 205–15
Hasty, Will, ed. *A Companion to Gottfried von Strassburg's Tristan*. New York, 2003
Hebron, Malcolm. *The Medieval Siege: Theme and Image in Middle English Romance*. Oxford, 1997
Horobin, Simon. '"In London and in Opelond": the Dialect and Circulation of the C version of *Piers Plowman*'. *Medium Aevum* 74 (2005) 248–69
Hunt, R. W., W. A. Pantin, and R.W. Southern, eds. *Studies in Medieval History Presented to Frederick Maurice Powicke*. Oxford, 1948
Huppé, Bernard F., and D. W. Robertson. *Fruyt and Chaf: Studies in Chaucer's Allegories*. Princeton, 1963
Jenkins, Priscilla. 'Conscience: The Frustration of Allegory'. *Piers Plowman: Critical Approaches*. Ed. S. S. Hussey. London, 1969. 125–43
Johnson, Lynn Staley. *The Voice of the Gawain-Poet*. Madison, 1984
Johnson, Sidney M. '"This Drink Will Be the Death of You": Interpreting the Love Potion in Gottfried's *Tristan*'. *A Companion to Gottfried von Strassburg's Tristan*. Ed. Will Hasty. New York, 2003. 87–113

Jones, Terry. *Chaucer's Knight: the Portrait of a Medieval Mercenary*. London, 1994
Justice, Steven. *Writing and Rebellion: England in 1381*. Berkeley, 1994
Kaeuper, Richard W. *Chivalry and Violence in Medieval Europe*. Oxford, 1999
Kane, George. *Chaucer and Langland: Historical and Textual Approaches*. London, 1989
Kean, P. M. 'Love, Law and *Lewte* in *Piers Plowman*'. *The Review of English Studies* 15 (1964) 241–61
——. *The Pearl: An Interpretation*. London, 1967
Kittredge, George Lyman. *Chaucer and His Poetry*. 1915; reprint Cambridge, MA, 1967
——. 'Troilus'. *Chaucer's Troilus: Essays in Criticism*. Ed. Stephen A. Barney. London, 1980. 1–25
Lacy, Norris, ed. *The New Arthurian Encyclopedia*. New York, 1996
Lawlor, J., ed. *Patterns of Love and Courtesy: Essays in Memory of C. S. Lewis*. Evanston, 1966
Lawton, David, ed. *Middle English Alliterative Poetry and Its Literary Background: Seven Essays*. Cambridge, 1982
Lewis, C. S. 'What Chaucer Really Did to *Il Filostrato*'. *Essays and Studies* 17 (1932) 56–75
——. *The Allegory of Love*. Oxford, 1936
——. *The Discarded Image*. Cambridge, 1964
Macaulay, G. C. 'The *Confessio Amantis*'. *Gower's* Confessio Amantis: *A Critical Anthology*. Ed. Peter Nicholson. Cambridge, 1991. 6–15
Mann, Jill. *Chaucer and Medieval Estates Satire: The Literature of Social Classes and the General Prologue to* The Canterbury Tales. Cambridge, 1973
——. 'Chance and Destiny in *Troilus and Criseyde* and the *Knight's Tale*'. *The Cambridge Companion to Chaucer*. Eds Piero Boitani and Jill Mann. Cambridge, 2003. 93–112
Matsuda, Takami, Richard A. Linenthal, and John Scahill, eds. *The Medieval Book and a Modern Collector: Essays in Honour of Toshiyuki Takamiya*. Cambridge, 2004
Matthews, Gervase. 'Ideals of Knighthood in Late Fourteenth-Century England'. *Studies in Medieval History Presented to Frederick Maurice Powicke*. Eds R. W. Hunt, W. A. Pantin and R. W. Southern. Oxford, 1948. 354–62
Mehl, Dieter. *English Literature in the Age of Chaucer*. London, 2001
Middleton, Anne. 'The Idea of Public Poetry in the Reign of Richard II'. *Speculum* 53 (1978) 94–114
——. 'The Audience and Public of *Piers Plowman*'. *Middle English Alliterative Poetry and its Literary Background: Seven Essays*. Ed. David Lawton. Cambridge, 1982. 101–24
Miller, Robert P., ed. *Chaucer: Sources and Backgrounds*. New York, 1977
Minnis, A. J., ed. *Gower's* Confessio Amantis: *Responses and Reassessments*. Cambridge, 1983
——, Charlotte C. Morse and Thorlac Turville-Petre, eds. *Essays on Ricardian Literature in Honour of J. A. Burrow*. Oxford, 1997
Morse, Charlotte C. 'From *Ricardian Poetry* to Ricardian Studies'. *Essays on Ricardian Literature in Honour of J. A. Burrow*. Eds A. J. Minnis, Charlotte C. Morse and Thorlac Turville-Petre. Oxford, 1997. 316–45
Murphy, James J. 'John Gower's *Confessio Amantis* and the First Discussion of Rhetoric in the English Language'. *Philological Quarterly* 41 (1962) 401–11
Muscatine, Charles. *Chaucer and the French Tradition*. Berkeley, 1957

———. *Poetry and Crisis in the Age of Chaucer*. Notre Dame, IN, 1972
———. *Medieval Literature, Style and Culture*. Columbia, SC, 1999
Natali, Giulis. 'A Lyrical Version: Bocccaccio's *Filostrato*'. *The European Tragedy of Troilus*. Ed. Piero Boitani. Oxford, 1989. 49–75
Nederman, Cary J., and Kate Langdon Forhan, eds. *Medieval Political Theory: A Reader*. London, 1993
Nicholls, Jonathan. *The Matter of Courtesy: Medieval Courtesy Books and the Gawain-Poet*. Woodbridge, 1985
Nicholson, Peter, ed. *Gower's* Confessio Amantis: *A Critical Anthology*. Cambridge, 1991
Olsson, Kurt. *John Gower and the Structures of Conversion: A Reading of the* Confessio Amantis. Cambridge, 1992
Palmer, J. J. N. 'The Historical Context of the *Book of the Duchess*: A Revision'. *Chaucer Review* 8.4 (1974) 253–61
Patterson, Lee. *Negotiating the Past: The Historical Understanding of Medieval Literature*. Madison, 1987
———. *Chaucer and the Subject of History*. Madison, 1991
Pearsall, Derek. *The Canterbury Tales*. London, 1985
———. 'Gower's Narrative Art'. *Gower's* Confessio Amantis: *A Critical Anthology*. Ed. Peter Nicholson. Cambridge, 1991. 62–81
———. *The Life of Geoffrey Chaucer*. Oxford, 1992
———. *The Canterbury Tales*. London, 1993
———. 'The Organisation of the Latin Apparatus in Gower's *Confessio Amantis*: The Scribes and their Problems'. *The Medieval Book and a Modern Collector: Essays in Honour of Toshiyuki Takamiya*. Eds Takami Matsuda, Richard A. Linenthal and John Scahill. Cambridge, 2004. 99–112
Peck, Russell M. *Kingship and Common Profit in Gower's* Confessio Amantis. Carbondale and Edwardsville, 1978
———. 'The Politics and Psychology of Governance in Gower: Ideas of Kingship and Real Kings'. *A Companion to Gower*. Ed. Siân Echard. Cambridge, 2004. 215–39
Perkins, Nicholas. *Hoccleve's* Regiment of Princes: *Counsel and Complaint*. Cambridge, 2001
Phillips, Helen, ed. *Langland, the Mystics and the Medieval English Religious Tradition: Essays in Honour of S. S. Hussey*. Cambridge, 1990
———, and Nick Havely, eds. *Chaucer's Dream Poetry*. London, 1997
———. *An Introduction to* The Canterbury Tales: *Reading, Fiction, Context*. Basingstoke, 2000
———. 'Register, Politics and the *Legend of Good Women*'. *Chaucer Review* 37 (2002) 101–28
———. 'Love'. *A Companion to Chaucer*. Ed. Peter Brown. Oxford, 2002. 281–96
———. 'The French Background'. *Chaucer: An Oxford Guide*. Ed. Steve Ellis. Oxford, 2005. 292–313
Pickles, J. D., and J. L. Dawson, eds. *A Concordance to John Gower's* Confessio Amantis. Cambridge, 1987
Porter, Elizabeth. 'Gower's Ethical Microcosm and Political Macrocosm'. *Gower's* Confessio Amantis: *Responses and Reassessments*. Ed. A. J. Minnis. Cambridge, 1983. 135–63
Putter, Ad. *An Introduction to the Gawain-Poet*. London, 1996
Riddy, Felicity. 'Jewels in *Pearl*'. *A Companion to the Gawain-Poet*. Eds Derek Brewer and Jonathan Gibson. Cambridge, 1997. 143–57

Rigby, S. H. 'Society and Politics'. *An Oxford Guide: Chaucer*. Ed. Steve Ellis. Oxford, 2005. 26–50
Runacres, Charles. 'Art and Ethics in the *Exempla* of *Confessio Amantis*'. *Gower's Confessio Amantis: Responses and Reassessments*. Ed. A. J. Minnis. Cambridge, 1983. 106–35
Russell, J. Stephen. *The English Dream Vision: Anatomy of a Form*. Columbus, 1988
Salter, Elizabeth. *Fourteenth-Century English Poetry: Contexts and Readings*. Oxford, 1983
Samuels, M. L. 'Dialect and Grammar'. *A Companion to* Piers Plowman. Ed. John A. Alford. Berkeley, 1988. 201–21
Saul, Nigel. *Richard II*. New Haven and London, 1997
——. 'The Kingship of Richard II'. *Richard II: The Art of Kingship*. Eds Anthony Goodman and James L. Gillespie. Oxford, 1999. 37–59
Scanlon, Larry. *Narrative, Authority and Power: The Medieval Exemplum and the Chaucerian Tradition*. Cambridge, 1994
Scattergood, V. J., and J. W. Sherborne, eds. *English Court Culture in the Later Middle Ages*. London, 1983
Schama, Simon. *Landscape and Memory*. London, 1995
Schlauch, Margaret. 'Chaucer's Doctrine of Kings and Tyrants'. *Speculum* 20 (1945) 133–56
Schless, Howard. 'A Dating for the *Book of the Duchess*: line 1314'. *Chaucer Review* 19.4 (1985) 273–6
Scott-MacNab, David. 'A Re-Examination of Octovyen's Hunt in the *Book of the Duchess*'. *Medium Aevum* 56 (1987) 183–99
Simpson, James. *Piers Plowman: An Introduction to the B-Text*. London, 1990
——. *Sciences and the Self in Medieval Poetry: Alan of Lille's* Anticlaudianus *and John Gower's* Confessio Amantis. Cambridge, 1995
Sisam, K., ed. *Fourteenth-Century Verse and Prose*. Oxford, 1921
Smith, George D. *The Teaching of the Catholic Church*. London, 1952
Spearing, A. C. *The Gawain-Poet: A Critical Study*. Cambridge, 1970
——. *Medieval Dream Poetry*. Cambridge, 1976
——. 'The *Canterbury Tales* IV: Exemplum and Fable'. *The Cambridge Companion to Chaucer*. Eds Piero Boitani and Jill Mann. Cambridge, 2003. 195–214
Speirs, John. *Chaucer the Maker*. London, 1951
Staley, Lynn. 'Translating "Communitas"'. *Imagining a Medieval Nation*. Ed. Kathy Lavezzo. Minneapolis, 2004
——. *The Languages of Power in the Age of Richard II*. University Park, PA, 2005
Stevens, John. *Medieval Romance*. London, 1973
Stokes, Myra. *Justice and Mercy in* Piers Plowman: *A Reading of the B-Text Visio*. London, 1984
Strohm, Paul. 'A Note on Gower's Persona'. *Acts of Interpretation: The Text in its Contexts 700–1600*. Eds Mary J. Carruthers and Elizabeth D. Kirk. Norman, OK, 1982. 293–9
——. *Social Chaucer*. Cambridge, MA, 1989
——. *Hochon's Arrow*. Princeton, 1992
Swanson, Robert. 'Social Structures'. *A Companion to Chaucer*. Ed. Peter Brown. Oxford, 2002. 397–414
Tasioulas, J. A. 'Science'. *Chaucer: An Oxford Guide*. Ed. Steve Ellis. Oxford, 2005. 174–90

Wallace, David. *Chaucerian Polity: Absolutist Lineages and Associational Forms in England and Italy*. Stanford, 1997
——, ed. *The Cambridge History of Medieval English Literature*. Cambridge, 1999
Watt, Diane. *Amoral Gower: Language, Sex, and Politics*. Minneapolis, 2003
——. 'Gender and Sexuality in *Confessio Amantis*'. *A Companion to Gower*. Ed. Siân Echard. 197–215
Whitaker, M. '*Pearl* and Some Illustrated Apocalypse Manuscripts'. *Viator* 12 (1981) 183–201
Williams, D. J. 'Alliterative Poetry in the Fourteenth and Fifteenth Centuries'. *The Middle Ages*. Ed. W. F. Bolton. London, 1980. 119–69
Windeatt, Barry. *Oxford Guides to Chaucer: Troilus and Criseyde*. Oxford, 1992
Yeager, R. F., ed. *John Gower: Recent Readings*. Kalamazoo, 1989
——. *John Gower's Poetic: The Search for a New Arion*. Cambridge, 1990

Index

Abraham 57, 73
Achilles 118
advice *see* counsellors
Aeneas *see* Aeneid
Aeneid 110
Agag (King) 23, 47
Albertanus of Brescia 146
Alceste 102–4, 106, 108, 109, 134, 153
Alcyone *see* Seys
Alexander (King) 8, 9, 21, 27, 31, 139, 149, 150
Anglo-Norman *Chronicle* 132
Anne of Bohemia 98, 100, 101–3, 106, 108
Ambrose 58
angel 37, 38, 41
Antenor 116
Appollonius 161
Aristotle 8, 25, 27, 31
Arthur (King) 4, 76–82, 110, 119, 128
Astell, Ann 149–50, 156
Augustine 58

Baillie, Harry 123
Barber, Richard 41
Barron, W. R. J. 105
belling of the cat 38–9, 45, 47, 124
Belshazarr (King) 72, 74
Bembre, Nicholas 122
Benoit 110, 116, 118, 120
  Le Roman de Troie 110
Benson, Larry 80
Beowulf 70
Bertilak de Hautdesert *see* Green Knight
Bible 23, 51, 52, 68, 147, 149
  Ecclesiastes 37
  Genesis 100, 110
  Isaiah 39
  Matthew 38, 73
  Revelation 43, 66, 69, 71, 96
  Vulgate Bible 67
birds, images of 89, 99, 105, 127, 140
  eagles 97, 99, 100–1, 114
Bishop Brinton 38
Black Prince 45, 85

Blanche, Duchess of Lancaster 68, 85–6, 91, 93–7, 102
boar 30
boat (image of, relating to body) 52
Boccaccio 67, 112–13, 115–16, 120–1, 124
  Olympia 67
  Il Filostrato 110, 118
body (image of, relating to rule) 10
Boethius 97, 107, 146
  De Consolatione 97, 146
Boffey, Julia 102
books 6, 55, 88, 103
Brewer, Derek 73
Bromyard, John 152
  Summa praedicantium 152
Burrow, John 1, 2–3, 4, 86, 160, 162
  Ricardian Poetry 160

Castile, Constance of 85
Castile, Peter of 45
Caxton 5
Chastity 10, 12, 27–34
Chaucer, Geoffrey 4, 6, 32, 36, 60, 71, 83–159, 160–2
  Ballad to Fortune 84
  Book of the Duchess 85–97, 102, 115, 117, 122
  Canterbury Tales 5, 12, 84, 122–59
    Clerk's Tale 129, 134–6
    Franklin's Tale 129–32, 135
    General Prologue 122–3, 130
    Knight's Tale 53, 71, 123–7, 134, 151
    Man of Law's Tale 132–4
    Manciple's Tale 136, 138–40
    Merchant's Tale 136–8, 140
    Monk's Tale 136, 145, 146, 149–50, 151, 156, 157
    Nuns' Priest's Tale 101, 136, 145, 146, 149, 150, 151–9
    Parson's Tale 12, 128, 136, 138, 140–5, 156
    Physician's Tale 132, 136
    Prioress's Tale 156

Sir Thopas 149
Squire's Tale 127, 128, 138
Tabard Inn 36
Tale of Melibee 130, 136, 145, 146–9
Wife of Bath's Tale 127, 128–9, 130, 131
  compared to Gawain-poet 61, 62, 68, 89
  compared to Gower 12–13, 33, 84, 86, 95, 128, 131, 139
  compared to Langland 56, 60
  Complaint of Chaucer to his Purse 84
  House of Fame 97–8, 101
  Lak of Stedfastnesse 83
  Legend of Good Women 99, 101–10, 124, 134, 138
  Parliament of Fowls 98–101, 105, 106
  Troilus and Criseyde 84, 110–22
chess 88, 94, 96
Christ 40, 41, 42, 47, 49, 50, 52, 57, 58, 60, 65, 128, 144, 161
Cicero 107
compilatio 7, 22, 34, 146
comun / commune/ commons 30, 37, 38, 49
consolatio 88–9
coronation 26, 149
  oath 26
Cotton Manuscript Nero A.x. 61, 64
counsellor, counsellors 24, 25, 104, 136–59
court 36, 65, 66, 71, 73–4, 76–80, 87, 100, 102, 106, 109, 110–11, 127, 137
courtesy 64–5, 71, 77–8, 87, 105, 109
courtly love 33, 34
crown 13–14, 36, 43, 103–4, 109
Crucifixion 57

Daniel 72
Dante 67
  Divina Commedia 67
Daunger 104–6, 109
David, King 27
De Charny, Geoffroi 41
Derby, Henry of *see* Henry IV
De Regimine Principum see under Giles of Rome
Donaldson, E. Talbot 121
dream vision 34, 35, 62, 68, 102
Duchess of Lancaster *see* Blanche

Echard, Sian 6
Ector 70, 114–8
Edmund (King) 57, 66

education of kings 8, 25, 139
Edward I 132
Edward II 45, 149–50
Edward III 39, 45, 46, 85, 108
Edward the Confessor 57, 66, 149
Edwards, A. S. G. 102
Eleanor, Queen 110, 119
elegy 68, 86
Elizabeth I 3
Elizabeth II 26
Eltham 101
Epstein, Robert 6
Esther 106
exemplum 38, 150

fable 38
fabliau 137
Ferster, Judith 147
Fisher, John 6
Forest *see* trees
Fortitude 36
Froissart 85, 90
  Paradys d'amours 88, 89

Gaunt, John of 84, 85–6, 90–2, 96, 98
Gawain 70, 76–82, 95
Gawain-poet 4, 6, 60, 61–82, 160–2
  compared to Chaucer 61, 62, 68, 89
  compared to Gower 61, 68
  compared to Langland 61, 62, 66, 68, 81
  Cleanness 69, 72–5, 77
  Patience 69, 73, 75–6
  Pearl 62–72, 73, 89
  Sir Gawain and the Green Knight 68, 69, 71, 73, 74, 76–82, 95, 127
Geoffrey of Monmouth 110
  Historia regum Britanniae 110
generosity *see* largesse
Giles of Rome 7, 13
  De Regimine Principum 7, 9, 37, 107
Goodman, Anthony 86
Gower, John 5–34, 60, 107, 119, 144, 160–2
  compared to Chaucer 12–13, 33, 84, 86, 95, 128, 131, 139
  compared to Gawain-poet 61, 68
  compared to Langland 35, 49, 55, 60
  Confessio Amantis 4, 5–34, 53, 68, 86, 99, 103, 104, 105, 141, 147
  Ahab (King) 17
  Amans 5–34, 53, 161
  Antigonus (King) 15
  Aristippus 15
  Armenia (King of) 21

Arpaghes 14
Arrons 25, 28–9
Brutus 28–30
Cambyses (King) 19
Camidotirus 19
Cinichus 15
Claudius 30
Codrus (King of Athens) 21
Collatin 29–30
Darius, Sultan of Persia 14
Diogenes 16
Dionys 22
Emperor Antonius 25
Emperor Maximin 18
Gaius Fabricius 18
Genius 5–34, 161
Gideon 23
Joab 23
Lichaon 22
Livius 30
Lucrece 28–30
Lycurgus 19, 20
Manachaz 14
Marsagete (Queen of) 22
Micah (Micaiah) 17
Nectanabus 9
Pompeius (Emperor of Rome) 21
Sadana Pallus (King of Asyrria) 27
Samuel 23
Sara 31
Sedechie 17
Siculus 22
Spertachus 22
Tarquin 25, 28
Thamarsis *see above,* Marsagete
Tobias 31
Virginia 30
Zorobabel 14
Prologue 6
Mirour de L'Omme 5
Vox Clamantis 5
Green, Richard Firth 102
Green Knight 77–82, 127
Guenevere 119
Guichard d'Angle 67
Guido delle Colonne 110

Harrowing of hell 57
Henry I 40
Henry II 110, 119
Henry IV 5, 84
Hocclève, Thomas 85
Regiment of Princes 85
hunt 90–1

Iliad 110

Jeroboam 27
Jerome 58
Jesus *see* Christ
John the Baptist 66, 68
Jonah 70, 75
Joseph 52, 89
Julius Caesar 11, 15, 16–17, 149
justice 17–21, 30, 33, 36, 42, 59, 107

Kittredge, George Lyman 119–20
Knighthood 36, 41, 70–1
Kynde (*see also* Kind *under* Langland, *Piers Plowman*) 113, 118

Lamb of God 43, 66, 68–9, 70–1
Lancaster, Duke of *see* Gaunt, John of
Langland, William 4, 26, 32, 35, 37, 44, 47–9, 51, 52, 55, 60, 71, 124, 160–2
 A Text 36, 39
 B Text 36, 39
 compared to Chaucer 56, 60
 compared to Gawain-poet 60, 62, 66, 68, 81
 compared to Gower 35, 49, 55, 60
 Piers Plowman 4, 35–60, 62, 76, 161
  Anima 53, 57
  Clergy 53, 56
  Conscience 45–9, 56, 58–9
  Dame Study 53
  Dowel, Dobet, Dobest 35, 52–3, 55–6
  Dreamer 36, 41, 42, 43, 44, 49, 51, 53–4, 56–9
  False Fickle Tongue 43
  Fortune 54
  Fortitude 59
  Grace 58–9
  Haukyn 56–7
  Holy Church 40, 41–3
  Hope 57
  Hunger 50
  Intelligence 47
  Inwit 53
  Kind 53, 55, 59
  Kind Wit 37, 40
  Lewtee 54
  Mede 43–50, 66
  Patience 56–7
  pardon 51
  Peace 47–8
  Piers Plowman 35, 49–50, 51–2, 57–9, 71
  Prudence 59

Reason   47–9
  Scripture   46–7, 53–4
  Truth   50, 51
  Visio   35, 52, 60
  Vita   35, 52, 57
  Waster   50
  Will   54, 56, 58–9
  Wit   53
  Worldly Knowledge   47–8
  Worldly Wise   48
  Wrong   47–9
lapidaries   68, 69
largesse   12, 14, 33
Launcelot   70
Latini, Bruno   7, 26
  Tresor   7, 22, 26, 107
Lewis, C.S.   7, 105, 118
lion   23, 30, 70–1, 107
Llull, Raimon   41
Lucifer   42

Macaulay   7, 13
Machaut   89, 90, 91
  Fonteinne Amoreuse   92
  Le Jugement dou roy de Behaingne   89, 91
  Le Dit dou Lyon   89
Macrobius   89, 107
Malory, Sir Thomas   70
Mann, Jill   126
Marie de France   129
Mary, Mother of God   64, 65, 103–4
Meed *see* reward
Merciless Parliament   26, 121
Mercury   20
Mirrors for Princes   4, 8, 34, 107, 123, 139, 148, 161
Mordred   119
Morgan Le Fay   79, 80
Morse, Charlotte   4
Moses   20, 54, 57
Muscatine, Charles   160

Narcissus   92–3
Nebuchadnezzar   52, 72
Nero   149

Octavian (Emperor)   90–1, 117
Olsson, Kurt   7, 11
Ovid   88

Pandarus   115, 117
parable
  Prodigal Son   80
  Rich man's feast   77
  Samaritan   57
  Vineyard   65
Patterson, Lee   1
Pearsall, Derek   143
Peasant's Revolt   121, 154–5
Peck, Russell   11, 12, 13, 27
Penelope   106
Perrers, Alice   45
Peter of Cyprus   149
Peter of Spain   149
Petrarch   124
Philippa, Queen   108
pity   12, 20, 21–4, 25
Plaint of Nature   101
pope   36, 54, 111, 144
Priam, King   116, 117, 120
Prudence   36

queen, queens   23, 64, 106, 108, 128

Rehoboam   2, 24, 25, 27
reward   37, 51
rhetoric   11
Ricardian   3, 34, 35, 60, 141, 160–2
Richard II   1–2, 3, 4, 24–8, 36, 39, 57, 65, 67, 68, 82–4, 98, 100, 101, 106, 107, 108, 117, 121, 122, 140, 143, 144, 146, 147, 148, 150, 153, 154, 155–7, 160
Riddy, Felicity   62
Roman de la Rose   67, 68, 90, 92, 104, 105
Roman de Renart   151, 154

Saint Gregory   54–5, 58
Saint James   42
Saint Kenelm   155–6
Saint Paul   158
Saint Peter   36
Sapientia *see* Wisdom
Saul   23, 46
Saul, Nigel   3–4, 25
Scanlon, Larry   144, 147–8
Schmidt, A.V.C.   35
Scipio   99
  Somnium Scipionis   101
Secreta Secretorum   7, 9, 95, 107
Seneca   26
sermon   37, 49
seven deadly sins   7, 34, 44, 49, 141
Seys and Alcyone   88, 90
Shakespeare, William   1, 2, 5
  Richard II   1, 2
Sheen   101
Simpson, James   33
Solomon   2, 23–4, 25, 27, 45, 136

Spearing, A. C.   80, 102
Staley, Lynn   6
Stokes, Myra   25, 39
Strode   119
Strohm, Paul   1–2, 84, 108, 120

temperance   36
Thomas Aquinas   37
Trajan   54–5, 60
Trawthe   76, 81
Treaty of Aquitaine   46
trees   92–3
Trevet, Nicholas   132
Trojan War   110, 118–20
truth   12, 13, 14, 40, 42, 44
tyrants, tyranny   3, 30, 80, 107, 109, 132–6

Ugolino of Pisa   149–50
Ulysses   11
universe   10–11
Usk, Thomas   122

Valentine's Day   98, 99, 104
Vincent of Beauvais   22
Visconti, Barnabo   149
Vitalis, Oderic   40–1
Vulgate Bible *see* Bible

Wace   119
   Brut   119
Wallace, David   1
Walsingham, Thomas of   85
wheel of fate, fortune   16, 149–50
William I   40
Wilton Diptych   2, 65–6, 107, 108, 149, 153
wisdom   24, 33
   sapientia   7
Wyclif, John   3, 86

CHAUCER STUDIES

I	MUSIC IN THE AGE OF CHAUCER, *Nigel Wilkins*
II	CHAUCER'S LANGUAGE AND THE PHILOSOPHERS' TRADITION, *J. D. Burnley*
III	ESSAYS ON TROILUS AND CRISEYDE, *edited by Mary Salu*
IV	CHAUCER SONGS, *Nigel Wilkins*
V	CHAUCER'S BOCCACCIO: Sources of Troilus and the Knight's and Franklin's Tales, *edited and translated by N. R. Havely*
VI	SYNTAX AND STYLE IN CHAUCER'S POETRY, *G. H. Roscow*
VII	CHAUCER'S DREAM POETRY: Sources and Analogues, *B. A. Windeatt*
VIII	CHAUCER AND PAGAN ANTIQUITY, *Alastair Minnis*
IX	CHAUCER AND THE POEMS OF 'CH' in University of Pennsylvania MS French 15, *James I. Wimsatt*
X	CHAUCER AND THE IMAGINARY WORLD OF FAME, *Piero Boitani*
XI	INTRODUCTION TO CHAUCERIAN ENGLISH, *Arthur O. Sandved*
XII	CHAUCER AND THE EARLY WRITINGS OF BOCCACCIO, *David Wallace*
XIII	CHAUCER'S NARRATORS, *David Lawton*
XIV	CHAUCER: COMPLAINT AND NARRATIVE, *W. A. Davenport*
XV	CHAUCER'S RELIGIOUS TALES, *edited by C. David Benson and Elizabeth Robertson*
XVI	EIGHTEENTH-CENTURY MODERNIZATIONS FROM THE *CANTERBURY TALES*, *edited by Betsy Bowden*
XVII	THE MANUSCRIPTS OF THE *CANTERBURY TALES*, *Charles A. Owen Jr*
XVIII	CHAUCER'S BOECE AND THE MEDIEVAL TRADITION OF BOETHIUS, *edited by A. J. Minnis*
XIX	THE AUTHORSHIP OF *THE EQUATORIE OF THE PLANETIS*, *Kari Anne Rand Schmidt*
XX	CHAUCERIAN REALISM, *Robert Myles*
XXI	CHAUCER ON LOVE, KNOWLEDGE AND SIGHT, *Norman Klassen*
XXII	CONQUERING THE REIGN OF FEMENY: GENDER AND GENRE IN CHAUCER'S ROMANCE, *Angela Jane Weisl*
XXIII	CHAUCER'S APPROACH TO GENDER IN THE *CANTERBURY TALES*, *Anne Laskaya*
XXIV	CHAUCERIAN TRAGEDY, *Henry Ansgar Kelly*
XXV	MASCULINITIES IN CHAUCER: Approaches to Maleness in the *Canterbury Tales and Troilus and Criseyde*, *edited by Peter G. Beidler*
XXVI	CHAUCER AND COSTUME: The Secular Pilgrims in the General Prologue, *Laura F. Hodges*
XXVII	CHAUCER'S PHILOSOPHICAL VISIONS, *Kathryn L. Lynch*
XXVIII	SOURCES AND ANALOGUES OF THE CANTERBURY TALES [I], *edited by Robert M. Correale with Mary Hamel*
XXX	FEMINIZING CHAUCER, *Jill Mann*
XXXI	NEW READINGS OF CHAUCER'S POETRY, *edited by Robert G. Benson and Susan J. Ridyard*

XXXII	THE LANGUAGE OF THE CHAUCER TRADITION, *Simon Horobin*
XXXIII	ETHICS AND EXEMPLARY NARRATIVE IN CHAUCER AND GOWER, *J. Allan Mitchell*
XXXIV	CHAUCER AND CLOTHING: Clerical and Academic Costume in the General Prologue to the *Canterbury Tales*, *Laura F. Hodges*
XXXV	SOURCES AND ANALOGUES OF THE *CANTERBURY TALES* [II], *edited by Robert M. Correale with Mary Hamel*
XXXVI	*THE LEGEND OF GOOD WOMEN*: Context and Reception, *edited by Carolyn P. Collette*
XXXVII	CHAUCER AND THE CITY, *edited by Ardis Butterfield*
XXXVIII	MEN AND MASCULINITIES IN CHAUCER'S *TROILUS AND CRISEYDE*, *edited by Tison Pugh and Marcia Smith Marzec*